Beginning Philosophy

Baruch A. Brody
Rice University

BEGINNING PHILOSOPHY

PRENTICE-HALL, INC., *Englewood Cliffs, New Jersey* 07632

Library of Congress Cataloging in Publication Data

BRODY, BARUCH A
   Beginning philosophy.

   Includes bibliographical references and index.
   1. Philosophy—Introductions. I. Title.
BD21.B73 100   76-26673
ISBN 0-13-073882-4

© 1977 by PRENTICE-HALL, INC.,
Englewood Cliffs, New Jersey

All rights reserved.
No part of this book may be reproduced
in any form or by any means without
permission in writing from the publisher.

Printed in the United States of America

10 9 8 7 6 5 4 3 2

PRENTICE-HALL INTERNATIONAL, INC., *London*
PRENTICE-HALL OF AUSTRALIA, PTY. LTD., *Sydney*
PRENTICE-HALL OF CANADA, LTD., *Toronto*
PRENTICE-HALL OF INDIA PRIVATE LIMITED, *New Delhi*
PRENTICE-HALL OF JAPAN, INC., *Tokyo*
PRENTICE-HALL OF SOUTHEAST ASIA (PTE.) LTD., *Singapore*
WHITEHALL BOOKS LIMITED, *Wellington, New Zealand*

Contents

PREFACE *ix*

**INTRODUCTION—
THE NATURE OF PHILOSOPHY** *1*

    I.1 The Nature of Philosophical Problems *1*
    I.2 The Nature of Philosophical Answers *6*
    I.3 The Nature of this Book *10*

I MORAL RULES AND THEIR EXCEPTIONS *11*

    1.1 Moral Rules and their Problems *12*
    1.2 Consequentialism *18*
    1.3 Ideal Utilitarianism and its Difficulties *24*
    1.4 A Return to Moral Rules *28*

2 MORALITY AND RATIONAL SELF-INTEREST — 33

    2.1 The Conventional Answers 35
    2.2 Two Philosophical Theories 37
    2.3 More Radical Approaches 46
    2.4 What Really are our Motives? 51
    2.5 Reasons and Motives 54

3 JUSTICE AND EQUALITY — 56

    3.1 Some Preliminary Distinctions 57
    3.2 Justice and Equality 59
    3.3 Some Classical Formulas 62
    3.4 Two Forward-Looking Theories of Justice 67
    3.5 Sketch of a Theory 75

4 THE EXISTENCE OF THE STATE AND THE OBLIGATION TO OBEY ITS LAWS — 78

    4.1 The Anarchist Argument 80
    4.2 Social Contract Theory 82
    4.3 Tacit Consent and Hypothetical Consent 87
    4.4 Obedience vs. Disobedience 91

5 THE EXISTENCE OF GOD — 100

    5.1 The Judao-Christian Conception of God 100
    5.2 The Arguments for Divine Existence 104
    5.3 The Arguments against Divine Existence 112
    5.4 Faith 118

6 THE IMPLICATIONS OF RELIGIOUS BELIEF — 121

    6.1 Does Morality Need Religion? 122
    6.2 Can Religion Make a Difference to Morality? 128
    6.3 Religion and the Meaning of Life 131
    6.4 Religion and Ritual 135

7 MAN AND HIS PLACE IN NATURE — 139

    7.1 Mind-Body Dualism *142*
    7.2 Behaviorism *153*
    7.3 The Brain-State Theory *157*

8 RESPONSIBILITY FOR OUR ACTIONS — 162

    8.1 Acts and their Effects *163*
    8.2 Liability *169*
    8.3 Punishment and Freedom *175*

9 TRUTH — 188

    9.1 Some Inadequate Definitions *190*
    9.2 The Pragmatic Theory of Truth *193*
    9.3 The Coherence Theory of Truth *196*
    9.4 The Correspondence Theory of Truth *199*
    9.5 A Recent Theory *204*
    9.6 Types of Truth *206*

10 KNOWING AND BELIEVING — 211

    10.1 The Nature of Knowledge *212*
    10.2 Two Skeptical Arguments *216*
    10.3 Rationalism vs. Empiricism *220*
    10.4 Some Suggestions *229*

CONCLUSION — 234

QUESTIONS FOR FURTHER THOUGHT — 237

Preface

Most philosophers find that they have to spend a fair amount of time teaching introductory philosophy. This should, in theory, be an exciting course to teach and an enjoyable course for students to take. As a matter of fact, however, many faculty members and students find it otherwise.

I believe that this is due in large measure to the books currently used in such courses. The texts in question are either complete original works or anthologies. In either case, the material in question was written for a philosophically more sophisticated audience. Both in organization and content, it is often too difficult for even very good students, and much of the time in class is spent just explaining to the students what the author said. Neither the teacher nor the student has the chance to explore these fascinating ideas and issues in any depth.

This text was written with the needs of the average student in mind. It tries, in a straightforward way, to explain some of the main philosophical issues and some of the classical positions on those issues. I also try to set out my own views on the topic. There are then questions for further thought. If the text works in the way it was designed to, the student should be able to come to class with a good grasp of the issues, the various opinions, and the questions. Classroom time can then be devoted to the enjoyable part of philosophy, trying to figure out which opinion (if any) is really right.

In writing this book, I was able to enjoy the feedback from teaching such a course at the Harvard University Extension Division for six years. The students in those courses ranged from Cambridge street-people to senior citizens with advanced professional degrees. Their enthusiastic participation in, and response to, the classes upon which this book is based encouraged me to write it, and I should like to take this opportunity to thank them for their many helpful suggestions.

BARUCH BRODY
Rice University
July 12, 1976

Introduction— The Nature of Philosophy

When you begin the study of a new subject, it is natural to wonder what you are getting into. What sort of questions will you be considering? Why are they important? How will you try to answer them? What answers can you reasonably expect from a beginning book like this one? This introduction is an attempt to answer these first, very natural, questions. In effect, it will give you reasons for staying in this course and reading this book.

This book is an introduction to the study of philosophy. One might expect it to begin with a definition of that subject. But such definitions are usually either too trivial to be helpful or too difficult to be understood at the beginning of the term. I hope that the answers to the above questions will take the place of such a definition.

I.1 THE NATURE OF PHILOSOPHICAL PROBLEMS

Think of the community where you grew up. Let us suppose that it was relatively homogeneous. Most of the people in such a community share certain basic beliefs about the values one ought to be pursuing in life and about the ways to pursue those values. No one lives his or her life entirely by those views (people are, after all, only human). But most of the people at least make some effort to do so. As a young person, you too are trained in those views, and you still find them attractive in many ways. Now suppose that you have recently come to wonder about these views. Perhaps you have encountered people who hold very different beliefs about the values you ought to pursue in life. Or perhaps you have recently encountered new situations, ones in which you felt uncomfortable following the views you grew up with.

Many young people have had this experience, in previous times and in our own. And often the experience has led them to ask difficult questions like these: What really is the difference between right and wrong? How can I tell the difference between the two? Will I gain or lose in life if I stick to trying to do what is right? When people ask such questions, they are asking philosophical questions. The first two chapters of this book are devoted to questions like these. They form the subject matter of that part of philosophy which is called ethics.

Every society has its own pattern of social organization. But, in these many different patterns, there are certain common features. For example, in any given society, the various goods are always distributed unequally. Some people have a lot more of what is thought of as desirable (wealth, power, prestige, leisure, etc.) than others. This pattern is normally accepted by all involved; it seems to them to be the natural way for things to be organized. But there are special situations in which this pattern comes to be challenged, either by those who have received less than what they consider to be their fair share and who want more or by those who have received more than they consider their fair share and who feel troubled about it. At such times, it is not unusual for people to consider such questions as: Should there be differentiations between people? If there should, which ones are just and which ones are unjust? At such times, people often recognize that the current legal system is devoted to protecting the interests of those who received the greatest gains. This leads them to ask still further questions like: Do I really have any obligation to obey the law? If I do, may I violate that obligation in the attempt to change the social order?

When people start asking questions like this, they are also asking philosophical questions. These questions form the subject matter of a second major area of philosophy: social and political philosophy. The third and fourth chapters in this book are devoted to a consideration of these questions.

Most people are brought up with beliefs about religious questions. In some cases, the beliefs taught are very extensive and call upon the believer to engage in a wide variety of religious practices. In other cases, the beliefs are far less extensive and seem to require very little by way of religious practices. Some people are brought up with antireligious beliefs.

However it is rare to find someone whose upbringing has had nothing at all to say about religion.

In earlier times, people in a given society usually shared the same religion. But, of course, our society is not homogeneous in that way. From early youth, we know of the wide variety of religious beliefs and practices that are common in our home communities, and as we grow older we encounter still other forms of belief and practice. Moreover, we encounter ways of thinking about the world—most notably the scientific standpoint—which leave out the religious element altogether. All of this leads us to wonder about our religious heritage. It is natural, then, for a person to ask such questions as: Is there any rational basis for holding my religious beliefs, or, for that matter, for holding any religious beliefs? If not, what should one believe about religion? What difference should religion make in life?

These questions are also philosophical questions, and they form the subject matter of a third part of philosophy: philosophy of religion. The fifth and sixth chapters of this book are devoted to a consideration of such questions.

Few things concern people more than the attempt to make sense of themselves and their fellow human beings. We have a sense of ourselves as being somehow special, and yet we know at the same time that we are, in many ways, just another part of the natural order surrounding us. One of the classic attempts to make sense of the duality of human nature claims that human beings are composed of two parts. One is a material object like all others. This is our body. The other is a nonmaterial substance. This is our soul. The soul is what truly makes us special. It differs from objects of the material world in that at least some of its actions are free. And it is the possibility of its survival that holds out the hope that we may survive the death of our material body.

This traditional picture of man has come under renewed challenge in recent years. There has been a revitalization of an alternative view of man, one that places man squarely in the material realm. This seems in any case to be the view of man that is most compatible with the findings of such sciences as biology and psychology. The development of this scientific view of man has forced us to confront such questions as: Is there really any way in which man is special? Is there any hope for our survival after death? Is there any place for human freedom and human responsibility? These are also important philosophical questions. They form part of the subject matter of a different branch of philosophy: metaphysics. We will consider these questions in chapters 7 and 8.

Much of the first third of our life is devoted to our education. We are taught some of what mankind knows to be true. Moreover, and most important, we are taught how to go out and discover new truths.

But, if our teachers are honest, they also teach us how hard it is to discover the truth, and how often people have been wrong when they thought that they knew the truth. The history of mankind could be written as the history of how people discovered that what they thought to be so really wasn't true after all. This is the case even in our own scientific era. Indeed, many have pointed out that one of the great merits of the scientific approach is that it never takes anything as certain. It always leaves open the possibility of revising any of our beliefs. When one learns this honest message, however, one cannot help but be troubled by it. And it naturally leads one to ask certain questions: Is there really such a thing as the truth? If so, how do we know when we have discovered it? Indeed, can we ever know that we have discovered the truth?

To ask these questions is to ask some very basic philosophical questions. These questions comprise that part of philosophy known as epistemology, or the theory of knowledge. The last two chapters of this book are devoted to these questions.

We have so far introduced a number of philosophical questions, the ones that we will be discussing in the rest of this book. But we have not said anything about what makes them philosophical questions, or what they all have in common. I think that there are a number of important characteristics of these questions that should be noted, characteristics that help explain the importance of these questions.

1. Each of these questions concerns itself with the nature and validity of some sphere of human life. The first set of questions concern our moral life, the second set our political life, the third our religious life, the fourth set have to do with the way in which we think about ourselves, and the fifth set have to do with our knowledge-gathering activities. This feature might lead one to suspect that there is an area of philosophy devoted to understanding the nature and validity of each major aspect of human existence. This suspicion is more or less accurate. In addition to the areas already mentioned, there is also a philosophy of art, a philosophy of science, and even a philosophy of philosophy (although some philosophers might share with you the suspicion that this looks dangerously like the beginning of a problem).

Philosophers have always prided themselves on the wide scope of their discipline. Philosophy seems to relate to so many other disciplines and to so many parts of human life. The first feature of philosophical problems, then, that they relate to major aspects of human existence, makes the broad scope of philosophy perfectly understandable. Philosophy is, in this way, a universal discipline.

This first feature of philosophical problems also helps explain why so many workers in other disciplines have turned to philosophy. Many eminent scientists have worked in the philosophy of science, many eminent artists have worried about the philosophy of art, many eminent jurists have written about the philosophy of law. They too have been troubled about the nature and validity of the activities that normally engage them, and this leads to philosophy.

2. The interest in a particular area of philosophy is usually proportional to the extent to which people feel troubled about the corresponding human activity. When, for example, religious people are satisfied with their religious life, they have very little real interest in philosophy of religion (except as a sort of abstract intellectual game). But during a period of religious turmoil and doubt, when even those who are religious are troubled about their religious lives and beliefs, interest in the philosophy of religion rises. The same thing is true about the philosophy of science. The development of whole new types of scientific theory (like the theory of relativity and quantum mechanics) has seemed very troubling to many working scientists. These new theories are often not of the kind scientists were looking for. And this has left many scientists troubled about their own work. This, in turn, has given rise to a considerable growth of interest in the philosophy of science. Examples like this can be multiplied for all the fields of human activity.

Philosophy has always been viewed with a certain amount of suspicion. Indeed, one of the first of the great philosophers, Socrates, was condemned and executed for his philosophical activities. There were many in his home city, Athens, who viewed him as a dangerous character, given to corrupting the young. In a way, this view of philosophy is perfectly understandable. As we have just seen, the philosopher is concerned with examining the nature and the validity of major human activities. This process often results in a negative evaluation. So those who are engaged in the activity in question may well be justified in viewing philosophy as a potential challenge to them.

Nevertheless, it would not be correct to view philosophy as intrinsically revolutionary. To begin with, not all philosophical argumentation ends up with a negative evaluation of some activity or practice. On many occasions, the result of the philosophical investigation is a reaffirmation. For example, while some philosophers of religion have been very critical of both religious belief and religious practice, there have been others whose work has reaffirmed these same aspects of religion. Two notable examples are the Jewish thinker Maimonides and the Christian philosopher St. Thomas Aquinas. Second, and perhaps even more important, it is not really the philosopher who raises the potentially challenging questions about the nature and validity of the practice in question. As we have seen, these questions are already felt by people engaged in the activity. All the philosopher does is to channel their questioning into a serious and rigorous discussion.

3. Philosophical investigation can make a great difference in the way we carry out these human activities and practices. Let us look at just a few examples of this.

Jeremy Bentham is one of the great figures in the history of ethics, social and political philosophy, and the philosophy of law. During his lifetime, he was engaged in a critical reexamination of the English legal system. He looked at the basic principles of that system, and found them wanting. He saw that the system failed to take into account the consequences of its own rules and practices. As a result, he called for a major revamping of the English legal system, including changes which would increase the general welfare of the people. As a matter of fact, the English legal system was never totally overhauled along the lines that Bentham suggested. But his ideas made a great difference in the long run, and the law was never the same because of his philosophical examination of its foundations.

St. Thomas Aquinas is one of the great figures in the history of the philosophy of religion. In his lifetime, traditional religious ideas were being challenged by many young people who had come under the influence of the newly discovered Greek philosophy. St. Thomas, as we pointed out above, was not a revolutionary religious thinker; his work was rather a defense of the basic validity of traditional religious beliefs. Still, in the course of his reexamination of the foundations of religious belief, he found it necessary to restate and reinterpret many traditional ideas about both religion and morality. Catholicism was without doubt significantly changed and enriched by his activities.

We have seen so far that the following can be said about philosophical questions and their importance. Philosophical questions probe the nature and validity of various human activities, beliefs, and institutions. They arise because the people who are engaged in these activities, who hold these beliefs, who are part of these institutions, are themselves troubled about the foundations of these activities, beliefs, and institutions. The result of the philosophical activity may be a challenge or a reaffirmation. But, whatever the result, these activities, beliefs, and institutions are never the same afterwards.

I.2 THE NATURE OF PHILOSOPHICAL ANSWERS

Is there a God? This is a typical philosophical question. It probes the validity of a belief that is fundamental to many religious traditions. Now there obviously are only two possible answers to this question: yes and no. One doesn't have to be much of a philosopher to come up with an answer. What then can the philosopher contribute?

What makes an action right? This is another typical philosophical

INTRODUCTION—THE NATURE OF PHILOSOPHY

question. It probes the nature of a distinction (the distinction between right and wrong actions) that is fundamental to our whole moral life. Here there is no short, complete list of answers. Still, it is not hard to think of many possible answers. An action is right if it is in accord with the will of God. An action is right if it promotes my own self-interest. An action is right if it promotes the interests of the oppressed. Many others could be suggested. It is not hard to come up with answers to these philosophical questions. What then does the philosopher contribute?

What the philosopher is concerned with is not merely finding an answer to his questions. He is concerned with finding an answer that he can rationally defend. In other words, the philosopher is concerned with finding reasons for thinking that one of the possible answers to the philosophical question is the correct one. Many people attempt to answer questions that we can recognize as philosophical. Some base their answers on tradition, some on revelation, some on personal feelings. What distinguishes the philosophical approach is that it attempts to answer these philosophical questions by an appeal to reason.

For example, St. Thomas Aquinas is not famous for his answer "yes" to the question of whether God exists. That answer had been given by many both before and after his time. What made St. Thomas such an important philosopher was that he attempted to provide reasons for accepting that answer, reasons that could be defended rationally. Again, Jeremy Bentham is not famous merely for saying that the English legal system required a major overhauling; that had been said very frequently. What made him so important were the reasons he gave in criticizing that system, reasons that he felt could be defended rationally.

This explains why much of philosophy is concerned with discussing *arguments*, and not just answers or positions. Although there certainly are cases in which people put forward strikingly new positions and answers to philosophical questions, what most philosophers contribute, and what becomes the basis for most philosophical discussions, are new rational arguments for or against traditional answers.

How does this affect what you will find in this book? We will, of course, raise certain philosophical questions. And we will introduce a variety of answers from those that have been offered by various philosophers. Most of our time, however, will be devoted to analyzing the arguments for and against these answers. This is not surprising, for it is these arguments that are the heart of the philosopher's contribution.

What is an argument and how does one go about deciding whether or not it is a good one? The purpose of every argument is to prove that something is true. Let us call the statement whose truth we are trying to prove the *conclusion* of the argument. In trying to prove the conclusion, we have to appeal to something else. Those other statements whose truth we appeal to are the *premises* of the argument. To put this another way, when one offers an argument, one sets out to prove the truth of the conclusion on the basis of the truth of the premises.

Let us look at an example of an argument. "Socrates must be mortal because he is a man and all men are mortal." Now this argument is an attempt to prove the truth of the statement that Socrates is mortal. So that statement is the conclusion of the argument. In trying to prove the truth of our conclusion, we appeal to the truth of two other statements: that all men are mortal and that Socrates is a man. So those two statements are the premises of our argument. We can then represent our argument in the following form, writing our conclusion under our premises:

> All men are mortal
> *Socrates is a man*
> Socrates is mortal

Now that we have some idea of what an argument is, let us turn to the question of what makes an argument a good argument. A short answer is that an argument is a good one if it proves the truth of the conclusion; that, after all, is the whole purpose of offering the argument in the first place. But that isn't much of an answer. It just raises the further question of when the argument proves the truth of the conclusion.

The logician says that an argument is a valid argument if there is no way in which the premises can be true while the conclusion is false. The above argument is valid: there is no way in which Socrates could be immortal (that is, there is no way our conclusion could be false) if all men are mortal and Socrates is a man (if our premises are true). On the other hand, the following argument is not a valid argument:

> *All men are mortal*
> All animals are mortal

This argument is invalid because it could be that the premise could be (and is) true while the conclusion is false (all that this would require is the existence of some immortal animals). Note by the way, that this argument is invalid even though, in fact, both its premise and conclusion are true. It is invalid because the premise does not *prove* the truth of the conclusion. Despite the truth of the premise, the conclusion might still be false.

Consider the following argument:

> All men are immortal
> *Socrates is a man*
> Socrates is immortal

This is a valid argument. There is no way in which the premises could be true and the conclusion false. Still, this argument does not prove the truth of its conclusion. The conclusion is, in fact, false. So the mere fact that an argument is valid is not enough for it to prove the truth of its conclusion. Something else is required. The logician says that the argument must also be sound; its premises must also be true. Only when an argument is both valid and sound does it prove the truth of its conclusion.

Let us see where we stand. We have seen that the philosopher does not merely attempt to provide answers to philosophical questions; the philosopher also tries to prove that his answers are the correct answers. He succeeds in doing so only if his arguments for his conclusions are both valid and sound.

Let us apply all of this to a simple philosophical argument. This is a simplified version of one of the standard arguments to prove the existence of God. It runs as follows: There must be a God, since everything has to have a cause. On analysis, this turns out to be the following argument:

Everything has a cause
There must be a First Cause, God

Confronted with this argument, as with any other, one must ask two questions. First, is the argument valid (does its conclusion follow from its premises)? And, secondly, is the argument sound (are its premises true)? There are considerable doubts here on both of these scores. To begin with, isn't there a possibility of the premise being true while the conclusion is false? Suppose that the universe has existed for an infinitely long period of time and that everything in it has been caused by something that existed before. This would be a case in which the premise of the argument is true while the conclusion is false. We do not know whether the universe really is that way, but that's not the point. The mere possibility of its being that way shows that the argument is *invalid*. Secondly, those who offer this argument cannot accept the truth of its premise, that everything has a cause, since they believe in a First Cause, which would have to be an Uncaused Cause. Ironically enough, the very people who offer this argument would have to reject it as *unsound*. In short, then, this argument has failed both of our tests, and it does not prove the truth of its conclusion.

This last example is extremely important. It has, of course, illustrated all of the points that we have been trying to make about evaluating arguments. More important, however, it has done so in connection with a real philosophical argument, and it therefore illustrates the sort of thing that we will be doing in the rest of this book.

I.3 THE NATURE OF THIS BOOK

We have so far talked about the nature of philosophy in general. We have outlined the nature of philosophical problems and the way to evaluate philosophical answers. We have, however, said very little about this philosophy book, other than to indicate which problems we will be covering.

This book is an introductory text, so it hopes to introduce you to a considerable number of problems and give you a real sense of what the whole field is like. But, at the same time, we cannot go too deeply into any one of the problems. Treatment in great depth would require skills beyond those possessed by the introductory student. Many writers of introductory texts try to solve this problem by merely introducing the various issues and not working towards any solution to them. This seems to me to be a real cop-out. I have tried in each case at least to outline a satisfactory theory which will serve as a solution to the problems raised. Because of the introductory nature of the text, I could not, of course, present a full defense of the theories I propose. I do believe, however, that they are correct and that the arguments I present are sound and valid. You will, however, have to evaluate them for yourselves.

A word about the Questions for Further Thought at the end of the book. These are not simple homework problems. They raise serious philosophical questions and call upon you to do a lot of serious philosophical thinking. I hope you enjoy them.

One final word. Philosophy is an exciting discipline. The questions that it raises are interesting and vital questions, and the method it employs can be very provocative. I hope that you will sense this excitement and want to go on to do more philosophy.

1

Moral Rules and Their Exceptions

In this chapter, our main concern will be with studying moral rules. Why do philosophers study moral rules? Primarily because these rules play a central role in the moral codes of most people. Consider, as an example, all those people who live by the Ten Commandments. What are the Ten Commandments? They are a set of moral rules telling us what we should do (honor they father and mother) and what we should not do (thou shall not kill). Or consider, as another example, all those people who live by the Golden Rule (do unto others as you would have them do unto you). As its very name implies, the Golden Rule is another moral rule. Many more examples could be given. In fact, try the following experiment in class: ask each of the students (and the teacher) to write down on a piece of paper some of the most important things that he or she thinks about when trying to resolve a moral dilemma. You will rapidly discover just how widespread the appeal to moral rules really is.

One of the reasons why there are so many widely accepted moral rules is that much of our moral education consists of being taught these moral rules. This is not surprising. Those who provide us with that moral education (our parents and teachers) want their teachings to extend beyond the immediate case, and one way to accomplish this is to teach rules that are supposed to cover all sorts of cases. Even if we are not explicitly taught a moral rule, even if we are only told what is right or wrong in a given case, we are encouraged to generalize and to act in the prescribed way in similar cases.

Given that these moral rules are so important to the moral life of most people, philosophers have studied them extensively. One thing that philosophers have done is to critically evaluate particular rules. Is the Golden Rule really such a good idea? After all, people have different tastes, and other people may not want you to do unto them what you would want them to do unto you. Or consider the rule against killing. Is self-defense a legitimate exception to that rule? Is capital punishment? In short, philosophers have spent a lot of time worrying about whether particular moral rules are appropriate and whether particular exceptions to these rules are legitimate. Another, and more fundamental, philosophical approach has been to raise certain general questions about moral rules, such as: What are the sources of moral rules? Which, if any, are dependable? Are there legitimate exceptions to these moral rules and how can we find out which exceptions are legitimate? What procedures should we adopt to determine which rule should be followed when two or more rules conflict with each other? It is this second, more general approach, that we shall adopt in this chapter. Nevertheless, we will apply our conclusions to one particular problem—whether euthanasia is a legitimate exception to the moral rule against killing—as a way of showing how our general conclusions work out in practice.

1.1 MORAL RULES AND THEIR PROBLEMS

There are a number of reasons for being skeptical about moral codes based on rules. Such moral codes often encounter difficulties when they confront the question of exceptions and the question of conflicting rules. An examination of a few examples should make this point clear.

example a

During World War II, the question of saturation bombing arose. In an attempt to meet the military challenge posed by the Axis powers, leading Allied military authorities suggested that the Allies bomb the major Axis population centers. This, they argued, would disrupt the Axis military effort by weakening the morale of the total population. These authorities knew that this policy would cause much harm to innocent civilians, but they offered a variety of arguments in its favor. To begin with, they argued that anything is legitimate in war. Then, they claimed that saturation bombing would shorten the war and actually save lives

MORAL RULES AND THEIR EXCEPTIONS

in the long run. Moreover, they said, there really are no innocent civilians in modern warfare. All civilians, in one way or another, contribute to the war effort. Finally, they argued that there really is no difference between saturation bombing and bombing military targets when you know that this will cause the death of innocent civilians who live nearby. This debate was intensified by the American decision to drop bombs on Hiroshima and Nagasaki, and it has continued in relation to the military tactics adopted in Vietnam.

We can best understand these issues by looking at them from the following perspective. There is a widely accepted moral rule that combatants should respect the right to life of innocent noncombatant civilians. This moral rule has become part of international law. Thus, Article 3 of the Geneva Convention of 1949, extending the principle even to armed conflicts within a country, says:

> Persons taking no active part in the hostilities, including members of armed forces who have laid down their arms . . . shall in all circumstances be treated humanely, without any adverse distinction founded on race, color, religion or faith, sex, birth or wealth, or any other similar criteria. To this end the following acts are and shall remain prohibited at any time and in any place whatsoever with respect to the above-mentioned persons: . . . violence to life and person, in particular murder of all kinds, mutilation, cruel treatment and torture.

This moral and legal principle clearly prohibits the sort of bombing that we are discussing. Now, as we look at the arguments *for* that bombing, we find that they are of different types. One, the claim that anything is legitimate in war, directly challenges the validity of our moral principle. The others do not. All that they claim is that some saturation bombing is a legitimate exception to this rule. The bombing should be thought legitimate because it will save more lives, or because it is like the admittedly legitimate exception of bombing military targets when civilians live nearby, or because there are no innocent civilians in modern total warfare.

How are we to decide whether these grounds are sufficient to justify an exception to our moral rule? How are we to decide whether the correct moral rule allows for such exceptions? People who follow moral rules have found these questions difficult to answer. And for many philosophers it has seemed attractive to say that the best solution to this problem is to perform that action (keeping the rule or breaking it) that will produce the best consequences. But saying this seems to suggest that rightness and wrongness ultimately depend upon consequences, what count are the consequences and not the moral rules.

example b

In 1841, the *William Brown,* a boat sailing from Liverpool to Philadelphia, struck an iceberg and sank. Two lifeboats, neither very safe, were lowered, but they became separated. One was so overloaded with passengers that it was barely able to move. It began to leak, and then a squall came up. The captain recognized that unless the load was lightened, everyone might die. But no one volunteered to jump overboard. What should he have done? If he threw some people overboard, he would be killing them. If he did not, he probably would have caused many more to die. In any case, if it were necessary to throw someone overboard, who should it be? Should he have drawn lots? Should he have saved the stronger, those with a better chance of surviving the ordeal?

The captain's dilemma was partially due to the fact that there were two moral rules involved. He accepted the validity of both, and they led to conflicting consequences. On the one hand, the fundamental rule against killing seemed to dictate that no one should be thrown overboard. On the other hand, there was the moral rule—particularly applicable to one in command—that one should choose the action that would save as many lives as possible. This seemed to dictate that he should throw some people overboard. So the first problem he faced was how to reconcile the conflict between two moral rules whose legitimacy and validity he accepted.

There are those who claim that one should never make an exception to a legitimate moral rule. Such people would presumably not be troubled by our bombing example, since they allow for no exceptions. But what would they have said to our captain? How can they deal with the problem of conflicting rules, a problem that can come up for practically all systems of rules that contain more than one rule? Philosophers, too, have found this problem very perplexing.

These problems about particular cases are not the only problems faced by believers in moral rules. There are many philosophers who feel that advances in developmental psychology and cultural anthropology have shown how irrational it is to base one's morality on a set of rules. Let us look at results from each of these fields separately.

Some philosophers claim that those who emphasize the importance of moral rules have simply failed to mature morally, that is, they have not reached the later stages of moral development. They point to the researches of the child psychologist Jean Piaget, who has shown that children emphasize rules between the ages of five and nine, but then begin to be more flexible. And they conclude from these facts that a correct morality for adults must de-emphasize rules. This is the argument of P. H. Nowell-Smith:

> Even Piaget's older children could not have played marbles without rules; but they treated them as adaptable, as subservient to the purpose of playing a game, which is what they wanted to do. They treated the rules as a wise man treats his motor car, not as an object of veneration but as a convenience. This, I suggest, is how we, as adults, should regard moral rules. . . . The life of love is, like a work of art, not a means to an end, but an end in itself. For this reason in all close human relationships there should be a flexibility in our attitude to rules characteristic to the expert artist, craftsman, or games player. ("Morality: Religious and Secular," *Rationalist Annual* [1961])

There are two difficulties with this sort of argument. To begin with, more recent psychological research has suggested that even at the "more mature" stages of moral development, moral rules play a central role in our moral thinking. To be sure, these rules are not the simple rules that we were taught as children, but they are nevertheless moral rules. Thus, Lawrence Kohlberg has defined the final stage of moral development as follows:

> The universal-ethical-principle orientation. Right is defined by the decision of conscience in accordance with self-chosen ethical principles appealing to logical comprehensiveness, universality, and consistency. These principles are abstract and ethical (the Golden Rule, the categorical imperative); they are not concrete moral rules like the Ten Commandments. At heart, these are universal principles of justice, of the reciprocity and equality of human rights, and of respect for the dignity of human beings as individual persons. ("From Is to Ought" in T. Mischel's *Cognitive Development and Epistemology*)

Second, and perhaps even more important, none of these facts about our moral development shows us what our attitude ought to be towards moral rules. For all we know, the child's "less developed" reverential attitude towards concrete moral rules might be more insightful than the "more mature" stages that Piaget and Kohlberg have praised.

Let us turn, then, to the argument from cultural anthropology. A striking fact that has been discovered by anthropologists is the way that moral rules vary from one society to another and from one culture to another. There are some moral rules (e.g., thou shall not kill) that are widely held across societies and cultures, but even here, there may be sharp disagreements about the extent of the rule. As the great cultural anthropologist E. Westermarck pointed out:

> In spite of the great similarity of moral commandments, there is at the same time a difference between the regard for life, property, truth, and the general well-being of a neighbour which displays itself in savage rules of morality and that which is found among ourselves. . . . Primitive peoples carefully distinguish between an act of homicide committed within their own community and one where the victim is a stranger: while the former is in ordinary circumstances disapproved of, the latter is in most cases allowed and often considered worthy of praise. (*Ethical Relativity*, p. 197)

And even if we consider only "more advanced" societies, you can find disagreement as to whether this principle extends to fetuses (consider the great dispute about abortion) and to higher animals (consider the dispute over vegetarianism). There are many other rules that different societies disagree about entirely.

These disagreements among societies and cultures about moral rules have led many to claim that the appeal to moral rules is irrational. We cannot know, they say, which moral rules are correct (the position of *moral skepticism*). Some even claim that there is really no such thing as a correct moral rule (the position of *moral nihilism*). Now it is obvious that the mere fact that societies disagree does not call for either moral skepticism or moral nihilism, but it does at least raise in our minds certain obvious questions: How can we tell which moral rules are correct? Do our moral beliefs rest solely upon our social training or can the moral rules we believe in be defended rationally? In trying to answer these questions, philosophers and moralists have appealed to self-evidence, to revelation, and to the general consequences of following these rules. Let us look at each of these answers separately.

The philosopher John Locke maintained that we can derive correct moral principles from self-evident truths. He wrote:

> I doubt not but from self-evident propositions, by necessary consequences, as incontestible as those in mathematics, the measures of right and wrong might be made out, to anyone that will apply himself with the same indifferency and attention to the one as he does to the other of these sciences. . . . 'Where there is no property there is no injustice' is a proposition as certain as any demonstration in Euclid: for the idea to which the name 'injustice' is given being the invasion or violation of that right, it is evident that these ideas, being thus established, and these names annexed to them, I can as certainly know this proposition to be true, as that a triangle has three angles equal to two right ones.

MORAL RULES AND THEIR EXCEPTIONS

But most philosophers have doubted that moral truths are self-evident. After all, in the light of anthropological findings, it would seem that what is self-evident to one society is not necessarily self-evident to another. And even within a given society, moral rules change over the centuries. What is thought at one time to be self-evidently true is challenged as false at another time. Consider sexual prohibitions. Those that were once thought to be appropriate, and self-evidently so, are now widely rejected. In the light of all this, does the fact that a rule *now* seems *to us* to be self-evidently true stand up as a proof that it really is true?

Moral rules have frequently been based on religious teachings and revelations. But it is hard to see how religion can philosophically validate our beliefs in moral rules. After all, the revelations of different religions, as well as their moral rules, often conflict. So it looks as though the revelations need validating as well. (We will return to this question in Chapter 6.)

Rejecting these sources then, many philosophers have found the validity of our moral rules in human experience. For, quite simply, human experience has taught us that following these rules leads to the best consequences. In other words, many philosophers have suggested that our moral rules are validated by the way they work. To quote John Stuart Mill:

> During all that time [the whole duration of the human species] mankind have been learning by experience the tendencies of action; on which all the prudence as well as the morality of life are dependent. People talk as if the commencement of this course of experience had hitherto been put off, and as if, at the moment when some man feels tempted to meddle with the property or life of another, he had to begin considering for the first time whether murder and theft are injurious to human happiness . . . mankind must by this time have acquired positive beliefs as to the effects of some actions on their happiness; and the beliefs which have thus come down are the rules of morality for the multitude. . . . (*Utilitarianism,* chapter 2).

Suppose we agree for now that moral rules are validated, if at all, if beneficial consequences result from following them. But now we will have to face the following claim: rules are not really fundamental to morality. The ultimate test of the rightness and wrongness of our actions is their consequences. If the consequences are good, then the action is right, no matter what moral rules may say. To quote J. J. C. Smart:

> Suppose that there is a rule R and that in 99 percent of the cases the best possible results are obtained by acting in accordance with

R. Then clearly R is a useful rule of thumb; if we have not time or are not impartial enough to assess the consequences of an action it is an extremely good bet that the thing to do is to act in accordance with R. But is it not monstrous to suppose that if we have worked out the consequences and if we have perfect faith in the impartiality of our calculations, and if we know that in this instance to break R will have better results than to keep it, we should nevertheless obey the rule? Is it not to erect R into a sort of idol if we keep it when breaking it will prevent, say, some avoidable misery? Is not this a form of superstitious rule-worship (easily explicable psychologically) and not the rational thought of a philosopher. ("Extreme and Restricted Utilitarianism," *Philosophical Quarterly* (1956)).

In order to summarize our discussion so far, we need to make some technical distinctions. Some moral systems are called *deontological* moral systems. These systems claim that the morality of an action depends upon its relation to a system of moral rules. Other moral systems are called *teleological,* or *consequentialist,* moral systems. They claim that the morality of an action ultimately rests upon its consequences. We have seen a number of reasons for preferring consequentialism. To begin with, consequentialism is able to deal with exceptions and conflicting rules. But we have seen another, perhaps more important reason, too. If, as it seems, moral rules are valid only according to their consequences, doesn't this show that consequences are the ultimate basis of rightness and wrongness?

1.2 CONSEQUENTIALISM

As we have seen, the basic thesis of consequentialism is that the rightness or wrongness of a particular action is ultimately determined by its consequences. But this means that a consequentialist has to commit himself or herself to several highly controversial beliefs. The first is that the end (the consequence) justifies the means (the action). As Joseph Fletcher once wrote:

> . . . it is amazing that Christian ethics down through the centuries should have accepted almost unanimously the sententious doctrine that "the end does not justify the means." We have to ask now, "if the end does not justify the means, what does?" The answer is, obviously, "Nothing!" Indeed, unless justified by some end in view, any action is literally meaning less—i.e., means-less, merely random, pointless. (*Moral Responsibility*, pp. 21-22)

MORAL RULES AND THEIR EXCEPTIONS

A second controversial belief is that rightness or wrongness depends upon the situation or circumstances surrounding the act. For the same action performed in different circumstances will have different consequences. For this reason consequentialism is often called *situation ethics*. To quote Fletcher once more:

> Only the obligation is absolute—the obligation to stand by our decision—but the decisions themselves are relative to the situation. The metaphysical moralist with his intrinsic values and laws says, "Do what is right and let the chips fall where they may." The situational moralist says, "Whether what you do is right or not depends precisely upon where the chips fall." (*ibid.*, p. 26)

In the light of all this, it is clear that consequentialism gets close to the roots of morality. It is therefore deserving of a very careful evaluation. To do this, we must first examine its theses more carefully.

According to the consequentialist, when we face a moral dilemma, we have to evaluate the different actions open to us. Each of these actions has certain consequences. And the right action is the one with the best consequences. Two questions then arise: Best for whom? Best by what standard? Let us look at these questions.

Best for whom? There are two common answers to this question. One, the *egoist* answer, is: "best for the individual who has to perform the action." According to the egoists, the right action for you to perform in a given case is the action that will yield the best consequences for you. The other answer which may be called the *altruist* answer, is: "best for *all* individuals affected by the action." According to the altruists, the right action for you to perform in a given case is the action that will yield the best consequences for all concerned.

A good expression of the egoist position has been given by Nathaniel Brandon:

> The clash between egoism and altruism lies in their conflicting answers to these questions. Egoism holds that man is an end in himself; altruism holds that man is a means to the ends of others. Egoism holds, that, morally, the beneficiary of an action should be the person who acts; altruism holds that, morally, the beneficiary of an action should be someone other than the person who acts. . . . Because a genuinely selfish man chooses his goals by the guidance of reason—and because the interests of rational men do not clash—other men may often benefit from his actions. But the benefit of other men is not his primary purpose or goal; his *own* benefit is his primary purpose and the conscious goal directing his action. (in Ayn Rand's *Virtue of Selfishness*, pp. 57-8)

This quotation hints at a deeper reason why egoists oppose altruism. They feel that altruism commands our servitude to others; we must benefit others at a cost to ourselves.

There are two common objections to egoism. The first claims that, as a selfish morality it leads to unacceptable consequences. Richard Garner and Bernard Rosen state this objection:

> Suppose that it is to S's interest to refrain from paying his debts, to kill his wife and children, or even to annihilate the citizens of the United States; according to statement 5 [the version of egoism they are considering] he would have the right to do all these things. Certainly no one who was not blinded by an adherence to ethical egoism would be willing to assert that S did in fact have the right to do these things. (*Moral Philosophy,* p. 51)

Egoists would, of course, deny that their theory has such consequences. They would insist that a proper understanding of self-interest would show that such a case is not at all possible. But most philosophers have felt otherwise.

The other objection to egoism is that it breaks the good into fragments. It is irrational to claim that one part of the good (the good for me) is worthwhile and should be pursued while another part of the good (the good for others) is not worthwhile and should not be pursued. As Henry Sidgwick put it:

> . . . by considering the relation of the integrant parts to the whole and to each other, I obtain the self-evident principle that the good of any one individual is of no more importance, from the point of view (if I may say so) of the Universe, than the good of any others; unless, that is, there are special grounds for believing that more good is likely to be realised in the one case than in the other. And it is evident to me that as a rational being I am bound to aim at good generally,—not merely at a particular part of it. (*Methods of Ethics,* Book III)

For these reasons, most philosophers have been altruists and have maintained that one must consider the consequences of one's actions for all involved. But it must be remembered that this is not a doctrine of total self-sacrifice. After all, you are affected by your actions, so the consequences for you certainly count. John Stuart Mill, in discussing utilitarianism, a version of altruism that we shall discuss below, put this point as follows:

> The utilitarian morality does recognize in human beings the power

of sacrificing their own greatest good for the good of others. It only refuses to admit that the sacrifice is itself a good. A sacrifice that does not increase or tend to increase the sum total of happiness, it considers as wasted. . . . As between his own happiness and that of others, utilitarianism requires him to be as strictly impartial as a disinterested and benevolent spectator. (*Utilitarianism,* chapter 2)

When altruists talk about taking into account the consequences of one's actions for all affected by them, they normally have in mind the consequences for people now living. But some of the more perceptive altruists have seen that this may be a mistake. Henry Sidgwick, for example, wrote:

Are we to extend our concern to all the beings capable of pleasure and pain whose feelings are affected by our conduct or are we to confine our view to human happiness? The former view is the one adopted by Bentham and Mill, and (I believe) by the Utilitarian school generally: and it is obviously most in accordance with the universality that is characteristic of their principle. . . . But even if we limit our attention to human beings, the extent of the subjects of happiness is not yet quite determinate. In the first place, it may be asked, how far are we to consider the interests of posterity when they seem to conflict with those of existing human beings? It seems, however, clear . . . that the interests of posterity must concern a Utilitarian as much as those of his contemporaries, except insofar as the effect of his actions upon posterity—and even the existence of human beings to be affected—must necessarily be more uncertain. (*Methods of Ethics,* Book IV)

These two groups, animals and future generations, were neglected in traditional moral thinking, and Sidgwick is certainly right in suggesting that the altruist may have to consider their interests as well.

It should be noted, moreover, that these questions are no longer of merely theoretical interest. It may well be the case, for example, that one of the roots of the environmental crisis is precisely the attitude that fails to take into account the interests of future generations. The attitude encourages the use of our natural resources at a wasteful pace and the pollution of the environment without any concern for what it will be like in the future. It may well be the case, then, that the altruist claim, the claim that we should consider the consequences of our actions for all affected by them, must be understood in a far wider sense than it has been in the past.

Best by what standard? What standard do we use in evaluating the consequences—whether for ourselves or others—of our actions? To put the question another way, what, precisely, is the good that the consequentialist would have us maximize when we perform our actions?

One classical answer is given by *hedonism*. This is a belief that the one and only standard to be used in evaluating consequences is the pleasure produced. In other words, pleasure is the one and only good. The thesis of hedonism has been one of the most controversial in the history of philosophy, so let us look at it carefully.

At first glance, the hedonistic thesis is absurd. Aren't there many other goods besides pleasure? Isn't health a good? How about knowledge and beauty? And so on. Hedonists are well aware of this obvious objection, and they attempt to meet it by distinguishing between intrinsic goods (ends) and extrinsic goods (means). According to the hedonist, when he says that the one and only good is pleasure, he means that it is the only intrinsic good. All of these other goods are extrinsic goods (means). They are good ony because they are means to pleasure.

Perhaps a few examples will make this clearer. Suppose that a doctor cures a patient. We would in most cases suppose that his action was morally right. The hedonistic consequentialist would say that this is so only because such an action leads to the best consequence. But the consequence he has in mind is not the patient's being restored to health; it is instead the resulting pleasure experienced by the patient, his family, etc. The patient's being restored to health is merely an instrument for the achievement of good. It is merely a means to the pleasure that follows.

Hedonists would say knowledge is a similar kind of good. For the hedonist, knowledge is merely an instrumental good. But it is a valuable instrumental good (1) because knowledge can be used in life to produce much pleasure and (2) because we get pleasure from the very act of acquiring knowledge. The hedonist says similar things about the appreciation of beauty, the experience of love, and so forth.

In short, then, the hedonistic consequentialist says that the right action is the one that produces the most intrinsic good, which he identifies with the most pleasure. Such a view seems to assume that different pleasures can be compared with one another, that one can conceive of one pleasure as greater than another. That is exactly how the classical hedonists conceived of pleasure. One of them, Jeremy Bentham, even proposed a "calculus" of pleasures:

> To a person considered by himself, the value of a pleasure or pain considered by itself, will be greater or less, according to the four following circumstances: 1. Its intensity. 2. Its duration. 3. Its certainty or uncertainty. 4. Its propinquity or remoteness. . . . When the value of any pleasure or pain is considered for the purpose of estimating the tendency of any act by which it is produced, there

> are two other circumstances that are to be taken into the account; these are, 5. Its fecundity, or the chance it has of being followed by sensations of the same kind. . . . 6. Its purity, or the chance it has of not being followed by sensations of the opposite kind. . . . Take an account 1. of the value of each distinguishable pleasure which appears to be produced by it in the first instance. 2. of the value of each pain which appears to be produced by it in the first instance. 3. of the value of each pleasure which appears to be produced by it after the first. . . . 4. of the value of each pain which appears to be produced by it after the first. . . . Sum up all the values of all the pleasures on the one side and those of all the pains on the others. (*Principles of Morals and Legislation*, chapter 4)

Other hedonists, like Henry Sidgwick, were more skeptical about the possibility of such calculations.

> Is there any reason to suppose that the mind is ever in such a state as to be a perfectly neutral and colourless medium for imagining all kinds of pleasures? . . . Is it not probable that there is always some bias of the kind? that we are always more in tune for some pleasures? . . . It must, I think, be admitted that the exact cognition of the place of each kind of feeling in a scale of desirability, measured positively and negatively from a zero of perfect indifference, is at best an ideal to which we can never tell how closely we approximate. (*Methods of Ethics*, Book II, chapter 3)

Not all consequentialists have been hedonists. Those who have opposed hedonism have raised two fundamental objections to it. First, they have claimed, there are pleasures that are not at all good. Consider, for example, a sadist who is beating up his victim. We can all agree that the sadist's action is wrong. But why? According to the hedonist, the answer is that although the pleasure the sadist gets is intrinsically good, the action is wrong because the pain he inflicts outweighs the pleasure he gets. It is just this point that the nonhedonist objects to. He feels that the sadist's pleasure is intrinsically bad, not intrinsically good, and that hedonism is therefore incorrect. W. D. Ross presented a version of this argument:

> We have a decided conviction that there are bad pleasures and (though this is less obvious) that there are good pains. We think that the pleasure taken either by the agent or by a spectator in, for instance, a lustful or cruel action is bad; and we think it a good thing that people should be pained rather than pleased by contemplating vice or misery. (*The Right and the Good*, pp. 136-37)

The second objection to hedonism is that there are other intrinsic goods besides pleasure. In particular, nonhedonists claim that knowledge, beauty, and virtue are among the intrinsic goods, and are not just the extrinsic goods that the hedonist pictures them as being. This is a difficult dispute to settle, since both sides agree that the things in question are good. They merely disagree about why they are good. There seems to be some force in Ross's presentation of this argument:

> If anyone is inclined to doubt this and to think that, say, pleasure alone is intrinsically good, it seems to me enough to ask the question whether, of two states of the universe holding equal amounts of pleasure, we should really think no better of one in which the actions and dispositions of all the persons in it were thoroughly virtuous than of one in which they were highly vicious. To this there can be only one answer . . . even if we could not imagine any circumstances in which two states of the universe equal in pleasantness but unequal in virtue could exist, the supposition is a legitimate one, since it is only intended to bring before us in a vivid way what is really self-evident, that virtue is good apart from its consequences. (*ibid.*, pp. 134-35)

Let us see where we stand. We have considered, in this section, the two fundamental questions faced by all consequentialists: in judging actions by their consequences, what standard of value do we use and whose interests are we concerned with? We have seen the advantages of altruism over egoism and of nonhedonism over hedonism. We can combine all of these results into the position of *ideal utilitarianism*. In this view, the right action is the one that will produce the most intrinsic good (here, this is not necessarily the most pleasure) taking into account the interests of all concerned. It is this version of consequentialism that we will look at next.

1.3 IDEAL UTILITARIANISM AND ITS DIFFICULTIES

Ideal utilitarianism is in many ways a very attractive doctrine. It combines all of the advantages of consequentialism, altruism, and nonhedonism. As a version of consequentialism, it can deal with the problems posed by exceptions to moral rules and by conflicting moral rules. As a version of altruism, it does not lead to the objectionably selfish features of egoism, yet it does allow the individual to consider his own interests as well as the interests of others. And as a version of nonhedonism, it is not committed to saying that pleasures alone—and all of them—are intrinsi-

MORAL RULES AND THEIR EXCEPTIONS

cally good. The acceptance of ideal utilitarianism in recent years is not surprising.

Despite its deserved popularity, it is not without difficulties. In particular, three serious objections have been raised against it. In this section, we will examine each of them.

1. *The objection from cases where other actions count.* Consider an example. We normally believe that a citizen in a democratic society has a moral obligation to vote, and that it is wrong to refrain from voting unless there is a serious reason (e.g., sickness). Now suppose that we try to defend this moral belief by using ideal utilitarianism. Difficulties immediately come up. After all, imagine someone who could vote but feels lazy and would prefer to stay home and rest. Two options are open to him. He can stay home or he can vote. The good consequences of the former are apparent; he would be satisfying his desire to rest. But what are the good consequences of the latter? Voting doesn't seem to have any obvious ones. After all, unless it is a very special election, his vote will make absolutely no difference to the outcome. So it seems that ideal utilitarians, like other consequentialists, would have to conclude that the right thing to do is to stay home. It is this kind of conclusion that leads many to reject ideal utilitarianism.

Utilitarians have tried to meet this objection, however. The objection, as stated, fails to take into account certain subtle consequences, they say. For example, your not voting may lead many others to stay home as well, and the total effect could be very bad. The democratic system itself might be weakened. The trouble with this response is that it only applies in some cases. For example, if you are a leading citizen and your failure to vote is heavily publicized, then these bad results may occur. They will not occur in other cases. Yet a moral obligation to vote seems to remain. So this reply won't do.

There is an important thing to notice about the voting case, and others like it. If everyone refrained from voting, terrible consequences would indeed occur. Our whole democratic system would collapse. Yet, when a particular individual refrains from voting, his action has none of these bad consequences. According to ideal utilitarianism, then, it seems permissible for him to refrain from voting. The trouble with ideal utilitarianism (and indeed with all consequentialism) is that it allows us to consider the consequences only of the *particular* action. It does not allow us to consider the consequences of the whole *class* of actions to which the particular one belongs. As Jonathan Harrison has written:

> There are some actions which we think we have a duty to do, although they themselves produce no good consequences, because such actions would produce good consequences if they were gener-

ally practiced. There are some actions which we think we have a duty to refrain from doing, even though they themselves produce no harmful consequences, because such actions would produce harmful consequences if the performance of them became the general rule. . . . These two duties cannot be derived from the duty of setting a good example, or of refraining from setting a bad example, for I should still feel them incumbent upon me, even if no one were to know. . . . Such facts, if they are facts, have not been entirely neglected by utilitarians. . . . But utilitarians have not always realized that, in admitting that the performance of such actions is a duty, they are departing from, or at least modifying, utilitarianism. ("Utilitarianism, Universalization, and our duty to be just." *Proceedings of the Aristotelean Society* (1952-53))

2. *The objection from justice and right.* Utilitarianism is concerned with producing the most intrinsic good. It doesn't, however, have anything to say about how that good is to be distributed. This fact about utilitarianism gives rise to an additional set of objections to it. Let us begin once more with a few examples.

example a

There is an ongoing debate in our society about the minimal assets to which each citizen is entitled. The basic idea is that justice demands that each citizen share equally in certain basic goods. There is general agreement that these should include certain basic freedoms (e.g., freedom from enslavement) and certain basic necessities (e.g., food). The disagreement is about what else should be involved. We will be considering such disputes in a later chapter, also. All we need to notice now is that these ideas of justice and equality seem to be based upon other moral considerations and not upon the question of maximizing the total amount of intrinsic good. It seems, therefore, that ideal utilitarianism (and all consequentialism) is at best an incomplete moral theory.

example b

When awards—for example, grades or salary raises—are handed out, we naturally feel that they should be distributed according to merit. The notion of merit is complicated, but it probably should include such features as results achieved, effort expended, improvement over a period of time, and so on. We feel that an individual has a right to the awards he merits. It would be wrong to take them away from him to give to others. But this, again, seems to be a moral consideration which is independent of the question of maximizing the total amount of intrinsic good.

Now, utilitarians have generally claimed that such moral considerations are misleading. According to utilitarianism, these considerations of justice and equal rights are really based upon maximizing the total amount of intrinsic good. And, in fact, we *ought* to distribute basic goods equally, according to the utilitarian, because doing so maximizes intrinsic good. When the slave is deprived of his basic freedoms, the resulting gain to the slaveholder does not make up for the loss of intrinsic goods suffered by the slave. Similarly, we ought to distribute awards according to merit because doing so maximizes intrinsic good. After all, says the utilitarian, the merit system encourages people to produce better results by rewarding them for doing so. In short, then, utilitarians feel that they can provide a utilitarian basis for these other moral considerations.

Most philosophers have felt, however, that this position is inadequate. They have felt, for example, that slavery is wrong whether or not the loss to the slave is greater than the gain to the slaveholder. In fact, they would say, the gain to the slaveholder is morally irrelevant. One philosopher, John Rawls, has put the point as follows:

> I am not, of course, suggesting the absurdity that the classical utilitarians approved of slavery. I am only rejecting a type of argument which their view allows them to use in support of their disapproval of it. The conception of justice as derivative from efficiency [i.e., from maximizing intrinsic good] . . . cannot account for the fact that slavery is always unjust, nor for the fact that it would be recognized as irrelevant in defeating the accusation of injustice for one person to say to another . . . that nevertheless it allowed of the greatest satisfaction of desire. ("Justice as Reciprocity" in *Mill's Utilitarianism*, p. 264)

3. *The objection from special obligations.* Suppose that you promise to give me a sum of money on a certain date and that I rely on that promise. Normally, your promise is binding. You would not be relieved of your obligation to give me that money merely because you can produce more good by giving it to someone else. Philosophers put this point by saying that you have a special obligation to the person to whom you have made a promise. Such an obligation takes precedence over other possible demands. All this does not mean that you must always keep a promise. In case of certain emergencies, of course, you would be relieved of such an obligation. A special obligation simply means an obligation with a high priority, an obligation that we only owe to some people, and an obligation that we are relieved of only by real emergencies.

There are many kinds of special obligation. There are the obligations of the parent to the child and of the child to the parent. Friends have special obligations to each other, and there is the special obligation of gratitude to those who have aided us. Naturally there are questions about each of these special obligations—about their extent, their force, and so on. We are not now concerned with these questions. What we are concerned with here is whether the existence of special obligations challenges ideal utilitarianism.

The existence of these obligations certainly seems to conflict with ideal utilitarianism (and, indeed, with all types of consequentialism). After all, another way of stating the utilitarian position is this: that our moral obligation is to maximize intrinsic good, and any unit of intrinsic good must count equally, no matter who has it. But, if this is so, how can we give precedence to some of our obligations? Moreover, as we saw in the case of promises, the mere fact that we can produce more intrinsic good by breaking our promise does not relieve us from the obligation. This is in direct conflict with the utilitarian view that we should always maximize the good. A. I. Melden puts this point very well by the use of a graphic example:

> Two explorers are at the North Pole. One has been badly injured and cannot make it back to his base. For the other to attempt to bring him back is to preclude any possibility for his own survival. The injured person persuades his companion that he ought to be left to his fate; but, before he is left to die, he gives his partner a sum of money and makes him promise to use it, upon his return to civilization, to pay for his son's education. The survivor returns to civilization. What obligation, if any, does he have by virtue of his promise? Now, if utilitarianism is correct, the obligation to keep one's promise is determined wholly by the experience—goods produced or likely to be produced by the action. It would seem therefore that nothing that has happened in the past and only what can be expected in the future is relevant. . . . Hence the survivor ought (since ought is wholly determined by consequences) to ignore the promise and act in just the way he ought to act if he were suddenly to come upon the money through sheerest accident. But this does violence to our moral sensibilities. ("Two Comments on Utilitarianism," *Philosophical Review* (1951))

1.4 A RETURN TO MORAL RULES

Let us see where we stand. In the first two sections of this chapter, we used a process of elimination to arrive at a moral theory, ideal utilitarianism, that seemed satisfactory. But despite its many attractive features, we have found serious objections to it. What shall we do?

There are some philosophers who feel that we should stick to utilitarianism, anyway. They feel that the objections raised in section 1.3 are not really convincing. After all, they argue, all these objections show is that utilitarianism conflicts with some of our views—about such things as justice and special obligations. But the most that can show is that one side of the conflict is wrong. And perhaps it is the commonly held views which are mistaken while utilitarianism is correct.

One such philosopher is J. J. C. Smart. In a famous passage, he argues very strongly for keeping utilitarianism in the face of these objections.

> I wish to repudiate at the outset that milk and water approach which describes itself sometimes as "investigating what is implicit in the in the common moral consciousness" and sometimes as "investigating how people normally talk about morality." We have only to read the newspaper correspondence about capital punishment . . . to realise that the common moral consciousness is in part made up of superstitious elements, of morally bad elements, and of logically confused elements. . . . "This obligation to obey a rule" says Nowell-Smith [*Ethics*, p. 239] "does not, *in the opinion of ordinary men*" [my italics] "rest on the beneficial consequences of obeying it in a particular case." What does this prove? Surely it is more than likely that ordinary men are confused here. Philosophers should be able to examine the question more rationally.

Smart has not, however, carried the day. Philosophers generally have felt far more sure of our intuitions and commonly held beliefs than about the rationality of any moral theory. In short, they have felt the force of the objections we discussed above, and have rejected utilitarianism. But what does this mean for moral theory?

Well, going back to the objections, we see that they apply to every form of consequentialism. It follows therefore that what must be rejected is the whole consequentialist approach. What is needed is a non-consequentialist morality.

We must be careful about drawing conclusions that are too extreme. It does not follow from anything we have said that a consideration of consequences is irrelevant in morality. But, we should see that, even if it is relevant, other factors must be relevant as well. From what we have said, it must follow that maximizing intrinsic good is not the whole of morality and that questions of justice, special obligations, and so on, are also part of morality.

In recent years, philosophers have turned to these other factors and have tried to see how all factors can be combined in a single moral system. But, so far, no widely accepted solution has emerged. What we shall see in the rest of this chapter is just one attempt at sketching such a solution.

Suppose that we give up consequentialism and return to the deontological approach to morality. This, we hope, will contain rules that can take these different factors into account. What are the main problems that we will face? As we saw in the first section of this chapter, there will be two main problems: the problem of the source of our moral rules and the problem of exceptional cases (especially those involving conflicting rules). I think we will ultimately find that Locke was right and that both of these problems can be—and usually are—resolved by self-evident truths which we can learn through intuition. We shall argue that, by truly understanding moral intuition, we can construct a deontological system that avoids the difficulties of consequentialism.

Let's begin to sketch our theory by outlining a set of moral views on one important problem: the problem of euthanasia. Our concern here is not with their correctness (although I believe that they are correct). Our main concern will be with the way this set of views illustrate the role of intuition in constructing a moral system.

The main problems surrounding euthanasia arise because any act of euthanasia deprives the person being killed of something to which he has a right, namely, his life. Now, in general, people can willingly give up something to which they have a right, and, in fact, they can request that they be so deprived. Unless there are special circumstances, the person who carries out such a request has done no wrong. Returning then to the issue of euthanasia, if an individual consents to giving up his life, or actively requests that his life be taken, then (unless there are special circumstances) the taking of his life is permissible. Let me just add that in order for the consent or request to be in effect, the individual must be competent and he cannot have been forced or deceived when he gave his permission. All of this means that the standard notions about euthanasia have to be rethought. It is not relevant for us to consider whether the individual gains or loses, because it is his choice and not ours. For the same reason, the possibility of an unusual recovery or the use of pain-killing drugs are also irrelevant here. Nor need we consider the particular means of ending the person's life (direct vs. indirect). The legitimacy of the means will be determined by the nature of his consent. Our sole concern in determining the permissibility of the act of euthanasia is whether there has been an *efficacious consent*.

But what if the individual is unable to request or consent to euthanasia? Does our approach mean that euthanasia would not be permissible in such cases? What about the use of pain-killing drugs in such cases? That, too, may shorten the life of the individual. Won't we have to appeal to some different principles to solve these problems? I do not think so, for there are two additional points to be noted. First of all, individuals can, and often do, give consent in advance to the loss of something to which they have a right. This at least suggests the possibility of arranging for euthanasia in advance. Secondly, we should consider—but more hesitantly—the possibility of relying upon hypothetical consent, that is, upon our judgment that the individual would consent if he could. It is, after all, that type of consent that is assumed in treating emergency patients whose consent to being treated cannot be obtained.

What do we learn about the role of moral intuitions by examining these views about euthanasia? It seems to be that two crucial lessons emerge.

1. We must distinguish two types of moral intuitions: intuitions about the truth of certain general claims and intuitions about what is right or wrong in particular cases. The first type of intuition is our source of knowledge of such basic truths as the fact that each human being has a right to life and that it is very wrong to deprive a person of that right. The role played by the second type of intuition is more subtle, so we must look at it more carefully. To begin with, we can collect intuitions about particular cases and use them to derive certain general propositions that cannot themselves be found by intuition. Thus, for example, it is not intuitively evident that people can consent to being deprived of their rights or that those who then deprive them do not act wrongly. But as one reflects on particular cases that *are* evident (e.g., I can take your book if you consent), such principles become more and more plausible. Second, we can use these intuitions about particular cases to refine our already accepted general principles. In this way, we use intuition to refine intuition. Thus, we can use our intuition to find that it is okay for a doctor to operate on an unconscious patient on the grounds that the patient would consent if he could. Then, we can use that intuition as the basis for saying that hypothetical consent is all that may be required in certain cases.

2. In approaching a particular moral problem, even one involving exceptions and conflicting rules, we should first collect all relevant data. This includes, besides factual information, such things as self-evident general truths, general principles derived from intuitively clear cases, and any intuition-based changes in these principles. This should provide sufficient data to resolve the moral issues. In the case of euthanasia, what will be relevant are the principles concerning an individual's *efficacious*

consent to being deprived of his rights. Taking note of these, we can see our way to an argument justifying certain acts of euthanasia. Usually, however, there will be unresolved aspects of the moral issues. In such cases, we must seek out still further intuitions from analogous cases. These will enable us to resolve our problems by a further refinement of our principles. This is the very process that helped us see certain acts of euthanasia as being justified by hypothetical consent.

In short, then, we see emerging here a methodology for a deontological moral system, a methodology grounded on moral intuition. The set of rules that will emerge will no doubt be very complicated, far more so than the simple-minded rules that we normally think of. But it may well be the case that only such complicated sets of rules can deal with the many tricky problems of exceptions and conflicting moral rules. In any event, we have the outline of an answer to the problems that are supposed to be so troublesome for a deontological system.

There are, no doubt, many who will object to this dependence upon moral intuitions. Moral intuitions, they will say, vary too much among people and change too much over time. Such intuitions could not, therefore, be a reliable source of moral knowledge.

I freely concede that there is a problem here, but I feel that its importance can be overestimated. To begin with, if there are conflicting intuitions, we can always search out other ones which will enable us to resolve the issues at hand. (More experiences will also help, since they play such an important role in sharpening our intuitions.) If we cannot find the intuitions we need, then, at least for the moment, the issues will have to remain unresolved. But this method will often work. Secondly, the fact that intuitions change should bother only those who are seeking a final and infallible source of moral knowledge. Others, who are seeking a more experientially based source of moral understanding, may welcome this fact about moral intuitions. That moral intuitions change is often a reflection of the fact that our intuitions are responsive to new situations and to the better understanding that arises out of new experiences.

We can tentatively conclude with this summary of what we have found: Morality must be understood as a complex set of rules, based upon intuition, that determine the rightness and wrongness of our actions, so consequentialist approaches, such as situation ethics, are fundamentally in error.

2

Morality and Rational Self-Interest

Suppose for a moment that you are competing for a very important job. This job would advance your career considerably. The final choice is between you and one other candidate. Suppose, moreover, that you have an opportunity to spread a vicious lie about your opponent. If the lie is believed, you'll get the job. Why shouldn't you spread the lie? No doubt doing so would be morally wrong. But isn't it foolish to be concerned with morality when your career and so much of your own happiness is at stake? If it is not foolish to be concerned about morality in this situation, why isn't it?

In situations like this, one course of action seems to be morally correct while a different course of action seems to be in one's own self-interest. The question that naturally arises, then, is which course of action to follow. Should one do the right action even at a great cost to onself? If so why? What rational purpose can there be for sacrificing one's self-interest?

Philosophers have been troubled by this question for a long time. It is not surprising, because this is a dilemma faced by all of us on many occasions throughout our lives. Indeed, this problem is at the root of the first great philosophical classic, Plato's *Republic*. At the beginning of that book, one of the main characters makes the following claim:

> All men believe in their hearts that injustice is far more profitable to the individual than justice. . . . If you could imagine anyone

obtaining the power of becoming invisible, and never doing any wrong or taking what was another's, he would be thought by the onlookers to be a most wretched idiot, although they would praise him to one another's face.

In order to strengthen this argument, a mythical story is told, the story of Gyges the Lydian.

> They relate that he was a shepherd in the service of the ruler at that time of Lydia, and that after a great deluge of rain and an earthquake the ground opened and a chasm appeared in the place where he was pasturing, and they say that he saw and wondered and went down into the chasm. And the story goes that he beheld other marvels there and a hollow bronze horse with little doors, and that he peeped in and saw a corpse within, as it seemed, of more than mortal stature, and that there was nothing else but a gold ring on its hand, which he took off, and so went forth. And when the shepherds held their customary assembly to make their monthly report to the king about the flocks, he also attended, wearing the ring. So as he sat there it chanced that he turned the collet of the ring toward himself, toward the inner part of his hand, and when this took place they say that he became invisible to those who sat by him and they spoke of him as absent, and that he was amazed, and again fumbling with the ring turned the collet outward and so became visible. On noting this he experimented with the ring to see if it possessed this virtue, and he found the result to be that when he turned the collet inward he became invisible, and when outward visible, and becoming aware of this, he immediately managed things so that he became one of the messengers who went up to the king, and on coming there he seduced the king's wife and with her aid set upon the king and slew him and possessed his kingdom.

> If now there should be two such rings, and the just man should put on one and the unjust the other, no one could be found, it would seem, of such adamantine temper as to persevere in justice and endure to refrain his hands from the possessions of others and not touch them, though he might with impunity take what he wished even from the market place, and enter into houses and lie with whom he pleased, and slay and loose from bonds whomsoever he would, and in all other things conduct himself among mankind as the equal of a god. And in so acting he would do no differently from the other man, but both would pursue the same course. And yet this is a great proof, one might argue, that no one is just of his own will but only from constraint, in the belief that justice is not his personal good, inasmuch as every man, does wrong. For that there is far more profit for him personally in injustice than in justice is what every man believes, and believes truly, as the proponent of this theory will maintain.

Obviously, no one possesses Gyges' magic ring. But we all have opportunities to profit by acting immorally. In all of these cases, we have to ask ourselves "why should I be moral?"

2.1 THE CONVENTIONAL ANSWERS

There are a variety of conventional attempts to meet this problem. The simplest is the plain denial that it exists. Consider, for example, the familiar maxim "Honesty is the best policy." This and other such sayings essentially claim that, if we look at the matter fully, considering long-range as well as short-range considerations, we will see that our self-interest is best served by doing the right thing. There is clearly some truth to these maxims. There are cases in which doing the wrong action will clearly hurt us in the long run.

For example, many students know that it is often possible to get a good grade, with much less work, by cheating on an exam. And this dishonest course of action might at first seem to be in their self-interest. But look carefully at the long-range consequences of cheating. Suppose, for example, you really need to know the material you were being tested on at some later time, perhaps in another course, or outside of school. You may lose out then because you cheat now. Marital infidelity is another example. Many people have found they can be unfaithful to their spouses and "get away with it." The immediate pleasures obtained from doing so have made it seem as though this dishonest act is really in their self-interest. But again, one should carefully examine the long-range consequences, for example, the psychological effects on one's relationship with one's spouse. This might well reveal that faithfulness is really in one's true interest.

There may well be many such cases in which "honesty pays." But it would be rash to conclude that this is true in all cases. At first glance, in fact, it would seem that there are many cases in which the opposite is true. Consider some of your actions that you know to have been wrong. Did you really always lose because you did them? If you didn't lose, then wasn't it the smart thing to do? Why shouldn't we perform the wrong action in such cases?

Let's consider these questions more closely. First of all, does the fear of being caught and punished enter into the issue? Perhaps we shouldn't do the wrong action because the punishment we will receive for doing it outweighs any gain we receive? I suspect that this answer is widely believed. It seems, for example, to lie behind the belief that a strong system of criminal justice will deter crime. The trouble with this answer is that it assumes that we will always be caught and punished.

It doesn't address itself to the cases in which we have a good chance of getting away with our wrongdoings. When the probability of being caught is low enough, and the gain from wrongdoing large enough, it would seem rational to gamble on getting away with the wrong action.

The moral training which many parents give their children unfortunately emphasizes just this possibility of being caught and punished. This leads children, not unreasonably, to conclude that there is an eleventh commandment: "Thou shall not get caught." Children conclude that being moral is appropriate only when there is little chance of getting away with being immoral. If we don't want children to draw that conclusion, we must train them otherwise. But we must be able to give them a different reason for behaving morally—so we return to our basic question.

Things would be very different, of course, if we knew that we would *always* be caught and punished. However, the opposite is true; all too often, we have a good chance of avoiding punishment, at least the ordinary forms of punishment. This last remark will suggest to many that there may be other forms of punishment, ones that always work, and that our problem can be solved if we will turn our attention to them.

What could these super-effective forms of punishment be? One is the internal pangs of conscience. After all, say some moralists, we always know when we do wrong, and our conscience bothers us about it. The reason then for doing the right action, even if we could get away with wrongdoing, is that we will be punished by our consciences for doing the wrong action. Another kind of punishment is divine retribution. According to some religious moralists, we shouldn't do wrong, even if we can get away with it, because God will always know about it. He will punish us, if not in this life, then in the afterlife.

There is no doubt that some wrongdoers suffer greatly from pangs of conscience. But as a general solution to the question of why one should be moral, this appeal to the pangs of conscience is insufficient because: (1) it does not apply to all people, since the voice of conscience seems to be weak in many people; (2) it does not apply to all cases, since in many cases one's conscience is not particularly bothered and the gain from wrongdoing may outweigh the slight stirrings of conscience; (3) it does not take into account the way our consciences come to terms with our shortcomings. As I think we all know from our own experience, we tend to find justifications for our shortcomings, especially when they are repeated. After a while, our consciences no longer bother us. It is this malleability of conscience that makes it an uncertain basis for doing the right action.

The appeal to divine punishment is a different matter. For if God does exist and does punish all evildoers, then we always have a powerful reason—and one based on self-interest—for doing the right action. However, most philosophers have not wanted to rest the case for being moral on our desire to avoid divine retribution. To begin with, no matter how sound that case may be logically, it does not seem to be psychologically effective. Perhaps this is because divine punishment seems so far away, belonging to some unknown existence after death. At any rate, the fear of divine punishment does not deter even religious people from doing at times what they know to be wrong. Secondly, if we were to take this approach, then we would be justified in making moral sacrifices only if we could prove (or make it likely) that God exists. As we shall see in chapter 5, doing that is not so easy. It seems preferable, then, to find another basis for acting morally. Finally, and perhaps most important, this type of argument would force us to reevaluate our feelings about the nobility of moral behavior. If the reason for behaving morally is just to avoid punishment (even divine punishment), then we have no reason to treat moral self-sacrifice as a noble form of behavior.

This last point is extremely important, and we will examine other aspects of it later in this chapter and also in chapter 6. But it has a special significance in the religious context, one that should be noted now. Let us begin with an example. Suppose that someone gives a very large sum of money to a noble cause. We would normally approve of that action and think highly of the person who gave the money. The action, so to speak, raises his moral worth. But now suppose that we discover that he gave the money because (1) he was promised even more in return if he gave it, and (2) he was told that he would be severely punished if he didn't give it. We would still be glad that he gave the money (it is good, after all, for the cause to have the funds). But we would no longer think so highly of the donor. The action no longer raises his moral worth in our view. Now when the religious person says we should act out of a fear of divine punishment and a desire for divine reward, that person is advocating that we all act with motives similar to those of our "pseudo-philanthropist." And this seems a terrible thing to advocate. In short, while religious moralists may believe that God will punish the evil and reward the good, they should oppose the view that these rewards and punishments give us our reason for behaving morally.

2.2 TWO PHILOSOPHICAL THEORIES

There have been, in the history of philosophy, two especially notable attempts to deal with our problem. One is to be found in Plato's *Republic*, and the other is found in Thomas Hobbes's *Leviathan*. While these two attempts are very different, they share the theme that a proper solution to the problem must begin with an understanding of human nature.

Plato's analysis of human nature begins with a phenomenon that we are all familiar with, self-conflict. Consider the person who desires something but who recognizes that satisfying this desire would be a great mistake. Such a person both wants and doesn't want to satisfy his desire. How is this phenomenon to be explained? Plato felt that we can explain it only by supposing that the human psyche, or soul, is not a simple, unified thing. It must be composed, Plato felt, out of several potentially conflicting elements. Self-conflict comes about when these potentially conflicting elements actually do come into conflict with each other.

What different elements does Plato find in our psyche? There are three of them: desire, reason, and spirited feelings. The first two are easy to understand. Take as an example a person who wants to be unfaithful to his spouse but who knows that unbearable marital conflicts will result. This person is moved to commit adultery by desire but is moved to refrain from it by reason. This, of course, is a familiar pattern. The third element is harder to understand, but Plato seemed to have felt that it must be present in those cases where we have a spirited nonrational (not necessarily irrational) opposition to our own desires. His example of this is a person who feels a morbid desire (e.g., to see dead bodies) and a feeling of disgust at his own desire.

Plato is not alone in thinking that self-conflict can only be understood by reference to different parts of the human psyche. Indeed, a very similar approach is to be found in Freud's theory of the structure of the human personality. Freud's *id* is like Plato's desire; it is a faculty of passions and desires. Freud's *superego* is like Plato' spirited element, a faculty of strong feelings of opposition to various desires. And Freud's ego is like Plato's reason, the factor forced to consider things rationally, including the reality surrounding the person. Without overdoing the analogy, then, I think it does point out that Plato's theory of human nature is still today an appealing one.

Such a conception of human nature obviously gives rise to the question of how these different elements should relate to each other. Plato felt that this relation must be hierarchical, that reason must with the aid of our spirited element rule over desire. And he felt that this should be so because it was in the interest of the individual. Why does Plato believe this? He offers three reasons. First of all, in this way, the individual "sets in order his own inner life, and is his own master and his own law, and at peace with himself." The point seems to be this: when desires rule, a person never knows any peace. On one day, one desire rules and the person follows one course of action. The next day, a different desire rules and the person pursues still a different course of action. On still other days, no desire rules over the others, they all conflict, and the person cannot follow any consistent course of action.

The second argument for reason's ruling over desire is that the person in whom reason rules would pursue intellectual pleasures. And the pursuit of such pleasures would be in his self-interest. It would be in his self-interest because those who have experienced all the different pleasures perceive from their experiences that these intellectual pleasures are not only the most rewarding but the most pleasurable. To quote Plato:

> The three parts [of the soul] have also, it appears to me, three kinds of pleasure, one peculiar to each, and similarly three appetites and controls.
>
> What do you mean? he said.
>
> One part, we say, is that with which a man learns, one is that with which he feels anger. But the third part, owing to its manifold forms, we could not easily designate by any one distinctive name, but gave it the name of its chief and strongest element, for we called it the appetitive part because of the intensity of its appetites concerned with food and drink and love and their accompaniments, and likewise the money-loving part, because money is the chief instrument for the gratification of such desires.
>
> And rightly, he said.
>
> And if we should also say that its pleasure and its love were for gain or profit, should we not thus best bring it together under one head in our discourse so as to understand each other when we speak of this part of the soul, and justify our calling it the money-loving and gain-loving part?
>
> I, at any rate, think so, he said.
>
> And, again of the high spirited element, do we not say that it is wholly set on predominance and victory and good repute?
>
> Yes, indeed.
>
> And might we not appropriately designate it as the ambitious part and that which is covetous of honor?
>
> Most appropriately.
>
> But surely it is obvious to everyone that all the endeavor of the part by which we learn is ever toward knowledge of the truth of things, and that it least of the three is concerned for wealth and reputation.

Much the least.

Lover of learning and lover of wisdom would be suitable designations for that.

. . . . . .

Are you aware, then, said I that if you should choose to ask men of these three classes, each in turn, which is the most pleasurable of these lives, each will chiefly commend his own? The financier will affirm that in comparison with profit the pleasures of honor or of learning are of no value except in so far as they produce money.

True, he said.

And what of the lover of honor? said I. Does he not regard the pleasure that comes from money as vulgar and low, and again that of learning, save in so far as the knowledge confers honor, mere fume and moonshine.

It is so, he said.

And what, said I, are we to suppose the philosopher thinks of the other pleasures compared with the delight of knowing the truth and the reality, and being always occupied with that while he learns? Will he not think them far removed from true pleasure, and call them literally the pleasures of necessity, since he would have no use for them if necessity were not laid upon him?

We may be sure of that, he said.

Since, then, there is contention between the several types of pleasure and the lives themselves, not merely as to which is the more honorable or the more base, or the worse or the better, but which is actually the more pleasurable or free from pain, how could we determine which of them speaks most truly?

In faith, I cannot tell, he said.

Well, consider it thus. By what are things to be judged, if they are to be judged rightly? Is it not by experience, intelligence, and discussion? Or could anyone name a better criterion than these?

How could he? he said.

Observe, then. Of our three types of men, which has had the most experience of all the pleasures we mentioned? Do you think that the lover of gain by study of the very nature of truth has more experience of the pleasure that knowledge yields than the philosopher has of that which results from gain?

There is a vast difference, he said, for the one, the philosopher, must needs taste of the other two kinds of pleasure from childhood, but the lover of gain is not only under no necessity of tasting or experiencing the sweetness of the pleasure of learning the true natures of things, but he cannot easily do so even if he desires and is eager for it.

The lover of wisdom, then, said I, far surpasses the lover of gain in experience of both kinds of pleasure.

Yes, far.

And how does he compare with the lover of honor? Is he more unacquainted with the pleasure of being honored than that other with that which comes from knowledge?

Nay, honor, he said, if they achieve their several objects, attends them all, for the rich man is honored by many and the brave man and the wise, so that all are acquainted with the kind of pleasure that honor brings, but it is impossible for anyone except the lover of wisdom to have savored the delight that the contemplation of true being and reality brings.

Then, said I, so far as experience goes, he is the best judge of the three.

. . . .

There being, then, three kinds of pleasure, the pleasure of that part of the soul whereby we learn is the sweetest, and the life of the man in whom that part dominates is the most pleasurable.

How could it be otherwise? he said.

At any rate the man of intelligence speaks with authority when he commends his own life (*Republic*, Book IX)

Plato had one final argument for the claim that we are best off if reason rules our soul. It too is an argument designed to show that the pleasures we will then pursue are the ones most worthy of being pursued. But he does not now appeal to our experiences of the different pleasures; instead, he appeals to an analysis of their intrinsic nature.

The argument that he offers is very hard to follow, and scholars have disputed its exact meaning. The crux of it seems to be that the intellectual pleasures, which are based on acquiring truth and pursuing an understanding of reality, are themselves the *true* pleasures, the ones most worthy of pursuit. Plato puts his argument as follows:

In *this* way, then, consider it. Are not hunger and thirst and similar states inanitions or emptinesses of the bodily habit?

Surely.

And is not ignorance and folly in turn a kind of emptiness of the habit of the soul?

It is indeed.

And he who partakes of nourishment and he who gets wisdom fills the void and is filled?

Of course.

And which is the truer filling and fulfillment, that of the less or of the more real being?

Evidently that of the more real.

And which of the two groups or kinds do you think has a greater part in pure essence, the class of foods, drinks, and relishes and nourishment generally, or the kind of true opinion, knowledge and reason, and, in sum, all the things that are more excellent? (*ibid.*)

Suppose, then, that on the basis of all these arguments we agree with Plato's conception of how the ideal soul works. Suppose that we agree that we are best off when reason rules. What follows from this? Plato felt that this provided a reason, based on self-interest, for acting morally. After all, he argued, a man in whom reason rules would never act immorally. A person who acts immorally must not have his psyche in proper working order. But we have just seen how disadvantageous such a psychic disorder is. So a life of moral behavior must be truly in our own self-interest.

The Platonic argument is a fascinating one. Plato, in effect, claimed that we must turn our attention from the particular action to the type of personality that lies behind its performance. It is only when we do that, said Plato, that we can see the reason for behaving morally. For the real shortcoming of immoral behavior lies in the type of person we have to be in order to behave immorally.

Although this idea is attractive, there is a serious difficulty with the argument as Plato actually presented it. Plato's argument clearly rests on the assumption that a person in whom reason rules, a person whose psyche is well-ordered, will not behave immorally. Is there any reason to believe that this is so? As we look back at the text of Plato, we find that he treated that assumption as self-evident.

Will the just man [the man in whom reason rules] or citizens ever be guilty of sacrilege or theft, or treachery either to his friends or to his country?

Never.

Neither will he ever break faith where there have been oaths.

Impossible.

> No one will be less likely to commit adultery or to dishonor his father and mother, or to fail in his religious duties?
>
> No one.
>
> And the reason is that each part of him is doing his own business, whether in ruling or being ruled? (*Republic*, Book IV)

One can even see why Plato thought that this was so. His idea of the thief or the adulterer was of a person who was swept away by desire and did what reason forbade. But why couldn't there be a calm and rational thief or adulterer, one in whom reason rules but whose reason tells him to perform the immoral action? Unless Plato can rule out this possibility—and it is hard to see how he can—then the rational life and the moral life are not necessarily identical. In terms of self-interest, the benefits of the former are not the same as the benefits of the latter. To quote David Sachs:

> It will be recalled that Thrasymachus [Socrates' opponent], in stating his position, mentioned among unjust acts temple-robbing, kidnapping, swindling, thieving, and so forth This list, again, was enlarged by Glaucon's mention of sexual relations with whom one pleases, killing, freeing from bonds anyone one wishes, and so forth; that is, acts commonly judged immoral or criminal. The man of whom it was to be proven that his life will be happier than other lives is the man who does not commit such acts.
>
> What Plato tries to establish, however, is that a man each of the parts of whose soul performs its own task, and who conducts himself throughout his days in such a way that this condition will remain unaltered, leads a happier life than any men whose souls are not thus ordered. Regardless of Plato's success or failure in this endeavor, for it to be at all relevant he has to prove that his conception of the just man precludes behavior commonly judged immoral or criminal; that is, he must prove that the conduct of his just man also conforms to the ordinary or vulgar canons of justice. Second, he has to prove that his conceptions of the just man applies to—is exemplified by—every man who is just according to the vulgar conception. For, short of this last, he will not have shown it impossible for men to conform to vulgar justice and still be less happy than men who do not. Plato had to meet both of these requirements if his conclusions about happiness and justice are to bear successfully against Thrasymachus' contentions and satisfy Glaucon's and Adeimantus' demands of Socrates. There are passages in the *Republic* which show that Plato thought there was no problem about the first requirement; there are, however, no passages which indicate that he was aware of the second. In any event, the fact is that

he met neither requirement; nor is it plausible to suppose that he could have met either of them. ("A Fallacy in Plato's Republic," *Philosophical Review* (1963))

We turn now to the argument offered by Thomas Hobbes. Hobbes begins with a fundamental assumption about human nature: that human beings are essentially self-interested agents, each acting to obtain what he thinks is in his self-interest and prepared to harm other human beings in order to obtain it. Now this would be okay if there were enough goods to completely satisfy everyone. But since there are not, human beings compete for what is available and come into armed conflict with each other. Hobbes calls this state of human conflict the state of nature.

Now there are those who would say that Hobbes's picture of human nature is too bleak, and that he is not justified in supposing that human beings would actually behave in that way. Hobbes felt, however, that he could justify his pessimistic views by reference to facts that we could all observe.

> It may seem strong to some man that has not well weighed these things that Nature should thus dissociate and render men apt to invade and destroy one another; and he may therefore desire . . . to have the same confirmed by experience. Let him, therefore, consider with himself: when taking a journey, he arms himself and seeks to go well accompanied; when going to sleep, he locks his doors; when even in his house he locks his chests: and this when he knows there be laws and public officers. . . . Does he not there as much accuse mankind by his actions as I do by my words? (*Leviathan*, chapter 13)

Now, said Hobbes, it is clear that no rational person would want to live in the state of nature. It would not be so bad if we could be sure of winning. But no person is so strong that he doesn't have to fear conflicts with other people (or groups of people). So the state of nature is something we should want to avoid.

The basic idea behind Hobbes's argument for acting morally is then very simple: the rational self-interested person should agree to abide by certain moral principles, which would regulate his relations with other human beings, in order to be able to live without this fear of conflict. Or, to put this point another way, if we are to live with other people, we must follow certain moral rules respecting the rights and interests of other people. Only in that way can people live in peace with one another.

Hobbes clearly has an important point. Even if we do give up something by behaving morally, and even if we would in a particular case gain by behaving immorally, we know that we would lose even more if everyone behaved immorally. And it is this knowledge that leads us to behave morally.

But isn't there a confusion here? Hobbes is right in saying that we would be better off if everyone behaved morally than if everyone pursued his own self-interest without regard to morality. But wouldn't *I* be better off if I could follow my own self-interest while others worried about morality? And if so, isn't it rational for me to do just that? Shouldn't I try to get away with advantageous acts of immorality while urging others to be moral?

We began this chapter by imagining just such an immoral but advantageous act spreading a vicious lie in order to get a lucrative position. What would Hobbes say to a person considering such an act? Presumably, Hobbes would say to him that he would be better off if no one did that than if everyone did that sort of thing. And no doubt that claim of Hobbes is true. After all, if everyone went around spreading such lies, our would-be liar could certainly be harmed by them as well. But couldn't our person then reply to Hobbes by saying that he would gain if he spread such lies while others did not and that *that* is exactly what he hopes to do by surreptitiously spreading lies while encouraging others to be moral. How could Hobbes meet that reply?

Hobbes was very aware of such questions and problems. He preferred, however, to think of them as follows. Suppose that I decide to behave morally and not pursue my immediate self-interest. Suppose, for example, I decide not to spread the lie about my competitor. This will be fine if others also decide to behave that way, if, for example, my competitor also decides not to spread lies about me. But suppose that other people then decide to treat me immorally. Suppose my competitor decides to tell the lies about me, after all. Then I will really be in trouble. My interests will suffer greatly if I obey the restrictions of morality while others do not. How, asked Hobbes, can I be sure that this won't happen? How can I take the chance of behaving morally when I know that others may decide not to follow suit?

Hobbes's own solution to all of these problems is that we should institute a very powerful state, one that has almost absolute power. This sort of state will ensure that everyone obeys the restrictions of morality.

> The only way to erect such a common power, as may be able to defend them from the invasion of foreigners, and the injuries of one another, and thereby to secure them in such sort as that by their own industry and by the fruits of the earth they may nourish themselves and live contentedly, is to confer all their strength and

power upon one man, or upon one assembly of men, that they may reduce all their wills, by plurality of voices, onto one will. (*Leviathan,* chapter 17)

There are many who feel that such a solution is unacceptable because we would have to give up too many of our liberties to the state. The price, they would say, is too high. And if we won't have Hobbes's state his solution apparently collapses. Some of these philosophers have claimed, however, that Hobbes's absolute state is not required to ensure moral behavior. Kurt Baier, for example, claimed that:

> . . . reason can support morality, only when the presumption about other people's behavior is reversed. Hobbes thought that this could be achieved only by the creation of an absolute ruler with absolute power to enforce his laws. We have already seen that this is not true and that it can also be achieved if people live in a society, that is, if they have common ways of life, which are taught to all members and somehow enforced by the group. Its members have reason to expect their fellows generally to obey its rules, that is, its religion, morality, customs, and law, even when doing so is not, on certain occasions, in their interest. Hence they too have reason to follow these rules (*The Moral Point of View,* chapter 7, section 3)

This claim is not, however, entirely convincing. To begin with, it seems to be overly optimistic about the extent to which moral training and social pressure lead people to behave morally. Second, and more important, even if we could expect most people to behave morally in most cases, not all of our problems would be solved. It's true that we wouldn't need to worry about others cheating if we behaved morally. But the question would still remain as to why we should behave morally if we could get away with advantageous immoral acts. Without something like Hobbes's absolute government, there will be cases in which we could get away with advantageous immoralities. Baier doesn't really explain why we should not gain personal advantages by performing those actions.

2.3 MORE RADICAL APPROACHES

We have so far examined several attempts to show that being moral is always in our self-interest. These we have found lacking. This leads us to wonder if it's even possible to connect morality and self-interest. Suppose that it's not. What does that mean?

There are philosophers who feel that this failure is not really very important. Some believe, in fact, that the whole attempt was a mistake. One such philosopher was H. A. Prichard. He wrote:

> A general but not very critical familiarity with the literature of Moral Philosophy might well lead to the remark that much of it is occupied with attempts either to prove that there is a necessary connexion between duty and interest or in certain cases even to exhibit the connexion as something self-evident. . . . When we read the attempts referred to we naturally cannot help in a way wishing them to succeed; and we might express our wish in the form that we should all like to be able to believe that honesty is the best policy. At the same time we also cannot help feeling that somehow they are out of place, so that the real question is not so much whether they are successful, but whether they ought ever to have been made. (*Duty and Interest*)

Philosophers like Prichard feel there is no need to prove that morality is identical with self-interest because we have reason to be moral even if it is not in our self-interest. They say that Plato, Hobbes, and others were mistaken in claiming that self-interest is ultimately the only reason for acting. Prichard and his followers believe that there are other reasons for acting morally. And, they say, since there are these other reasons, it is not very important if we cannot prove that morality is in our self-interest.

What are these other reasons? Prichard says, for one thing, that we want to do the right thing:

> We obviously are referring to a fact when we speak of someone as possessing a sense of duty and, again, a strong sense of duty. And if we consider what we are thinking of in these individuals whom we think of as possessing it, we find that we cannot exclude from it a desire to do what is a duty, as such, for its own sake, or, more simply, a desire to do what is a duty . . . if we admit the existence of a desire to do what is right, then there is no longer any reason for maintaining as a general thesis that in any case in which a man knows some action to be right, he must, if he is to be led to do it, be convinced that he will gain by doing it. For we shall be able to maintain that his desire to do what is right, if strong enough, will lead him to do the action in question in spite of any aversion from doing it which he may feel on account of its disadvantages. (*ibid.*)

Other philosophers have said the reason is that we have a concern for the welfare of others. Francis Hutcheson, for example, said that the true reason for virtuous action is "some determination of our nature to study the good of others, or some instinct, antecedent to all reason from interest, which influences us to the love of others."

Let us return now to our case of the two competitors for the one job. According to Prichard, the one competitor should not spread the damaging lie about the other because doing so will fly in the face of his desire to do the right thing. According to Hutcheson, the one competitor should not spread the damaging lie about the other because doing so will fly in the face of his concern for the well-being of others.

This whole approach, if accepted, would certainly affect our ideas about moral training. We have already remarked that in the moral training of a child, it is a mistake to emphasize the personal benefits that come from being moral. If we do emphasize this, of course, we do not provide the child with a reason for being moral in cases where morality and self-interest conflict. Prichard's theory suggests, as an alternative, that moral training should develop in the child a desire to do the right thing. Hutcheson's views suggest that moral training should develop the child's concern for the well-being of others. John Stuart Mill envisaged just this kind of moral training.

> In an improving state of the human mind, the influences are constantly on the increase, which tend to generate in each individual a feeling of unity with all the rest; which, if perfect, would make him never think of, or desire, any beneficial condition for himself, in the benefits of which they are not included. If we now suppose this feeling of unity to be taught as a religion, and the whole force of education, of institutions, and of opinion, directed . . . to make every person grow up from infancy surrounded on all sides both by the profession and the practice of it, I think that no one, who can realise this conception, will feel any misgiving about the sufficiency of the ultimate sanction. (*Utilitarianism,* chapter 3)

The Prichard-Hutcheson view also helps explain an important fact about morality. Because of their motives, we often distinguish between two people who have performed the same action, praising one while not praising the other. A philanthropist who gives to gain public acclaim is not as praiseworthy as one who gives for truly charitable motives. Now if self-interest were really the only motive for human action, there could be no such distinction. All actions would be selfishly motivated and no one would deserve praise for moral behavior. But if Prichard or Hutcheson is right, we can distinguish those who deserve praise from those who do not. Those who act with motives other than self-interest will clearly be the ones deserving praise.

Some philosophers have taken this point one step further. According to them, the only truly praiseworthy action is one done from a sense of duty. No person deserves any true praise for any action done from any desire, even the desire to aid others. Immanuel Kant put it as follows (using the term "esteem" for what we refer to as "true praise"):

> To be beneficent when we can is a duty; and besides this, there are many minds so sympathetically constituted that, without any other motive of vanity or self-interest, they find a pleasure in spreading joy around them and can take delight in the satisfaction of others so far as it is their own work. But I maintain that in such a case an action of this kind, however proper, however amiable it may be, has nevertheless no true moral worth, but is on a level with other inclinations, e.g., the inclination to honor, which, if it is happily directed to that which is in fact of public utility and accordant with duty and consequently honorable, deserves praise and encouragement, but not esteem. (First section of the *Foundations of the Metaphysics of Morals*)

In making this claim, of course, Kant was strongly disagreeing with the Hutcheson version of the thesis that we are considering.

Kant went on to draw certain conclusions which have startled many of his readers.

> . . . assume that the mind of that friend to mankind was clouded by a sorrow of his own which extinguished all sympathy with the lot of others and that he still had the power to benefit others in distress, but that their need left him untouched because he was preoccupied with his own need. And now suppose him to tear himself, unsolicited by inclination, out of this dead insensibility and to perform this action only from duty and without any inclination—then for the first time his action has genuine moral worth. Furthermore, if nature has put little sympathy in the heart of a man, and if he, though an honest man, is by temperament cold and indifferent to the sufferings of others, perhaps because he is provided with special gifts of patience and fortitude and expects or even requires that others should have the same—and such a man would certainly not be the meanest product of nature—would not he find in himself a source from which to give himself a far higher worth than he could have got by having a good-natured temperament? This is unquestionably true even though nature did not make him philanthropic, for it is just here that the worth of the character is brought out, which is morally and incomparably the highest of all: he is beneficent not from inclination but from duty. (*ibid.*)

Most philosophers have felt that this is going too far, that a person who acts from benevolent motives, and not from self-interest, is already deserving of praise. This more balanced view is expressed by W. D. Ross:

> Kant's distrust of desire leads him to hold that all actions springing from desire are quite lacking in moral value—that an action done from kindness or love, unaccompanied by the sense of duty, is worth no more than the most selfish or the most cruel action. We can agree with him in thinking that the sense of duty is the highest motive, without following him in putting all other motives on the same dead level. Kant simplifies the moral life too much in making it a contest between one element which alone has worth and a multitude of others which have none; the truth rather is that it is a struggle between a multiplicity of desires having various degrees of worth.

We have seen attractive features in the views of Prichard and Hutcheson. They seem to provide us with a reason for being moral even against our own self-interest. They offer us an interesting approach to moral training and education. And they provide us with a satisfactory account of when actions and people are truly praiseworthy. There are, nevertheless, two large problems which they must face:

1. Assume that one of their theories is true. That means that we have at least two radically different types of motives: self-interest, on the one hand, and, on the other, duty or benevolence. How then are we to choose between them when they conflict? No doubt these theories provide us with a reason for being moral. But we are also left with a reason for being immoral. What rational basis is there for choosing between these reasons? Consider again the competitors for the job. If either Hutcheson or Prichard is right, then the competitors have a reason for not spreading the lie (concern for the "good of others," or the "desire to do what is right"). But they also have a reason for spreading it (self-interest). So how shall they decide between these two reasons?

2. Are their theories correct? Do we ever really act from any motive other than self-interest? From our own experiences we all are painfully aware of people who seem to be acting from the loftiest of motives but who are really acting out of self-interest. Maybe that is true in all cases.

In the final sections of this chapter, we will deal with these two objections.

2.4 WHAT REALLY ARE OUR MOTIVES?

Let us begin with the second objection, which raises the question of human motives. Hutcheson and Prichard are attacking the thesis of *psychological egoism,* the view that the only reason or motive for any action is self-interest. They insist that there must be other reasons for human actions.

What arguments do they offer for their views? To begin with, they think that the truth of their views is something that we can experience in our own feelings. Thus, Hutcheson writes:

> But what will most effectually convince us of the truth on this point is reflection upon our own hearts, whether we have not a desire of the good of others, generally without any consideration or intention of obtaining these pleasant reflections on our own virtue.

Secondly, they feel that we can see in the actions of others clear examples of actions not based on self-interest. Finally, they appeal to the fact that only their views explain (as we saw above) the fact that some people are praiseworthy.

Prichard and Hutcheson certainly recognize that those who act out of nonselfish motives are often motivated by self-interest, too. All that they want to claim is that this does leave a place open for the nonselfish motives:

> But it must be here observed that as all men have self-love as well as benevolence, these two principles may jointly excite a man to the same action, and then they are to be considered as two forces impelling the same body to motion. . . . Thus if a man has such strong benevolence as would have produced an action without any views of self-interest, that such a man has also in view private advantage, along with public good, as the effect of his action, does in no way diminish the benevolence of the action. When he would not have produced so much public good had it not been for prospect of self-interest, then the effect of self-love is to be deducted, and his benevolence is proportioned to the remainder of good, which pure benevolence would have produced. (Hutcheson, *op. cit.*)

Many people are skeptical about these claims. They suggest that the only thing that we really desire is what is in our own self-interest. Such people offer three arguments for this view:

1. When we look at examples of supposedly nonselfish actions, we often find that they are motivated by hidden considerations of self-interest.

2. People who supposedly act from benevolent motives or from a sense of duty are really acting to obtain the pleasure of seeing others happy or the pleasure of feeling that they are virtuous. So they are really acting to obtain their own pleasure, and that is a act motivated by self-interest.

3. In any case, we act to satisfy our desires, whatever they are, and that makes our action motivated by self-interest.

The first of these arguments has a great deal of intuitive appeal. After all, we have all been fooled that way. We have all admired people for their supposedly noble and generous actions only to discover the truly selfish motives that have moved them. Nevertheless, these experiences, while enough to make us somewhat skeptical about people's motives, are not enough to establish the general truth of egoism. They do not establish that people only act from selfish motives. And there is, after all, the evidence that Hutcheson and Prichard appeal to that suggests that egoism is not valid.

The second argument is more substantial. It concedes that there is some psychological truth in the Hutcheson-Prichard thesis, but it claims that the thesis distorts the nature of that truth. We are not moved, says this argument, by a desire to do what is right or to see others happy; what really moves us is the pleasure we get from thinking of ourselves as doing the right thing or from seeing others happy. Since it is this desire for our own pleasure that moves us, egoism is still correct. This view was forcefully presented by Moritz Schlick:

> The idea of personal destruction is, in general, one of the most terrifying; not the most terrifying, for there are enough miseries in comparison with which death is felt as a soothing relief. Yet we observe, in life and history, acts of will whose fatal and miserable consequences are not only inevitable for the performer, but are clearly seen by him to be involved as the goal of his action. The martyr accepts pain and death for the sake of an idea, a friend gives his life or "happiness" for his friend. Can any one in earnest say of such persons that their decisions are determined by the motives which possess the most pleasant or the least unpleasant emotional tones?
>
> According to my firm conviction, one cannot say anything else if one would tell the truth, for such are the facts. Let us then try to analyze and understand the motive of heroism. The hero acts "for the sake of a cause"; he desires to carry out an idea or realize a definite goal. It is clear that the thought of this goal or

that idea dominates his consciousness to such an extent that there is in it hardly room for any other thoughts. At least this holds in the case of inspiration, from which alone an heroic act can arise. It is true that the idea of his own painful destruction is present, but, however burdened with pain it may be in itself, it is inhibited and repressed by the predominant end-in-view, which finally triumphs in an "act of will," in an effort which becomes stronger and sharper the longer and more clearly the thought of the unavoidable catastrophe confronts him. What is the source of the astonishing force of the decisive end-in-view? Whence the power of this affect? Without doubt this is due to *emotion*. Inspiration is the greatest pleasure that can fall to the lot of man. To be inspired by something means to be overcome by the greatest joy in the thought of it. The man who, under the stress of inspiration, decides to help a friend or save another creature from pain and destruction, whatever the cost, finds the thought of this act so profoundly joyful, so overwhelmingly pleasant that, at the moment, the idea of the preservation of his own life and the avoidance of pain cannot compare with it. And he who fights for a cause with such inspiration that he accepts all persecution and insult realizes his idea with such elevated pure joy that neither the thought of his miseries nor their actual pain can prevail aught against it. The notion of giving up his purpose because of pain is, for him, more unpleasant than the pain itself. (*Problems of Ethics*, chapter 2)

Nevertheless, this second argument does not really succeed. To begin with, even if its claims were true, we would still have a reason for acting morally. After all, the pleasure we get from thinking of ourselves as righteous or from seeing others happy is just as much a reason for doing the right action as Prichard's sense of duty or Hutcheson's sense of benevolence. But more important, there is evidence from both introspection and our observations of others to suggest that these claims are false. Hutcheson, for example, seems correct when he writes:

Reflections in our minds again will best discover the truth. Many have never thought upon this connection; nor do we ordinarily intend the obtaining of any such pleasure when we do generous offices. We all often feel delight upon seeing others happy, but during our pursuit of their happiness we have no intention of obtaining this delight. We often feel the pain of compassion, but were our sole ultimate intention or desire the freeing ourselves from this pain, would the deity offer us either wholly to blot out all memory of the person in distress, or to take away this connection, so that we should be easy during the misery of our friend, on the one hand, or on the other would relieve him from his misery, we should be as ready to choose the former way as the latter, since either of them would free us from our pain, which upon this scheme is the sole end proposed by the compassionate person. Don't we find in ourselves that our desire does not terminate upon the removal of our own pain? Were this our sole intention, we would run away, shut our eyes, or divert our thoughts from the miserable object, as the readiest way of removing our pain. (*ibid.*)

The third of the arguments noted above rests on a common confusion. It supposes that if I do an action to satisfy some desire of mine, then, no matter what the nature of the desire, the action is based on self-interest. But this supposition is a mistake. A "self-interested action" is one done to satisfy certain interests of mine, or certain desires for my own happiness, and not merely one done to satisfy any desire.

This point can also be put as follows: Those who make this third objection have the following picture in mind:

self-interested	other
action done to satisfy a desire	action not done to satisfy a desire

Given this picture, and the plausible assumption that all actions satisfy a desire, they conclude that the "other" category is empty and that all actions are self-interested actions. The trouble with this argument is that they are working with the wrong picture. The correct picture of the distinction is rather this one:

self-interested	other
action done to satisfy a desire for my own well-being	action done to satisfy a desire for something other than my own well-being

Given this picture, we can agree that all actions are done to satisfy some desire of the agent and still claim that not all actions are self-interested. All we need to suppose is that the agent can have desires for something other than his own well-being. And this certainly seems reasonable.

2.5 REASONS AND MOTIVES

We can conclude, then, that the egoist's arguments have failed. There is no reason to doubt that we have reasons for action other than self-interest. Now, we have still to deal with the first objection which we were left with at the end of section 2.3: How can we decide between the reasons for action given by Hutcheson and Prichard, on the one hand, and self-interest, on the other?

This is a question that the Hutcheson-Prichard approach does not answer. It says instead that there is no basis for preferring one type of reason to the other. We may decide to follow the one type of reason or we may decide to follow the other. We may decide to follow self-interest or we may decide to be moral. Which we will decide to do depends primarily on the strength of our various desires. But whatever we do, we will have a reason for doing it, although we will not have a reason for letting *that* reason prevail.

Let us return one more time to the competitor for the job. He has a reason (his self-interested desires) for spreading the lie about his rival. He probably also has a reason (his benevolent desires or his desire to do what is right) for not doing so. Given these conflicting reasons, he will have to choose which course of action he will follow; presumably, that choice will be determined by the strength of his various desires. But if he does choose to be moral, his action will have been based upon a good reason; there will be a good answer to the question "why should he have behaved morally?"

Not everyone is satisfied with such a conclusion. There are many who feel that philosophy must provide us with an account of the reasons we have for all our choices. On this conception of the goals of philosophy, the Hutcheson-Prichard approach is unsatisfactory. It admits the existence of a choice for which we have no reasons: the choice between following our reasons for doing what is in our own interest and following our reasons for doing what is moral. The Hutcheson-Prichard approach seems to leave us with some choices that are decided solely upon the basis of the strength of our conflicting desires.

Those who follow the Hutcheson-Prichard approach are not persuaded by this objection, however. It is fundamental to that approach to accept the idea that our reasons for actions will be based on desires, and that conflicts between fundamental desires cannot be resolved by further reasons. We have, that approach says, reasons for our actions, whether they be moral or immoral. We do not have reasons for *preferring* some reasons over other reasons.

3

Justice and Equality

In this chapter we will be concerned with trying to understand the concepts of justice and equality. We will begin by distinguishing various types of injustice and by seeing their relationships to equality and inequality. Then, we will consider a variety of difficult moral problems that arise in connection with these different types of injustice.

There is one preliminary point that the reader should note. Many of the major social problems of our time arise in connection with claims about justice and injustice. Many members of minority groups have claimed that justice demands that they receive reparations for previous injustices done to them. Others claim that this cannot be done without doing injustices to other people. Employees often claim that they are not being justly paid for their work. Employers claim that they are not receiving a just profit from their labor and investment. Tenants claim that it is unjust for landlords to demand high rents for meager apartments, while landlords claim that it is unjust to expect them to keep up their houses when they receive low rentals. And so on.

We will not, unfortunately, be able to treat these problems here. Our concern is with the fundamental concepts involved in such discussions. If the reader is then able to apply these fundamental concepts to social problems, an important goal of this book will have been achieved.

3.1 SOME PRELIMINARY DISTINCTIONS

Let us begin by considering various cases of injustice:

1. B steals $100 that belongs to A and does not restore it to A.

2. B's car crashes into A's car, causing $100 worth of damage but B does not have to compensate A.

3. B promises to give A $100 and A spends it in advance, relying on B's promise, but B does not actually give the money to A.

4. A does a required assignment satisfactorily, but B gives him a failing grade anyway.

5. A submits the best essay in a competition but B gets the prize.

6. A does most of the work in building a rowboat but B gets to use it most of the time.

7. A needs medical treatment much more urgently than does B, but B gets treated first.

In each of these cases, there is something that is due to A and the injustice consists in his not getting it. In case 1, A is entitled to his $100 and the injustice consists in his not getting it. In case 2, A is entitled to compensation for the damages he suffered, and the injustice consists in his not getting it. In case 3, A is entitled to the money which B promised him, and the injustice consists in his not getting it. In case 4, A is entitled to the passing grade that he earned, and the injustice consists in his not getting it. In case 5, A deserves the winning prize, and the injustice consists in his not getting it. In case 6, A deserves the greater use of the boat and the injustice consists in his not getting it. In case 7, A deserves to be treated first, and the injustice consists in his not getting that priority.

Despite this similarity, there are important differences between these cases. To begin with, cases 1–4 are fundamentally different from cases 5–7. Joel Feinberg has summarized this kind of difference as follows:

> In all cases, of course, justice consists in giving a person his due, but in some cases one's due is determined independently of that of other people, while in other cases, a person's due is determined only by reference to his relations to other persons. I shall refer to

context, criteria, and principles of the former kind as noncomparative, and those of the latter kind as comparative. ("Noncomparative Justice," *Philosophical Review*, 1974)

Thus in case 1–3, A is due $100 from B, and this can be determined independently of what is due to anyone else. Similarly, in case 4, A is due a passing grade no matter what grade is due to anyone else. On the other hand, A deserves the prize in case 5 because he has written a *better* essay than has anyone else. So what is due to A in this case can only be determined by looking at the performance of others and deciding what is due to them. Similarly, in case 6, A deserves to use the boat more because he has done *more* work than has B. What is due to A in this case can also be determined only by reference to what is due to others on the basis of their performance. And again in case 7, A is entitled to priority of treatment because of his *greater* need. What is due to A in this case can only be determined by reference to what is due to others on the basis of their need. Cases 1–4 are then cases of *noncomparative* injustice while cases 5–7 are cases of *comparative* injustice.

A second kind of difference which exists among the cases is that A is due the thing in question for a different reason in *each* case. In case 1, A is entitled to the $100 because it was his originally. In case 2, A is entitled to the $100 as compensation for the damage caused by B. In case 3, A is entitled to the $100 because B promised to give it to him. In case 4, A is entitled to the passing grade because he met the requirements for that grade. In case 5, A deserves the prize because he wrote the best essay. In case 6, A deserves the greater use of the boat because he did more of the work. In case 7, A deserves priority of treatment because his need is greater. So there are a variety of ways in which claims for justice arise.

The two kinds of differences which can exist among our cases are obviously related to each other. In every case, there is a reason why the thing in question is due to A. As we have just seen, this reason can vary from case to case. In only one set of cases, however, do these reasons make reference to what is due to other people. Such cases are cases of noncomparative injustice.

There is still one more distinction that is very important and should be noted here. It emerges most clearly when we look at case 6. In case 6, there is something desirable, the use of the boat, that has to be distributed between A and B. A just distribution would be one in which A and B get that share of the use that is due to each of them. In our case, where A did more of the work than did B, the fair share for each (assuming all else about them to be equal) should be proportionate to the amount of work that each did. Case 6 is then a clear case of *proportionate* injustice.

How can we tell when we are dealing with this type of case? To begin with, there must be some good (or evil) to be distributed. Secondly, there must be several people with legitimate claims to a share of the good (or to a share of avoiding the evil). Aristotle describes this kind of case as follows:

> This, then, is what the just is—the proportional; the unjust is what violates the proportion. Hence one term becomes too great, the other too small, as indeed happens in practice; for the man who acts unjustly has too much, and the man who is unjustly treated too little, of what is good. In the case of evil the reverse is true; for the lesser evil is reckoned a good in comparison with the greater evil, since the lesser evil is rather to be chosen than the greater. (*Nicomachean Ethics*, Book 5)

There are two key points to be noted about such cases:

1. All cases of proportionate justice are cases of comparative justice. After all, what is due to each person in cases of proportionate justice is their proportionate share, something that must be determined by reference to what is due to other people. On the other hand, there are cases of comparative justice (like 5 and 7) that are not, strictly speaking, cases of proportionate justice. The good in question there (the prize or the priority of treatment) is not to be distributed among several people but is to be granted to a single person.

2. In one case of proportionate justice, case 6, the basis of the competing claims is the amount of work done. This is not true in all cases of proportionate justice. For example, when two deserving people request your aid, the just thing to do may be to apportion your aid in proportion to their need. This would be a case of proportionate justice. Here, need, not work accomplished, is the basis of the claim. Saying this raises, of course, the whole question of what is a legitimate basis for claims in such cases. We discuss this fundamental question at some length below.

3.2 JUSTICE AND EQUALITY

When people talk about justice, they often refer to equality as well, and there is a popular view that justice and equality are the same thing. This view holds that people are treated unjustly whenever they are treated unequally. We shall soon see that this view is in error, but let us first consider the more general question of the relation between justice and equality. This question arises in cases of comparative justice, so let us turn to these. And we shall examine cases of nonproportionate and proportionate justice separately.

In cases of nonproportionate justice, like 5 and 7, justice naturally demands that people be treated equally. But this doesn't mean that everyone should equally get the prize or that everyone should equally get priority of treatment. What it does mean is: (1) The prize should go to the *best* essay and priority of treatment should go to the person *most* in need. Other factors should be considered only if relevant. In particular, factors like race or sex, personal likings of the judge or doctor, etc., should not be considered. (2) everyone should have an equal opportunity to compete for the prize or to be considered for priority of treatment. This equality of opportunity should be denied only for relevant reasons.

This account of what justice demands is not very precise, and, obviously, many further questions can be raised. Looking at (1) first: what makes some factors relevant and others not? Is it relevant, for example, to consider in the case of medical treatment whether the individual in question can pay for the treatment? Is it relevant to consider the extent of the person's potential contribution to society? Should priority be given to those who would be missed more if they did not get treatment and died? Or in the case of the prize for the best essay, is it relevant to consider not merely the quality of the essay but also the disadvantages under which the various candidates struggled? And if that is not relevant to the award for the best essay, is it relevant when we are dealing with admissions to a university? This list of questions could go on and on, for we obviously have to say a lot more about what is relevant to judgments of equality.

Looking at (2), we see the same pattern emerging. What does equality of opportunity really mean and what reasons could be relevant to denying such equality? For example, suppose in the case of the essay that there are substantial expenses involved (research costs, for example). Does equality of opportunity require that each of the candidates be given an equal sum of money to use in preparing the essay? Or is it sufficient that the candidates be allowed to compete if they can raise the money they need on their own?

We will have to consider these questions more fully later on in the chapter. For the moment, however, let us tentatively say that justice in such cases does not require that everyone be treated equally in all ways.

In cases of proportionate justice, the notion of equality is crucial.

But it must be defined in terms of the relevant proportions. Thus, in a case like 6, if A and B had both done the *same* amount of work (and all other factors were equal), justice would demand that they both share *equally* in the use of the boat. But since one has done more work than the other (and all other things are presumably equal), justice demands that A, the person who has worked more, be able to use the boat more often.

This account is, once more, very imprecise. It can be pointed out that everyone's share should be proportionate to his legitimate claims. But what makes a claim legitimate? In the case of the construction of the boat, is it legitimate to consider who paid for the wood? And how much do we weigh that against the question of who did the labor? If the idea of building a boat originated with one of the builders, should that be given any weight?

Questions like these can be raised in most cases of proportionate justice, and we will have to consider such questions more fully later on. What we must note now, however, is that with proportionate justice, as in other cases of comparative justice, justice doesn't always require that everyone be treated equally in all ways. There seem to be, in fact, clear cases of "just inequalities." This shows us the error of a popular notion, the thesis of *radical egalitarianism*.

This thesis holds that all inequalities are unjustifiable and ought to be eliminated. If our analysis up to now is correct, then that thesis is in error. Some inequalities (like A's getting the prize he deserves or getting a greater share of the use of the boat) are justifiable and should not be eliminated. Indeed, we would have an injustice if they *were* eliminated, since then the deserving person would not be getting his due. As Hugo Bedau has stated:

> Other philosophers . . . have argued the more interesting position that certain inequalities are justified because they are just. Such maxims of distributive justice as "To each according to his merit", "To each according to his needs", "To each according to his work", and "To each according to his prior agreements", all appear to be anti-egalitarian maxims. Yet, there seem to be many occasions where conduct is justified by appeal to these maxims in order to override criticism based on egalitarian principles. We do constantly speak of one person deserving one thing and another deserving something else; and in doing so, we often rely on one or another of these maxims and think ourselves justified and just in doing so. So these inequalities are presumably thought of as just inequalities. ("Radical Egalitarianism," *Nomos*, vol. 9)

There are two important points that should be kept in mind here:

1. As our analysis and Bedau's argument point out, the failure of radical egalitarianism shows us that there are just inequalities. But which inequalities are the just ones? It is this question, which has come to dominate all discussions of comparative justice, that will be at the heart of the rest of this chapter.

2. Although radical egalitarianism is incorrect, it still has a serious message, both theoretical and practical, that we must remember. The legitimate theoretical insight at the base of egalitarianism is the claim that inequality of treatment has to be *justified* by showing that more is due to one person than to others. If this cannot be shown, then we must treat people equally. The serious practical point is the reminder that many existing inequalities cannot be so justified and should be abolished. It is probably these points which have given radical egalitarianism more of an appeal than it actually deserves.

3.3 SOME CLASSICAL FORMULAS

In this section, we will discuss "just inequalities." Let's begin by considering a series of classical formulas. Although these formulas deal only with cases of proportionate justice, and not with all cases of comparative justice, a consideration of them will be very helpful at this stage of our enquiry.

The formulas are:

1. To each according to his abilities
2. To each according to what he produces
3. To each according to the effort he expends
4. To each according to his need

These are all principles of proportionate justice. They are all concerned with a distribution of goods among a group of people in proportion to something. What do they say? Formula 1 says that these goods should be distributed in proportion to the abilities of the people in question. It is just to give one person more than another only in so far as the first has more ability. Formula 2 says that these goods should be distributed in proportion to what the people in question have produced. It is just to give one person more than another only in so far as the first has produced more than the second. Formula 3 says that these goods should be distributed in proportion to the effort the people in question have expended. It is just to give one person more than another only in so far as the first has expended more effort than the second. Formula 4 says that these goods should be distributed in proportion to the needs of the people in question. It is just to give one person more than another only in so far as the first needs more.

As we saw in section 3.2, the main demand of proportionate justice is that each individual should receive a share proportionate to his legitimate claim. The main problem was that it was not clear which claims would be legitimate. Each of the above formulas represent, in effect, a different attempt to solve this problem. Each formula, in effect, names something which could plausibly support a legitimate claim. Thus, the first important thing to note about these formulas is that, for each of them, we can think of situations for which they seem to be sound principles for proportionate justice. For example, formula 1 seems to be correct for the distribution of advanced education. That is, it seems just, in many cases, to distribute such training in proportion to the abilities of the candidates. To say this, let me hasten to add, is not to endorse the current methods of assessing such abilities (e.g., I.Q. testing, or College Board Examinations). There are, I believe, quite legitimate doubts about their ability to measure a student's potential. Moreover, there are certainly circumstances under which it would be just to consider factors other than ability as well. But, in many cases at least, it would seem just to distribute education in proportion to ability, and to follow formula 1.

Formula 2 seems more appropriate when we consider wages. The "piece work" system of wages—according to which wages are paid for by the "piece," or by the amount of work produced—has an element of justice to it. Again, to say this is not to advocate that system as the general system of wages. There may, after all, be drawbacks to this system, and there may well be cases in which factors other than productivity should be considered. All I am claiming is that, in many cases, a system of wages proportional to productivity (embodying formula 2) would seem to be just.

As for formula 3, it would seem just for parents to praise their children in proportion to their efforts, for it is the effort and not necessarily the result which counts in many cases. Again, there may be other factors which should justly play a role; all that we are saying is that formula 3 embodies a principle of proportionate justice for at least some cases.

Finally, and with similar reservations, formula 4 seems a sound principle for the distribution of basic necessities, such as food, shelter, and medical care.

The second important thing to note about these formulas is indicated by the very fact that each seems to be correct in some contexts. For, it appears that none of them will do as a general theory of justice. As Nicholas Rescher has said:

> One and the same shortcoming runs through all of the above canons of distributive justice: they are all monistic. They all recognize but one solitary, homogeneous claim made of production (be it need, effort, productivity or whatever), to the exclusion of all others. A single specific ground of claim establishment is canonized as uniquely authoritative, and all the others dismissed. As a result, these canons all suffer the aristocratic fault of hyperexclusiveness. (*Distributive Justice*, pp. 81–82)

This point can also be put as follows. We are looking for a general theory that will tell us which inequalities are just in a given case. Each of the formulas listed above tell us that certain inequalities are just. But they say, in effect, that it is the same type of inequality that is just in each case. Formula 1 says that only inequalities based on ability are just, and they are always just. Formula 2 says that only inequalities based on productivity are just, and they are always just. And so on. This does not seem correct. Inequalities based on abilities (or on productivity, or on effort, or on need) are sometimes just and sometimes unjust. What we need is a general theory of justice that will tell us *when* they are just and *when* they are unjust.

There is yet another problem about these famous formulas of proportionate justice that suggests that we must go beyond them. Despite their initial plausibility, there are reasons for hesitating about each of them. These reasons are so grave that only a general theory of justice can tell us whether we should retain these formulas at all.

In order to see the gravity of the problem, let us begin by considering formula 1. It is important to keep in mind that a person's abilities are, to a large extent, determined by his genetic endowment and early training, and that these are something for which he deserves neither praise nor blame. Given that this is so, why should anyone receive a greater share of goods simply because he has greater ability? Isn't this a case of rewarding people for the accidents of their birth? Is this just? As John Rawls has written:

> Perhaps some will think that the person with greater natural endowments deserves those assets and the superior character that made their development possible. Because he is more worthy in this sense, he deserves the greater advantages that he could achieve with them. This view, however, is surely incorrect. It seems to be

one of the fixed points of our considered judgments that no one deserves his place in the distribution of native endowments, any more than one deserves one's initial starting place in society. . . . (*A Theory of Justice,* pp. 103–4)

It might be thought that this problem is covered by formula 2, the claim that it is just to distribute goods in proportion to what a person produces. After all, it rewards a person not for his natural abilities but for what he does with those abilities. But this suggestion is wrong, too, for what someone produces is to a considerable extent determined by his natural abilities. A person with more abilities can produce more. So formula 2 still rewards people for their natural endowments, for the accidents of birth. Karl Marx saw this when he wrote the following, in objection to a version of formula 2.

But one man is superior to another physically or mentally and so supplies more labour in the same time, or can labour for a longer time; and labour, to serve as a measure, must be defined by its duration or intensity, otherwise it ceases to be a standard of measurement. This equal right [formula 2 and its variants] is an unequal right for unequal labour. It recognises no class differences, because everyone is only a worker like everyone else; but it tacitly recognises unequal individual endowment and thus productive capacity as natural privileges. (*Critique of the Gotha Program,* Part II)

Many of those who advocate formula 3 feel that their view avoids these difficulties. They feel that what should justly be rewarded is a person's efforts to use to the highest extent whatever abilities he has. Consider, for example, the case of the following two students: A is a student with a great deal of natural ability who does outstanding work with little effort. B does good work by using to the fullest extent his more limited abilities. If A gets the better grade, he will be rewarded primarily for his natural abilities. So why not reward B with the higher grade? Then rewards will distributed in proportion to what the two students really deserve.

The trouble with this claim is that it forgets that there are many different kinds of talent, and that one natural talent is the one possessed by B: perseverance and a disposition to try very hard. It may well be the case, then, that following formula 3 simply means rewarding in proportion to a different natural talent.

In short, then, formulas 1–3 are dubious. They all, in one way or another, involve rewarding people in proportion to natural talent, and there are serious reasons for doubting the justice of any system that does that. It is this sort of consideration that has led many thinkers to formula 4, the principle that justice consists in distributing goods in proportion to people's needs.

But there are also difficulties with this. To begin with, its adoption could result in everyone being worse off than before. Since formula 4 puts no requirement on what you must produce (or try to produce) in order to get your share of goods, its adoption would lead to a general lessening of the motive for working. A possible consequence might be that everyone would suffer from a resulting shortage of goods. Therefore, it is argued, formula 4 is unsound as a principle of justice. To quote John Hospers:

> It may be suggested that one's reward should depend on how much one needs; the one who needs the most should receive the most. Some would doubt that need should be used as a criterion at all, and some would say that it should be used only sparingly or in extreme situations; but few would suggest that it should be the only criterion. If it were, work would soon come to a standstill, and there would be nothing left with which to reward anyone. Doubtless the needy should not be allowed to starve—especially if they desire work but, through no fault of their own, can find none. Doubtless even those who are able to work but refuse to do so ("Society owes me a living") should not be allowed to starve and if possible should be sent to a psychiatrist. (Some would say that they *should* be permitted to starve. But should their families too?) But at least, reward cannot be based entirely upon need. If nonworkers were rewarded as much as workers, who would desire to work? Some doubtless would, but would then have to work much harder, to make up for the large mass of the indigent. (*Human Conduct*, chapter 9)

It is clearly possible, then, that the adoption of formula 4 could lead to some people working while others had the benefit of that work. Many feel that this is a form of injustice, akin to the injustice of slavery, rather than the essence of justice. Discussing a system of taxation which takes from those who produce to distribute to those who are needy, Robert Nozick writes:

> Taxation of earnings from labor is on a par with forced labor. Some persons find this claim obviously true: taking the earnings of n hours labor is like taking n hours from the person; it is like forcing the person to work n hours for another's purpose. Others find the claim absurd. But even these, *if* they object to forced labor, would oppose forcing unemployed hippies to work for the benefit of the needy. And they would also object to forcing each person to work five extra hours each week for the benefit of the needy. But a system

JUSTICE AND EQUALITY 67

that takes five hours' wages in taxes does not seem to them like one that forces someone to work five hours, since it offers the person forced a wider range of choice in activities than does taxation in kind with the particular labor specified. (But we can imagine a gradation of systems for forced labor, from one that specifies a particular activity, to one that gives a choice among two activities, to . . . ; and so on up.) Furthermore, people envisage a system with something like a proportional tax on everything above the amount necessary for basic needs. Some think this does not force someone to work extra hours, since there is no fixed number of extra hours he is forced to work, and since he can avoid the tax entirely by earning only enough to cover his basic needs. This is a very uncharacteristic view of forcing for those who *also* think people are forced to do something *whenever* the alternatives they face are considerably worse. However, *neither* view is correct. The fact that others intentionally intervene, in violation of a side constraint against aggression, to threaten force to limit the alternatives, in this case to paying taxes or (presumably the worse alternative) bare subsistence, makes the taxation system one of forced labor and distinguishes it from other cases of limited choices which are not forcings. (*Anarchy, State, and Utopia,* chapter 7)

We have seen, in this section, that each of the classical formulas of proportionate justice is subject to two kinds of criticism. To begin with, while they seem plausible in some cases, there are many other cases in which we have serious doubts about them. Moreover, there are serious theoretical objections that can be raised. Because of this, and the fact that these formulas do not even apply to cases of nonproportionate comparative justice, or to problems of equality of opportunity, most philosophers have rightly abandoned them in their search for some more general theory of comparative justice.

3.4 TWO FORWARD-LOOKING THEORIES OF JUSTICE

One attempt to articulate a fundamental theory of justice is to be found in the writings of the English utilitarian thinkers. We shall begin by looking briefly at the version of that theory put forward by John Stuart Mill.

Mill begins his discussion by correctly pointing out what distinguishes justice from all other aspects of morality. Justice uniquely involves people's receiving their due, receiving that to which they have a right:

> It seems to me that this feature in the case—a right in some person, correlative to the moral obligation—constitutes the specific difference between justice, and generosity or beneficence. Justice implies something which is not only right to do, and wrong not to do, but which some individual person can claim for us as his moral right. No one has a moral right to our generosity or beneficence, because we are not morally bound to practise those virtues towards any given individual. (*Utilitarianism*, chapter 5)

But what is it to have a right to something? And what is the basis for such rights? Mill provides the following utilitarian answer:

> When we call anything a person's right, we mean that he has a valid claim on society to protect him in the possession of it, either by the force of law, or by that of education and opinion. . . . Thus a person is said to have a right to what he can earn in fair professional competition; because society ought not to allow another person to hinder him from endeavouring to earn in that manner as much as he can. But he has not a right to three hundred [pounds] a year, though he may happen to be earning it; because society is not called on to provide that he shall earn that sum. . . . To have a right, then, is, I conceive, to have something which society ought to defend me in the possession of. If the objector goes on to ask, why it ought? I can give him no other reason than general utility. (*ibid.*)

In short, according to the utilitarian theory, justice consists in having each person possess those goods which the general interest says he should possess.

This theory at first seems very abstract. But Mill applied it to a series of practical issues, one of which we discussed in the last section:

> In a co-operative industrial association, is it just or not that talent or skill should give a title to superior renumeration? On the negative side of the question, it is argued that whoever does the best he can, deserves equally well. . . . On the contrary side it is contended, that society receives more from the more efficient labourer; that his services being more useful, society owes him a larger return for them. . . . any choice between them [. . . answers to this question], on grounds of justice, must be perfectly arbitrary. Social utility alone can decide the preference. (*ibid.*)

As a good utilitarian, Mill is telling us that justice consists in a distribution of goods that will result in the general good.

Since the time of Mill, utilitarians have tended to draw egalitarian conclusions from this theory of justice. They have argued that the general good is maximized when society is so organized as to result in a high degree of equality in the distribution of goods. This egalitarian version of the utilitarian theory is nicely summarized by Christopher Jencks:

> We begin with the premise that every individual's happiness is of equal value. From this it is a short step to Bentham's dictum that society should be organized so as to provide the greatest good for the greatest number. In addition, we assume that the law of diminishing returns applies to most of the good things in life. In economic terms this means that people with low incomes value extra income more than people with high incomes. It follows that if we want to maximize the satisfaction of the population, the best way to divide any given amount of money is to make everyone's income the same. Income disparities (except those based on variations in "need") will always reduce overall satisfaction, because individuals with low incomes will lose more than individuals with high incomes gain.
>
> The principal argument against equalizing incomes is that some people contribute more to the general welfare than others, and that they are therefore entitled to greater rewards. The most common version of this argument is that unless those who contribute more than their share are rewarded (and those who contribute less than their share punished) productivity will fall and everyone will be worse off. A more sophisticated version is that people will only share their incomes on an equal basis if all decisions that affect these incomes are made collectively. If people are left free to make decisions on an individual basis, their neighbors cannot be expected to pay the entire cost of their mistakes.
>
> We accept the validity of both these arguments. We believe that men need incentives to contribute to the common good, and we prefer monetary incentives to social or moral incentives, which tend to be inflexible and very coercive. We believe, in other words, that virtue should be rewarded, and we assume that there will be considerable variation in virtue from one individual to another. This does not, however, mean that incomes must remain as unequal as they are now. Even if we assume, for example, that the most productive fifth of all workers accounts for half the Gross National Product, it does not follow that they need receive half the income. A third or a quarter might well suffice to keep both them and others productive. (*Inequality*, chapter 1)

This utilitarian theory of justice merely extends the usual utilitarian argument to the topic of justice. Since we have already criticized utilitarianism in Chapter 1, we will not criticize it again here. Our purpose in reintroducing it is to contrast it to the recent general theory of justice put forward by John Rawls in his book *A Theory of Justice*. This theory has attracted considerable attention for it is one of the few attempts at a general, nonutilitarian theory of justice. We will therefore examine it very carefully.

There are two basic principles in Rawls's theory of justice. They are:

> First: Each person is to have an equal right to the most extensive basic liberty compatible with a similar liberty for others. Second: Social and economic inequalities are to be arranged so that they are both (a) reasonably expected to be to everyone's advantage, and (b) attached to positions and offices open to all. (*A Theory of Justice*, p. 60)

The first of these is a principle of equality, while the second determines what inequalities are just. Since our main concern is with the latter, we will focus on Rawls's second principle.

There are two main differences between Mill's principle of just inequalities—inequalities are just if they maximize the general good—and Rawls's principle. According to Mill, as long as the existence of some inequality maximizes the general good, it is a just inequality. It does not matter how goods are distributed or who has an opportunity to get them. According to Rawls, however, those two factors are very relevant; they are indeed the crux of the matter. For Rawls, an inequality is just only if the goods that it produces are distributed so that everybody gains, and only if everyone has an equal opportunity to be in the more favorable position.

Let us see, in a more concrete fashion, what Rawls's second principle comes to. Suppose we consider the familiar question: should we arrange our economic institutions so that, regardless of need, people are rewarded in proportion to their contribution? Is it just to have this kind of inequality in society? Rawls's second principle might yield the following answer to that question: if we have such a system, people will have a strong incentive to produce more, a much more powerful incentive than the one provided by the desire to aid others. This increased production would mean there is much more available. So everybody probably would gain. So, as long as everyone has an equal chance for getting the extra rewards by producing more, such a system is just.

This answer rests upon certain assumptions about the facts. The most crucial assumption is that the increased production will mean that everyone is better off. But suppose this isn't true? Suppose that such a system leads to some people—presumably nonproducers—being worse off? Then, according to Rawls, this type of inequality would be unjust: It involves sacrificing some so that others may gain. Mill would not agree with this conclusion. For Mill, if total human happiness is increased by such a system of rewards, it is just—despite the fact that it causes a hardship to some.

Rawls obviously requires a great deal before he will consider an inequality just. Why does he advocate such strong requirements for the justice of inequalities? He does so because he believes (1) that these are the only principles of justice that rational people would agree to in advance and (2) that a principle of justice is acceptable only if it would be accepted in advance by rational agents. As he puts it:

> The guiding idea is that the principles of justice for the basic structure of society are the object of the original agreement. They are the principles that free and rational persons concerned to further their own interests would accept in an initial position of equality as defining the fundamental terms of their association. (*ibid.*, p. 11)

Rawls has an extremely complicated argument to back up this claim, one that we cannot consider at this point. But there is another feature of his theory that deserves special attention. Rawls places great emphasis on equality of opportunity. An inequality is justified only if everyone has a real chance to obtain the more favorable position. Even if some social inequality would result in everyone benefitting, it would still be unjust if some people were not allowed to compete for the more favorable position.

Brian Barry, one of Rawls's most astute critics, has argued that Rawls's principle of just inequalities is fundamentally in error. Rawls's principle, says Barry, allows inequalities so long as they have certain consequences, namely, that everyone be better off. The trouble, according to Barry, is that this misses the whole point of principles of justice. Principles of justice, says Barry, tell us to reward or punish people, perhaps unequally, in accordance with what they have done and what they are:

> Justice is not a forward-looking virtue. Justice consists in some appropriate relationship between what a person has done or what he is now and the benefits that he receives or the costs that he bears. The size of incentive payments is not determined by the criteria of just distribution. It may be considered essential to pay someone a certain amount in order to get him to do something and it may also

be considered vital that he should do it. But the payment does not automatically become just when these two conditions obtain. ("On Social Justice," *The Oxford Review* (1967))

Barry's point can also be put as follows. Rawls's theory of just inequalities shares certain basic features with Mill's utilitarian theory of just inequalities. They both assert that the justice or injustice of an inequality is determined by the consequences of adopting that inequality into our social structure. They both assert, therefore, that the classical principles of justice, like the maxims of proportionate justice we listed above, should be followed only when it would lead to the appropriate consequences. (Mill and Rawls differ, of course, about the appropriate consequences, and about whether everyone must gain before an inequality is just). This is why Rawls would try to justify inequalities through what people produce. The existence of such an incentive yields benefits that come to everyone. Now, in this way, both Rawls's theory and utilitarianism differ from the classical view of justice—as embodied in such rules as our maxims. The classical view holds that the justice or injustice of an inequality is determined by the past and present actions, the character and condition of the individual person. It is determined by such things as a person's past actions and his present needs. Barry would therefore reject both Mill's and Rawls's accounts of justice, and return to principles that are not forward-looking.

A second objection can be raised against both the utilitarian theory and Rawls's more recent theory. This objection would first point out that there are several political ideals, and that justice is only one of them. Others would be equality, freedom, fraternity, and democracy. We have already seen, earlier in this chapter, that the ideal of equality is not identical with the ideal of justice. We saw, in fact, that there are such things as just inequalities. Now this second objection holds that, if we are to avoid tremendous conflicts between the ideals of justice and freedom, we must reject both the utilitarian and the Rawlsian conception of justice. The basic idea behind this argument is to be found in the following passage by Friedrich Hayek:

> We do not object to equality as such. It merely happens to be the case that a demand for equality is the professed motive of most of those who desire to impose upon society a preconceived pattern of distribution. Our objection is against all attempts to impress upon society a deliberately chosen pattern of distribution, whether it be an order of equality or of inequality. . . . If one objects to the use of coercion in order to bring about a more even or a more just distribution, this does not mean that one does not reward these as desirable. But if we wish to preserve a free society, it is essential that

we recognize that the desirability of a particular object is not sufficient justification for the use of coercion. (*Constitution of Liberty,* chapter 6)

Let us look at this argument more carefully, beginning with what is meant by freedom and liberty. Sometimes people who refer to freedom and liberty are referring to self-government via the democratic process. Sometimes they are referring to freedom of the will. But the proponents of this argument are referring to something different. When they use the term freedom they mean the human condition in which one person is not coerced by another person into acting in a certain way. The ideal of freedom that Hayek and others look to is the ideal of noncoercion.

What is it to coerce someone into acting in a certain way? If, for example, a person acts in the way that he does because he has been threatened by another person, we say he has been coerced. Thus, if A tells B that he will shoot B unless B drives A away from the scene of a crime, and B does drive A away because of that threat, then we think of B as having been coerced by A. Now, we have strong moral objections against coercion. We feel it is immoral to use threats to get people to behave in certain ways. This is not true in every case. Our system of criminal law uses threats of punishment as a way of getting people to do certain things but not other things. But there the person is being coerced into doing what he is supposed to do and refraining from doing that which he has no right to do (for example, killing or stealing). Normally, however, we think of coercion as illegitimate. The exact analysis of coercion, including this distinction between legitimate and illegitimate cases, is of great importance. However, we need not consider it now. We already have sufficient background to understand the objection being discussed—that the pursuit of justice, as understood by Mill or Rawls, leads to illegitimate coercion.

The main trouble seems to be that the principles of justice that they put forward are patterned principles of justice. Their principles say that a just distribution of goods should be in accordance with a certain pattern. The pattern may be a distribution in proportion to people's needs or efforts, or it may be a distribution that increases the total amount of goods. Whatever it may be, the important point is that there is a pattern. If society seriously pursues that ideal of justice, it will have to impose a pattern. And that means more governmental regulation and coercion. To quote Robert Nozick:

> No end-state principle or distributional pattern principle of justice can be continuously realized without continuous interference into people's lives. Any favored pattern would be transformed into one

> unfavored by the principle, by people choosing to act in various ways; e.g., by people exchanging goods and services with other people, or giving things to other people, things the transferrers are entitled to under the favored distributional pattern. To maintain a pattern one must either continuously interfere to stop people from transferring resources as they wish to, or continually (or periodically) interfere to take from some persons resources that others for some reason chose to transfer to them. (*Anarchy, State, and Utopia,* chapter 7)

Nozick argues that if we are to avoid excessive and illegitimate governmental coercion, which would deprive us of our freedom to use or transfer our assets as we please, we must not pursue any of the patterned ideals of justice.

What Nozick and others have shown is that there is a *conflict* between the patterned ideals of justice and the ideal of freedom to exchange and transfer goods without governmental regulation and coercion. They opt for this ideal of freedom and reject the patterned ideals of justice, but there are others—especially in the socialist camp—who argue for rejecting that ideal of freedom and for keeping the patterned ideals of justice. These thinkers believe that justice, in the patterned sense, lays the social foundation for a more important type of freedom.

> The freedoms to which Liberal Morality gives most attention . . . are of particular interest to three classes of men: entrepreneurs, professional consultants, and intellectuals. But there are, of course, other freedoms . . . of which the great mass of men are only too often deprived: in particular, the freedoms associated with leisure, freedom to obtain disinterested knowledge, to cultivate tastes of one's own, freedom or the genuine opportunity—to enjoy one's friendships and family life. . . . This freedom, freedom to be, cannot be legislated into existence; but it is our duty to ensure by whatever means we can devise, that the most obvious obstacles to it shall be removed. Among these are the economic waste and insecurity involved in every form of competitive (liberal) economy. ("Liberal and Socialist Morality," *Philosophy,* 1949)

A similar point was made by R. Tawney:

> It is constantly assumed by privileged classes that, when the State refrains from intervening in any department of economic or social affairs, what remains as the result of its inaction is liberty. In reality, as far as the mass of mankind are concerned, what remains is, not liberty, but tyranny. (*The Attack and Other Papers*)

JUSTICE AND EQUALITY

Nevertheless, despite this attempt to save a patterned conception of justice, it would seem better if we could find a theory of justice that did not involve so much coercion in its pursuit.

3.5 SKETCH OF A THEORY

There are a number of lessons to be learned from our analysis of the theories of justice that we have examined so far:

1. Justice is not the same ideal as equality; there exist just inequalities.

2. As Mill pointed out, the distinctive feature of justice is that it consists in each person's having that to which he has a right.

3. Various considerations are relevant in determining what is just, no one monolithic theory works, and what is relevant in some contexts is not relevant in others.

4. As Brian Barry has argued, these considerations are not forward-looking. They do not concern the consequences for society of certain social arrangements. Rather they are considerations having to do with the past and present situation, character, and actions of the agents involved.

5. Justice does not consist in some one overall pattern for the distribution of goods in society.

How can all of these lessons be put together into one comprehensive theory of justice? The following suggests itself as a first approximation. People have a variety of rights. They have these rights because of various factors of their past and present situation, their character and actions. They do not have them because of certain consequences of their having them. Different rights depend upon different factors. Justice consists in the satisfaction of these rights. This satisfaction results in certain equalities among people; these are the just equalities. It also results in certain inequalities among people; these are the just inequalities.

Naturally, there can be different versions of this theory of justice, each one based upon its own views of the rights of individuals. We will present such a version shortly. Before doing so, however, I want to say that even if one disagrees with some particular version of this theory, what one will be disagreeing with is a certain view of the rights that people have. One still may well agree with this general theory of justice, a theory that differs from the ones that we have considered until now.

What rights do people have? How are we to answer that question? Well, if our argument in chapter 1 is correct, we should appeal to our intuitions about general principles and particular cases. We cannot, however, present the whole argument from intuition here; all that we can do is to sketch its conclusion.

There seem to be four types of rights which people have:

1. *Rights to certain forbearances.* We have a right not to be killed, physically assaulted, coerced, libelled, etc. These are rights that all of us (at least initially) have equally.

2. *Rights based upon our basic needs.* We have a right to a certain level of nourishment, shelter, clothing, medical care, etc. These, too, are rights that all of us (at least initially) have equally.

3. *Rights based upon our acts.* We have the right to the results of our labor, and, in particular, we have the right to previously unowned natural resources that we have improved by laboring on them.

4. *Rights based upon the acts of others.* We have the right to all that has been promised to us, whether explicitly or implicitly. This right includes all that has been implicitly promised to us by our spouses (when we marry them), our parents (when they produce us), our fellow citizens (when they agree to live in a society with us), and so on. Since different promises are made to different people, these rights are never had equally by all.

There are at least two complications that have to be kept in mind here. The first is that there are many reasons why these rights need not be satisfied. Under certain circumstances, a person may be justly deprived of one of them. Thus, if A tries to assault B and B can prevent this only by assaulting A, B may justly do so for A has lost, in this context, his right not to be assaulted. They may be outweighed by considerations of great public gain or by the need to satisfy other rights. Thus, my property can be taken by the state if it needs it for the public welfare. In such cases, compensation is owed to the one who has been deprived of his rights. Again, one may be required to give up some rights in order to meet one's obligations to satisfy the rights of others. Thus, some of my property is taxed away from me to be used by the state to satisfy the rights of others.

The second complication is that these rights, particularly the rights of type 2, can be held valid to varying degrees. This greatly changes the practical implications of our theory of justice. The greater the extent of the rights of type 2, the greater the percentage of resources that must be devoted to satisfying them, and, since these are held equally by all, the greater the equality of distribution of the society's resources.

What, according to this picture, would the just society be like? This question cannot be fully answered. We know the society would be where everyone enjoys the rights of types 1 and 2 (with the exceptions of those who have waived or lost their rights, and of those who have received compensation for their being deprived of some of their rights). In other words, with these exceptions, it will be a society in which everyone has certain basic needs satisfied; it will also be a society where no one is killed, assaulted, coerced, etc. But the other features of the just society will depend partially on our actions (what work have we done) and partially upon the actions of others (what they have agreed to give us). These factors, of course, determine the other rights people have. In this way, then, there is no complete pattern of justice. Many of the demands of justice depend upon the free actions of people.

The sketch of justice we have here then is both incomplete and not entirely determined. But it is one that recommends itself to our intuitions the more we work it out.

4

The Existence of the State and the Obligation to Obey Its Laws

Suppose that you belonged to a group which had been oppressed for a long period of time. Your rights had constantly been infringed upon, you received extremely unfair treatment, and so on. As a result, you lived in conditions of poverty and deprivation. Suppose moreover that you had tried to change these conditions through the political system, by voting for favorable candidates and by appealing to the courts. But suppose also that you had failed—partially because members of your group weren't fully allowed to participate in the political system, and partially because the majority, which had more power, opposed your group. Finally, suppose you became convinced that there was a way to improve things—to demonstrate in front of those institutions that discriminated against you, to hold protest meetings in your city, etc.— but you also realized that such activities were illegal. What should you do? Is it permissible in such cases to violate the law?

Suppose that you felt your country was engaged in an illegal and immoral war, a war that was causing untold suffering to tens of thousands of innocent people. Suppose you had tried to stop this involvement through the normal political process. Again, suppose you had failed. And suppose finally that you were now ordered to join the army and fight in that war. You realize that your legal obligation is to obey that order, but, at the same time, you think it would be very immoral to fight in this war. What should you do? Is it permissible in such a case to violate the law?

THE EXISTENCE OF THE STATE

Questions like those rose to the center of attention with the civil-rights movement and the antiwar movement in the 1960s. Not surprisingly, these questions gave rise to diverse reactions. There were, on the one hand, many who were moved by Martin Luther King's claims:

> You express a great deal of anxiety over our willingness to break laws. This is certainly a legitimate concern. Since we so diligently urge people to obey the Supreme Court's decision of 1954 outlawing segregation in the public schools, it is rather strange and paradoxical to find us consciously breaking laws. One may well ask, "How can you advocate breaking some laws and obeying others?" The answer is found in the fact that there are two types of laws: There are just and there are unjust laws. I would agree with St. Augustine that "an unjust law is no law at all." . . . I hope you see the distinction I am trying to point out. In no sense do I advocate evading or defying the law as the rabid segregationist would do. This would lead to anarchy. One who breaks an unjust law must do it openly, lovingly, and with a willingness to accept the penalty. I submit that an individual who breaks a law that conscience tells him is unjust, and willingly accepts the penalty by staying in jail to arouse the conscience of the community over its injustice, is in reality expressing the very highest respect for law. ("Letter from Birmingham City Jail")

On the other hand, there were those who felt that this disobedience to the law was not merely illegal but also immoral:

> The country, therefore, cannot accept Dr. King's doctrine that he and his followers will pick and chose, knowing that it is illegal to do so. I say, such doctrine is not only illegal and for that reason alone should be abandoned, but that it is also immoral, destructive of the principles of democratic government, and a danger to the very civil rights Dr. King seeks to promote. (Louis Waldman, "Civil Rights—Yes: Civil Disobedience—No," *New York State Bar Journal,* 1965)

Behind this controversy lie fundamental philosophical questions about the nature and legitimacy of the state and its laws. These questons also concern the source and extent of our obligation to obey these laws. Those who were involved in the great debate of the 1960s about civil disobedience rarely dealt explicitly with these fundamental questions. Their arguments, however, were full of implicit assumptions about them. This is hardly surprising; basic philosophical issues are rarely discussed in an explicit and reasoned fashion during the heat of political arguments and practical political action. In this chapter, however, we will follow a more reflective approach. We will begin with these underlying questions about the legitimacy of the state and its laws and about the nature and extent of our obligation to obey them. It is only after we deal with these that we will return to the questions concerning civil disobedience.

4.1 THE ANARCHIST ARGUMENT

Our concern will be solely with the legitimacy of one type of law—the type that regulates behavior by prohibiting or requiring some action. Having grown up with such laws, we are all very used to their existence, and it is hard for us to conceive of what it would be like to live without them. But let us try to do so anyway. One thing is immediately clear: if these laws did not exist, we would have open to us many more options—some of which we might follow—than we do now. There are many things that we do not do (and others that we do do) only because of the threat of punishment for disobeying the law. In a way, therefore, the system of laws that we are considering is a coercive system; the state, through its laws and its penal institutions, coerces us into behaving in certain ways.

Our recognition of the coercive nature of the state and its legal system raises very clearly the fundamental problems about these institutions: what justifies the existence of this coercive state? Isn't coercion always wrong? If it is wrong, doesn't that mean that the state and its laws have no legitimacy?

There are many kinds of challenge to the legitimacy of the state and its laws. But most of these are challenges to specific states or to specific laws. And most presuppose the legitimacy of other states and other laws. For example, a challenge to a state on the grounds that it is a tyrannical oppressor of the people challenges only a specific state; it presupposes the legitimacy of other states, those which are ruled democratically and are run for the welfare of all. The challenge we are considering is more fundamental. For it challenges the legitimacy of all states which have laws regulating behavior and systems of enforcement backing up those laws (in effect, all states). In effect, our challenge is an argument for anarchism, for the view that all states are illegitimate. The anarchist approach is summarized by David Novick as follows:

> The essence of anarchist thought is the emphasis on the freedom of the individual, leading to the denial and condemnation of any authority which hinders his free and full development, particularly the State. The rejection of all authority represents the main contri-

bution of anarchism to political thought and distinguishes it from other political and social theories some of which, for example, liberalism, may have other features similar to anarchism, and may even start from the same basis. Bound up with these fundamental ideas are the theories and criticisms of law and government, of property, of the whole social and economic system and patterns of behavior prevalent in it, and of the ways and means suggested or preached as remedies or panaceas for the evils. ("The Place of Anarchism in the History of Political Thought," *Review of Politics,* 1958)

The crucial assumption of this argument is that it is always wrong to coerce people into behaving in certain ways. But is this assumption true? There seem to be at least two exceptions to this moral rule that might help meet the anarchist challenge.

1. There are some people (e.g., children, the mentally incompetent) whose behavior is legitimately regulated by those in the appropriate position (e.g., parents or guardians). Although we may object to particular cases, the general idea of such regulation—if done for the benefit of the children or the incompetent—seems appropriate and acceptable. Now there have been some who have responded to the anarchist argument by suggesting that the state is the guardian of its citizens, legitimately regulating and coercing their behavior for their own interest. However, this kind of paternalistic coercion seems objectionable when applied to competent adult citizens, whatever its merits as applied to children or the incompetent.

Although most of us would be quick to dismiss this kind of paternalism, its role in our own legal system is very great. There seem to be many laws whose goal is to protect us from ourselves, or somehow to coerce our behavior for our own benefit. Such laws include:

laws prohibiting suicide

laws requiring motorcyclists to wear safety helmets

laws requiring us to contribute to a retirement policy (Social Security laws)

laws prohibiting us from paying more than a certain rate of interest when we borrow money

laws regulating sexual behavior among consenting adults in private

laws regulating the use of drugs which do not lead to antisocial conduct

In each of these cases, the justification of the law seems to be that society is forcing us not to do certain things that might harm us. It is questionable whether any of these laws are just if we reject the view that it is permissible to coerce adult competent citizens for their benefit.

2. The second exception to the rule against coercion is of greater importance to political philosophy. Suppose that A is attempting to deprive B of something to which B has a right. Suppose, for example, that A is attempting to kill B. We would not object to the use of force, or the threat of force, as a way of preventing A from carrying out that action. We do not object to coercion when it serves to prevent the deprivation of rights. If this is so, then perhaps we can think of the state as a legitimate mechanism for carrying out the coercion that we need to protect our rights.

Just how extensive should such a state be? A lot depends on what rights you accept for legitimate protection. If the only right you believe in are certain forbearances, then the state should provide the coercive mechanism to prevent its citizens from being killed, assaulted, etc., and no more. If you accept rights to the fruits of labor and rights to what has been promised, then the state should also provide the coercive mechanism to prevent its citizens from being deprived of those rights. And finally, of course, if you accept rights to certain basic needs, then the state should provide the coercive mechanism to ensure the satisfaction of those needs.

Even if you take the most far-reaching of these alternatives, however, the resulting state will be far less extensive than any of the states we know today. It would not, presumably, provide highways or national forests. Nor would it regulate monopolies, or, indeed, carry out many other functions of the modern state. In short, it would use its coercive mechanism merely to protect rights. It would not go beyond that to promote the general welfare. To many, this seems like a very incomplete state. They would like to meet the anarchist challenge by showing that a much more extensive state can be justified. We turn therefore to attempts to justify the more extensive state.

4.2 SOCIAL CONTRACT THEORY

There is an important philosophical tradition which, if correct, would meet the challenge posed by the anarchist argument. This tradition says governmental coercion can be legitimate if it is based upon the consent of those being coerced. This is called the social contract theory because it sees governments arising and drawing their legitimacy from agreements between the people and the state. Perhaps the most familiar statement of this view is to be found near the opening of the Declaration of Independence:

THE EXISTENCE OF THE STATE

> We hold these truths to be self-evident, that all men are created equal; that they are endowed by their Creator with certain unalienable rights; that among these are life, liberty, and the pursuit of happiness. That, to secure these rights, governments are instituted among men, deriving their just powers from the consent of the governed.

This quotation contains the three fundamental claims of this tradition: (1) people have certain rights independently of any government, and these rights include the right of liberty (the right to do as one has decided and not be coerced); (2) people with such rights join together to form governments, for they have good reasons for preferring to live under a government than in a state of nature; (3) the government draws its legitimacy from the fact that each person has agreed to its existence and to its use of coercion to enforce its laws.

Versions of this tradition differ about how they understand these three claims, especially the second. Since the different interpretations of the second are so important, let us look at how a few versions understand it.

Plato advocates a view similar to at least part of the social contract theory in his fundamental work, the *Republic*. In the second book of that work, he sets out to discover the origins of the state. He sets out to discover why people join together to live in communities. He claims that they do so to gain material benefits. Living under some form of communal organization, they can benefit from joint effort and specialization of labor:

> A state, I said, arises, as I conceive, out of the needs of mankind; no one is self-sufficing, but all of us have many wants. Can any other origin of a State be imagined? There can be no other. Then, as we have many wants, and many persons are needed to supply them, one takes a helper for one purpose and another for another; and when these partners and helpers are gathered together in one habitation the body of inhabitants is termed a State. (*Republic*, Book II)

Thus Plato emphasizes gains in material goods. But, Hobbes and Locke—two very important modern social contract theorists—emphasize the role of the state as a protector of that to which we already have a right. Hobbes, as we saw in chapter 2, had a very pessimistic view of life in the state of nature. He felt it would be a life of fear and conflict. People, he said, join together to form an organized state to avoid that. They join together to preserve their security and their very lives:

> The final cause, end, or design of men (who naturally love liberty, and dominion over others) in the introduction of that restraint upon themselves, in which we see them live in commonwealths, is the foresight of their own preservation, and of a more contented life thereby; that is to say, of getting themselves out from that miserable condition of war which is necessarily consequent, as hath been shown, to the natural passions of men when there is no visible power to keep them in awe. (*Leviathan,* chapter 17)

Locke had a less pessimistic view of life in nature. Still, he felt that the existence of the state serves, in two very important ways, to preserve our rights, especially our property rights. First of all, the laws passed by state clarify and define the rights of each person, and court decisions peacefully settle questions and doubts about those rights. Secondly, the state can effectively protect us from those who try illegitimately to deprive us of that to which we have a right.

The social contract theory that we will be interested in here is closer to Plato's than to Locke's. We will be interested in the fact that people consent to the formation of the state because they want a coercive mechanism that can be used to promote the general welfare and not merely to protect their rights. Our only major difference with Plato is that he overemphasizes the material factors that contribute to the general well-being.

We have gone into these differences of opinion about the second claim of the social contract theory—about why people consent to the formation of a state—because these views will be very important when we come to consider questions of obedience to the law and civil disobedience. Let us now return to a more general examination of the social contract theory and the problems it faces.

The basic idea behind the social contract theory is this: governmental coercion is legitimate because those who will be subject to the coercion, the people, have consented to it in advance. They did so when they joined together to create the state. Because of their consent, they cannot object to being coerced later on.

The first question that we have to consider is whether their consent really does the job. Many philosophers have claimed that people cannot legitimately renounce their freedom, which is what they would be doing in consenting to state coercion. According to these philosophers, such renunciations are automatically null and void, and therefore the state would still be wrong in coercing its citizens even if they did consent. One such philosopher, Rousseau, put the argument as follows:

> To renounce freedom is to renounce one's humanity, one's rights as a man and equally one's duties. There is no possible *quid pro quo* [one thing in return for another] for one who renounces everything;

indeed such renunciation is contrary to man's very nature; for if you take away all freedom of the will, you strip a man's actions of all moral significance. (*The Social Contract*, I, 4)

The force of this objection will become clearer if we consider the following example. Suppose that someone voluntarily decides to become a slave, so that his master can coerce his behavior at will. Suppose moreover that the person who makes this decision is a mature responsible adult. Should we recognize his decision as being within his rights? Or wouldn't we want to say that that person's action is irrational, illegitimate, and void. But then why shouldn't we say the same thing about the citizen's consenting to being coerced by the government?

Defenders of the social contract theory insist, of course, that this is not a good analogy. They insist there are major differences between the slave and the citizen which explain why the slave's consent is illegitimate while the citizen's consent is not. The main differences are as follows:

1. The slave gives his master complete control over all of his actions. The citizen, by contrast, is consenting to a state that is severely limited in the types of coercive laws that it can pass, and these limitations protect the basic rights of the citizen.

2. The slave has no say at all in determining the orders that his master gives him. The citizen, on the other hand, is consenting to a state in which he can participate, through the democratic process. He can help decide which laws shall be passed so that he can help protect his rights and interests.

3. People gain a great deal by leaving the state of nature and forming a governed society. The major defenders of the social contract theory, particularly in their special defense of its second claim, have pointed out many such gains. It would be hard, they say, to imagine how civilized life could exist without a government. Consequently, the citizen's partial loss of freedom can be, and is, adequately compensated for. But the gains of the slave can hardly be commensurate with what the slave loses.

In short, the defenders of social contract theory feel that Rousseau's claim is a gross overstatement. Since the citizen consents to the formation of a democratic government whose powers are limited so as to protect the citizen's basic rights, and since such a government makes tremendous contributions to civilized life, the consent of the citizen is rational and legitimate. And it is this consent that justifies the existence of anything more than the most minimal state.

Note that this response strictly defines the form of a legitimate government. It must be a democratic state whose powers are so limited as to protect basic rights. This version of the social contract theory is then a defense of the liberal state. It should be pointed out that there were some social contract theorists, the most notable being Hobbes, who would not have agreed to these limits to the state's power. Hobbes and others felt that life in the state of nature is so bad, and the power needed to avoid that condition is so great, that the citizen should consent to an almost unlimited government. Let us focus our attention, however, on the more prevalent, liberal version of the social contract theory.

Let us suppose, at least for the sake of argument, that Rousseau is mistaken and that the consent of the governed would be enough to justify the state's coercive action. There are, nevertheless, a series of further objections against the social contract theory. David Hume put two of them as follows:

> But the contract on which government is founded is said to be the original contract, and consequently may be supposed too old to fall under the knowledge of the present generation. If the agreement by which savage men first associated and conjoined their forces be here meant, this is acknowledged to be real; but being so ancient and being obliterated by a thousand changes of government and princes, it cannot now be supposed to retain any authority. If we would say anything to the purpose, we must assert that every particular government which is lawful and which imposes any duty of allegiance on the subject was at first founded on consent and a voluntary compact. But besides that this supposes the consent of the fathers to bind the children, even to the most remote generations. . . . it is not justified by history or experience in any age or country of the world. ("Of the Original Contract")

Hume's objections are really very straightforward. The defenders of the social contract theory want to defend the state's use of coercion by referring to the citizens' consent. But, the consent in question must be consent to *that* state and not to some original state at the dawn of human history. Moreover, the consent in question had to be given at the time of the founding of the state in question. But, Hume argues, (1) most states began by the use of force and not by the consent of the citizens, and (2) even for those that began by the consent of citizens, coercive force is legitimate only when applied to those citizens who consented, and not to those (especially in future generations) who did not consent.

As we look over these two objections, we can see that they rest upon the fundamental assumption that the consent which justifies the existence of a state had to take place—if at all—at the time the state was actually founded. It is not surprising that Hume made that assumption. Those who put forward the social contract theory, philosophers like Plato, Hobbes, and Locke, called it a theory of the *origin* of the state.

THE EXISTENCE OF THE STATE

And it was sometimes even defended as a historical theory about how states began. Naturally, then, Hume just assumed that the consent in question had to occur when the state first began. But, of course, there is no reason why a contemporary defender of the social contract theory has to make that same assumption. There is no reason why he cannot say that states draw their legitimacy from some other consent. In the next section of this chapter, we will consider two attempts to defend the social contract along these lines.

4.3 TACIT CONSENT AND HYPOTHETICAL CONSENT

An obvious suggestion to begin with is that the state draws its legitimacy from the ongoing consent of the current generation of citizens. If such a consent exists it would solve both of Hume's problems. If the current citizens consent, we needn't be concerned with the origin of the state in question. Even if it originated through force or fraud, it is legitimate now if its citizens now consent to its existence. However, only if the next generation consents as well will it legitimately be able to coerce them. According to this version of the social contract theory, each generation is bound only by its own consent.

The trouble is, of course, that it is hard to see where and when the citizens of contemporary states would explicitly consent to the existence of their state. There are many tribal societies in which such consent is explicitly given by the young members of the tribe during their initiation into full membership in the tribe. Few states have such initiation rites. But perhaps such explicit consent isn't required. Perhaps all that is required is some implicit consent. And if that is all that is required then perhaps this theory will work. After all, don't we all consent to the existence of our state when we continue to live in it and derive benefits from doing so?

This version of the social contract theory was first suggested by Plato in his dialogue *Crito*. In that dialogue, Socrates is portrayed explaining why he will accept his unjust death sentence rather than disobey the law and escape. He says:

> Then the laws will say, Consider, Socrates, if we are speaking truly that in your present attempt you are going to do us an injury. For, having brought you into the world, and nurtured and educated you, and given you and every other citizen a share in every good which we have to give, we further proclaim to any Athenian by the liberty which we allow him, that if he does not like us when he has become of age and has seen the ways of the city, and made

our acquaintance, he may go where he pleases and take his goods with him. . . . Anyone who does not like us and the city, and who wants to emigrate to a colony or to any other city, may go where he likes, retaining his property. But he who has experience of the manner in which we order justice and administer the state, and still remains, has entered into an implied contract that he will do as we command him.

There are two points that should be noted about this tacit or implied consent. To begin with, its defenders usually say that the mere fact that a person does not leave the state is a source of tacit consent. But that needn't be the only way in which we tacitly consent to the state's existence. By engaging in a variety of political activities (for example, using the court system or voting in elections) we can also be said to be giving that tacit consent. And it might even be suggested that our obligation to obey the state's laws grows as we perform more of these civic actions. This suggestion has been developed by Michael Walzer. He offers, for example, the following analysis of the political obligation of oppressed minorities.

. . . oppressed persons simply have no political obligations, or rather, no obligations to the state. Slaves owe nothing to their masters and nothing again to the ruling committee of their masters. Nor do the relative numbers of slaves and masters make any difference, except in the strategic considerations of the two groups. Cases where the oppressed are recognized as citizens are much harder. Their votes are honestly counted, let us assume, but as it turns out they never win. They are free to organize, but they face a thousand petty difficulties and their attempts to sustain large-scale organizations regularly fail. Patterns of social and economic discrimination reinforce their minority political status (and their political weakness reinforces the social and economic patterns—it hardly matters which way the causal connections are worked). The pressure they can bring to bear within the political system is limited. . . . I want to argue more than this, beginning again with the special condition of the people I am considering: they are oppressed *citizens;* they are *formally* free and equal. I have suggested that activists working on their behalf ought to exploit the formal rules of the democratic system. Now insofar as they do this, or rather, insofar as they do it with some success, they begin the process of transforming their citizenship into something real (something valuable as well). That means also that they begin acquiring obligations within the democratic state where they work and to its citizens among whom they find allies and supporters. At the same time, however, their obligations continue to be mediated by the patterns of responsibility that exist within the world of the oppressed. (*Obligations,* chapter 3)

The second important point about tacit consent is this: To the extent that it results from a decision to stay in the state rather than to leave it, that consent can exist only if one is free and able to leave the state. A state that does not allow its citizens to emigrate can hardly claim afterwards that by not moving away its citizens have consented to the state's existence. This point is worth serious attention since it helps explain why the right to emigrate is of such fundamental importance. In many ways, the state that forbids emigration loses its very legitimacy. But this point also raises certain practical questions about the right to emigrate: (1) Does the citizen have the right to emigrate at any time or only during a given period of his life? In other words, is there a time after which it is considered that the citizen *has* consented to the existence of the state as well as to its right to prevent him from further emigrating? Can the state ever completely prohibit some people from emigrating (for example, those with access to security information)? (2) Does the state have to allow the citizen to take all of his property? Can it limit the amount that can be taken out? (3) Can the state insist that the citizen who emigrates must pay for his schooling, for previous benefits, etc.? Can it prohibit his emigration until he does so?

All of these questions are of great practical significance. But none of them touch at the heart of the theoretical difficulty with this proposal. The main difficulty with tacit consent has to do with whether it applies equally to all, that is, whether it explains the state's right to coerce *all* its citizens. David Hume put this objection as follows:

> Can we seriously say that a poor peasant or artisan has a free choice to leave his country when he knows no foreign language or manners and lives from day to day by the small wages which he acquires? We may as well assert that a man, by remaining in a vessel, freely consents to the dominion of the master, though he was carried on board while asleep and must leap into the ocean and perish the moment he leaves her. ("Of the Original Contract")

Those who defend the theory of tacit consent must recognize that the kind of objection Hume raises is a serious one. The most the defenders can do is to claim that it doesn't refute their theory. Instead, they say, Hume's objection merely shows that the state's right to coerce is stronger vis-à-vis some citizens (those who have a real opportunity to emigrate and who have tacitly consented in other ways).

Can this conclusion be avoided? Only if we can find some other consent. But which other consent? Not some actual consent at the time that the state was founded—for it might not have occurred—and not some actual present consent. Is there any other consent left?

These questions lead us to the final version of the social contract theory. This version says that the legitimacy of the state's coercive power rests upon a *hypothetical*, as opposed to an actual, consent. The leading advocate of this view is John Rawls. (This view, in fact, is closely related to Rawls's theory of justice, which we discussed in chapter 3.) Rawls puts it as follows:

> I believe that the appropriate conception, at least for an account of political obligation in a constitutional democracy, is that of the social contract theory from which so much of our political thought derives. If we are careful to interpret it in a suitably general way, I hold that this doctrine provides a satisfactory basis for political theory. . . . The interpretation I suggest is the following: that the principles to which social arrangements must conform, and in particular the principles of justice, are those which free and rational men would agree to in an original position of equal liberty; and similarly, the principles which govern men's relations to institutions and define their natural duties and obligations are the principles to which they would consent when so situated. It should be noted that in this interpretation of the contract theory the principles of justice are understood as the outcome of a hypothetical agreement. . . . There is no mention of an actual agreement nor need such an agreement ever be made. ("The Justification of Civil Disobedience")

At first glance, this hypothetical consent theory seems very strange. Rawls claims that a coercive social arrangement is justified if free and rational people in a position of equal liberty *would* agree to its existence. But of what importance is it that people under certain circumstances *would* consent to a social arrangement involving state coercion if no one in some actual state *has actually* consented to those coercive arrangements? Rawls maintains, however, that it is just this hypothetical type of consent which is morally most relevant. The *actual* failure of people to consent, due either to their not having an opportunity or to the fact that they do not satisfy the conditions of rationality, freedom, etc., is not morally relevant.

There are many difficult questions raised by such a hypothetical consent theory. To begin with, how exactly shall we specify the conditions under which the hypothetical choice would be made? Second, can we really be sure as to what social arrangements would be agreed to under these hypothetical circumstances? And finally, is Rawls right in supposing that this hypothetical consent is really more morally relevant than some actual consent or failure to consent?

Let us see where we now stand. We began with the anarchist's claim that the state could never be justified because it is a mechanism of coercion. That claim presupposed that coercion is never justified. However, that was easily refuted. But, the result of the refutation was not entirely satisfactory either, for all that we could easily show was that it was legitimate to have a coercive state as a mechanism for protecting rights. Just how extensive such a state would be would depend, of course, on what rights were to be protected. It seemed, then, that what we were looking for was a justification of a more extensive state. In trying to justify such a state, we turned to social contract theory. No version of that theory was entirely satisfactory, but a number of alternatives seemed possible, including the theory of tacit consent and the theory of hypothetical consent.

Let's assume, then, that the existence of an extensive but democratic state can be justified through the consent of its citizens. We shall try in the final section of this chapter to work out some of the implications of this view for the question of civil disobedience.

4.4 OBEDIENCE VS. DISOBEDIENCE

Social contract theory, at least in its more liberal form, has always had a revolutionary tinge to it. For example, John Locke ends his discussion with a defense of the right of the citizen to revolt. And it is just this feature of social contract theory which explains its appeal to America's Founding Fathers in justifying their revolt against George III.

It is important to understand what is revolutionary about this theory. One revolutionary argument might run as follows: Government is based on consent; as soon as the consent no longer exists, as soon as the citizens no longer desire the state, that state is illegitimate and its citizens have a right to revolt. But if this is the revolutionary argument it is a very weak one. After all, the citizens have agreed to the existence of the state and have benefitted from its existence. A group of them have no right to suddenly back out because the state's existence is suddenly disadvantageous. It would be as if you and I wanted to back out of a contract which suddenly turned disadvantageous.

Locke's revolutionary argument really runs as follows:

> There is therefore, secondly, another way whereby governments are dissolved, and that is; when the Legislative, or the Prince, either

of them act contrary to their Trust. . . . The Legislative acts against the Trust reposed in them, when they endeavour to invade the Property of the Subject, and to make themselves, or any part of the Community, Masters, or Arbitrary Disposers of the Lives, Liberties, or Fortunes of the People . . . since it can never be supposed to be the will of the Society, that the Legislative should have a Power to destroy that, which everyone designs to secure, by entering into Society, and for which the People submitted themselves to the Legislators of their own making; whenever the Legislators endeavour to take away, and destroy the Property of the People, or to reduce them to Slavery under Arbitrary Power, they put themselves into a state of War with the People who are thereupon absolved from any farther Obedience. ("Second Treatise," chapter 19)

The point of Locke's argument is that people consent to the state with certain goals in mind. In particular, they expect that the state will protect and secure their rights. This goal becomes a condition of their consent, a part of the social contract. When the state instead invades and destroys the rights of its citizens, it is the state that has broken a clause in the social contract. The state has not met a condition upon which the consent is given. Then, the citizen owes no obedience to the state much as we no longer have to obey a contract when the other party has failed to meet its obligations.

In Locke's day, as in our own, there were those who felt that the acceptance of this revolutionary message would lead to disastrous social conflict. Locke correctly saw that this prediction was too extreme.

I Answer, such Revolutions happen not upon every little mismanagement in public affairs. Great mistakes in the ruling part, many wrong and inconvenient Laws, and all the slips of humane frailty will be born by the People, without mutiny or murmur. . . . This Doctrine of a Power in the People of providing for their safety a-new by a new Legislative . . . is the best fence against Rebellion. . . . The properest way to prevent the evil [of oppression and rebellion] is to show them [the rulers] the danger and injustice of it. (*ibid.*)

The Lockean approach was fully accepted by our Founding Fathers, and we find it stated in the second paragraph of the Declaration of Independence. Notice, as you review those familiar lines, how the first half of the paragraph sets out the Lockean justification of revolution while the second half sets out the claim, similar to Locke's, that this theory would not lead to anarchy:

We hold these truths to be self-evident, that all men are created equal; that they are endowed by their Creator with certain unalienable rights; that among these are life, liberty, and the pursuit of happiness. That, to secure these rights, governments are instituted among men, deriving their just powers from the consent of the governed; that, whenever any form of government becomes destructive of these ends, it is the right of the people to alter or to abolish it, and to institute a new government, laying its foundation on such principles, and organizing its powers in such form, as to them shall seem most likely to effect their safety and happiness. Prudence, indeed, will dictate that governments long established should not be changed for light and transient causes; and, accordingly, all experience hath shown, that mankind are more disposed to suffer, while evils are sufferable, than to right themselves by abolishing the forms to which they are accustomed. But, when a long train of abuses and usurpations, pursuing invariably the same object, evinces a design to reduce them under absolute despotism, it is their right, it is their duty, to throw off such government, and to provide new guards for their future security. Such has been the patient sufferance of these colonies, and such is now the necessity which constrains them to alter their former systems of government. The history of the present King of Great Britain is a history of repeated injuries and usurpations, all having, in direct object, the establishment of an absolute tyranny over these states.

It is clear that Locke's discussion centers on the extreme case, one where the state violates so many of the rights of citizens that what is called for is a justifiable revolution. But what if the state only violates some of the rights of citizens, so that a revolution seems too extreme a response? Can the citizens disobey just those laws which violate their rights?

This question, of course, concerns the legitimacy of civil disobedience, which is our central concern in this section. It will be convenient to approach this question from two different points of view: the attitude of the citizen and the attitude of the state.

The attitude of the citizen. Some claim that it is implicit in the social contract that citizens can break laws if they are prepared to pay the penalties. Thus, Harris Wofford has argued as follows:

> Justice Holmes once argued even that a party to a private contract has a right to refuse to comply with the contract if he is ready to pay the penalty. I am not going that far. I do not say we have a right to break the social contract which is our legal system, except through constitutional amendments. But I am arguing that under our social contract man is to be free, and that a free man should

> look on each law not as a command but as a question, for implicit in each law is the alternative of obedience or of respectful civil disobedience and full acceptance of the consequences. Once men no longer believe that they as good citizens must obey any law passed by the legislature, no matter how bad, then they must ask themselves of each law, Is this a law that I should obey? Is it a just law? Is it so unjust that it needs to be resisted from the very inception, and cannot wait the slow process of parliamentary reform? This choice we always have to make. It is the choice which makes us free. I am talking about the freedom which Socrates felt on that morning when, having refused to obey the law abridging his freedom of speech but also refusing to evade the law by escaping from Athens, he peacefully drank the hemlock. ("Nonviolence and the Law," *Journal of Religious Thought*, 1957–58)

This argument is not entirely convincing. The whole purpose of the social contract is to create reasonable conditions where citizens trade some of their freedom for the benefits of living in a state. Can such a contract also provide that we maintain complete freedom—subject only to our paying a price for violating the law? One must not, of course, overdo the strength of the agreement which constitutes the social contract. One sees this fallacy in the argument against civil disobedience quoted from Louis Waldman at the beginning of this chapter. Waldman supposes that contract theory means that the laws of a democratic society must always be obeyed. This is simply a mistake. It is possible for democratic societies, as well as tyrannies, to violate the rights of citizens. John Stuart Mill reminds us of this.

> The will of the people, moreover, practically means the will of the most numerous or the most active part of the people; the majority, or those who succeed in making themselves accepted as the majority; the people, consequently may desire to oppress a part of their number. ("On Liberty," chapter I)

And social contract theory, at least the Lockean version, tells us that those oppressed citizens, rather than having an obligation to obey, have a right to revolt despite the fact that the state is a democratic state. What remains to be seen, however, is whether the right to revolt is selective. In other words, do citizens have a right to disobey *some* laws while not revolting completely and while accepting the general legitimacy of the state?

An attempt to answer this question is to be found in the following remarks of John Rawls:

> The difficulty is that we cannot frame a procedure which guar-

antees that only just and efficient legislation is enacted. Thus even under a just constitution unjust laws may be passed and unjust policies enforced. . . . In agreeing to a democratic constitution . . . one accepts at the same time the principle of majority rule. Assuming that the constitution is just and that we have accepted and plan to continue to accept its benefits, we then have both an obligation and a natural duty (and in any case the duty) to comply with what the majority enacts even though it may be unjust. In this way we become bound to follow unjust laws, not always, of course, but provided the injustice does not exceed certain limits. We recognize that we must run the risk of suffering from the defects of one another's sense of justice; this burden we are prepared to carry as long as it is more or less evenly distributed or does not weigh too heavily. ("The Justification of Civil Disobedience")

There are really two fundamentally sound points that Rawls is making here: (1) In agreeing to any state, given the imperfection of any constitution, we agree to put up with a certain amount of injustice. Consequently, not every act of injustice justifies disobedience. (2) There is a certain point, however, at which disobedience becomes justified even if the state is still basically just and no revolution is called for.

Rawls's answer is hardly a complete solution, for it does not settle the details as to when disobedience is justified and how much of it is justified. However, the basic framework for dealing with those details is there.

Let us agree with Rawls then, at least for the moment, that in an essentially just society, the mere fact that a law is unjust does not justify violating it. However, if the injustice in question were sufficiently great, breaking an unjust law *would* be justified. Now, what does this mean for the individual who legitimately violates the law and for the state that must deal with this violation? The conventional answer is that the individual must pay a penalty to the state for violating the law, despite the fact that the violation of the law was morally justified. Why must this penalty be paid? Marshall Cohen sets out the reasons in a very illuminating essay.

Cohen begins by rejecting the view that it is the acceptance of punishment that justifies the act of civil disobedience.

> It is in misinterpreting the role of punishment in the theory of civil disobedience that Ambassador Kennan makes one of his most conspicuous errors. For the theory of civil disobedience does not suggest (although such exponents as James Farmer and Harris Wofford have sometimes argued) that the disobedient's actions are justified by his willingness to pay the penalty that the law pre-

scribes. The idea that paying the penalty justifies breaking the law derives, not from Gandhi and the tradition of civil disobedience, but Oliver Wendell Holmes and the tradition of legal realism. According to Holmes and the legal realists the law characteristically presents us with an option—either to obey, or to suffer the consequences that attach to disobedience. This doctrine is indefensible even in the area of contract law where it arose, and where it has a fragile plausibility, but it is plainly absurd to suppose that the citizen has such an option in the area of criminal law. Criminal punishments are not a simple tax on criminal misconduct, and the citizen is not given the option of engaging in such conduct on the condition that he pay the tax. It is mindless to suppose that murder, rape, or arson would be justified if the criminal were willing to pay the penalty, and the civil disobedient is committed to no such mindlessness. ("Civil Disobedience in a Constitutional Democracy," *Philosophic Exchange* (1970))

Cohen's view is that what actually justifies the act of civil disobedience is the injustice of the law in question. Why then does Cohen think that the person who commits an act of civil disobedience should accept punishment? Some of the reasons for doing so are tactical. If the act of disobedience is to succeed in changing the laws of society, it is helpful to accept the punishment.

After openly breaking the law, the traditional disobedient willingly pays the penalty. This is one of the characteristics that serve to distinguish him from the typical criminal (his appeal to conscience is another) and it helps to establish the seriousness of his views and the depth of his commitment as well. Unfortunately, paying the penalty will not always demonstrate that his actions are in fact disinterested. For the youth protesting the draft, or the welfare recipient protesting poverty, has an obvious and substantial interest in the success of his cause. If the majority suspects that these interests color the disobedient's perception of the issues involved, its suspicions may prove fatal to his ultimate success. This is one reason why the practice of civil disobedience should not be limited to those who are directly injured by the government's immoral or lawless course (as Judge Wyzanski and others have suggested). A show of support by those who have no substantial interest in the matter may carry special weight with a confused, and even with an active sceptical, majority. The majority simply cannot dismiss those over thirty-five as draft-dodgers or those who earn over $35,000 a year as boondogglers. It may therefore consider the issues at stake, and this is the first objective of the civil disobedient. . . . The disobedient's willingness to suffer punishment has another purpose as well. It is meant to weaken the will of the transgressors and to dissuade them from a course of action that the dissenters consider immoral. For, if the transgressors do not draw back, they may be forced to punish some of the most scrupulous and dedicated members of the community. The fact that this is so will often persuade those who heedlessly supported the original measures, not to mention those who supported them with a dim sense of their injustice, to withdraw their support or even to join the opposition. Forcing others to suffer for their moral beliefs is a high price to pay for pursuing a questionable course of conduct and many will prefer not to pay it. (*ibid.*)

There are, moreover, nontactical reasons for being willing to accept the prescribed punishment. It must be remembered that the person who is committing civil disobedience is not a revolutionary. Although his beliefs do not allow him to obey a particular law, he is nevertheless committed to the rule of law and to the legitimacy of the state. His acceptance of the prescribed punishment is his way of reaffirming this commitment. As Cohen puts it:

> . . . by accepting the punishment prescribed by law the disobedient is able to emphasize his commitment to law, and it is especially important for him to do so in a democratic society. The values that the disobedient wishes to defend are, after all, precisely the values that are best served by a democracy under law, if only these laws remain within bounds. Should it come to a choice, the disobedient's ultimate commitment is certainly to justice, and not to the will of the majority. But his present purpose is to persuade the majority not to force this choice upon him and his present intention is to make the established system viable. It must not be supposed, incidentally, that the civil disobedient's position implies that he will never submit to the requirements of an unjust law. In fact, the citizen in a democracy often has a moral obligation to do just that. But there are limits to the injustice he will endure as there are limits to the injustice he will perpetuate. It is the civil disobedient's conviction that these limits have been reached. (*ibid.*)

The attitude of the state. In recent years, some have suggested that society would be wiser and juster if it did not impose penalties on civil disobedients. They have emphasized two factors that make the civil disobedient an unfit object of punishment: his motives (which certainly differ from the motives of the criminal) and our reactions to him (which certainly differ from our reactions to the criminal). Thus, Cohen writes:

> Of course, it does not follow from the fact that the disobedient is willing to pay the penalty that the government ought to exact it. The disobedient has been placed in an acute moral dilemma and he may have acted with good will toward the community. Certainly, his punishment may cause profound ruptures in the community. All these facts, and others, ought to be considered by the government in deciding whether to prosecute, and by the judiciary in deciding the terms of sentence. It will often be in the government's and, indeed, in the community's best interests to act with flexibility and discretion in these matters and it is a particularly barbarous fallacy to suppose that the government owes the disobedient his just portion of punishment. (*ibid.*)

There is still another consideration that might justify not punishing the civil disobedient. One important feature of our legal system provides that unjust laws can be challenged as unconstitutional. Unfortunately, in order to challenge a law, you must first break it. Would it be just, in such a context, to punish a citizen who breaks a law that he feels is unconstitutional and therefore invalid? This consideration is discussed by Ronald Dworkin.

> When the law is uncertain, in the sense that a plausible case can be made on both sides, then a citizen who follows his own judgment is not behaving unfairly. That privilege extends to those who believe that the law is clear, but also believe that it is deeply immoral because grossly unfair to some citizens. The argument we began by considering—that it would be unfair to tolerate draft dissenters because they are not "playing the game" of American society—is therefore invalid. On the contrary, this feature of our practices places on our government an affirmative responsibility of leniency, because if we believe that those who follow their own views are behaving properly, we ought to protect them.
>
> It does not follow that we are never justified in prosecuting and punishing dissenters. Obviously we could not follow the simple practice of acquitting everyone who thinks the law is on his side. But we can follow the more complex practice of attempting to accommodate those whose views of the law are plausible, even though our officials think they are wrong, so long as we can do this without great damage to other policies. ("Law and Civil Disobedience" in *Ethics and Social Justice*)

It seems reasonable to conclude, then, that although the civil disobedient should normally be prepared to accept punishment, society may well have good reasons for not actually applying that punishment.

So let us summarize. We began with the challenge of the anarchist, the claim that no state can be justified because, by its very nature, a state is a coercive mechanism. While this challenge could be met very easily if we were concerned only with justifying the existence of a minimal state, it is much harder to meet it if we try to justify the existence of a more extensive state. The social contract theory seemed the best way of justifying a more extensive state. We therefore adopted this approach, and in light of it, we examined the question of obedience and disobedience. We found that the social contract theory led to conclusions that were neither totally revolutionary nor totally obedient.

5

The Existence of God

The most important religious belief in the Judao-Christian tradition is the belief in the existence of God. In this chapter, we will try to evaluate that belief, that is, we will try to decide whether or not it is reasonable to believe that God exists. But before doing so, we must first make sure that we understand that belief, that we understand what the religious person is claiming when he says that God exists.

5.1 THE JUDAO-CHRISTIAN CONCEPTION OF GOD

Men have worshipped many kinds of things, ranging from sacred trees and animals to the ghosts of their ancestors. And they have called all these different things God. We are not concerned with these gods, however. We do want to understand the "God" of our own tradition, that is, the nature of the belief in the Judao-Christian God, Jehovah.

One way to understand that belief is by contrasting it with the ancient Greek belief in Zeus. The ancient Greeks believed that there existed a physical being, Zeus, who lived at the top of Mount Olympus with many other beings like him. These other beings were members of his family, and Zeus had come to power in that family by overthrowing his father. Zeus was very powerful, but neither his power nor his wisdom were unlimited. He was bound, for one thing, by the Fates. Nor was

Zeus all-just. He had, for example, often ravished or seduced young girls. Zeus made certain demands upon mankind, and the Greeks believed that a wise man should obey those demands.

The Jew or Christian who believes in Jehovah has a very different kind of belief. He believes in the existence of a noncorporeal being, Jehovah, who transcends space and time. This being is omnipotent (all-powerful), omniscient (all-knowing), and all-good. Jehovah has given man many commandments, and he will reward those who obey them and punish those who do not. But the religious person obeys those commandments out of love and reverence for the one who has commanded them.

In short, the belief that God exists is very different in the Judao-Christian tradition because of that tradition's special conception of God. The following are the main features of that conception:

1. God is noncorporeal; he has no body. He is therefore not found in some particular place. It should be noted that this idea seems to contradict the many Biblical passages in which God is portrayed as a corporeal being like Zeus. Thus, in the very beginning of Genesis, we read that: "They [Adam and Eve] heard the sound of God Jehovah as he was walking in the garden at the breezy time of day."

There have been some Jews and Christians who take such passages seriously and who think of God as embodied. But most have insisted that Jehovah is noncorporeal and that such passages should be understood symbolically or allegorically. It should also be noted that this doctrine of noncorporeality comes into apparent conflict with the Christian doctrine of Incarnation, the doctrine that God became a man. (One of the goals of classical Christian theology is to explain this apparent conflict.)

2. God is unique; there is nothing else like him. It is, of course, just this belief that constitutes the monotheism (belief in one God) of the Judao-Christian tradition. We are very used to this idea today, and we tend to forget just how revolutionary this idea—together with the idea of noncorporeality—seemed in its time. When the Romans accused the Jews and Christians of being atheists, they must have felt that having only one, noncorporeal God, in contrast to their many embodied divinities, was almost the same as having no God at all. Again, it should be noted that this belief comes into apparent conflict with the Christian doctrine of the Trinity. (And another of the goals of classical Christian theology is to explain away this apparent conflict.)

3. God is not limited in either his power or his knowledge; in particular, he is not bound by the Fates. These ideas are somewhat problematical, and much discussion has been devoted to paradoxes and problems that arise from them. For example, if God knows everything

then he knows what we will do, so how can we be free to choose how to behave? Again, if God is all-powerful, can he create a stone which is so heavy even *he* can't lift it? If he can create such a stone, he is not all-powerful (since he can't lift the stone). But if he can't create a stone that heavy, he is still, by that very limitation, not all-powerful. But we need not worry about these problems now.

4. God is all-good. He treats all of creation with a perfect combination of justice and mercy, much as a perfect father would treat his child. He desires to aid and comfort human beings in their distress, and he reaches out to them with his grace even if they don't first turn to him.

All of these features are part of the Judao-Christian conception of Jehovah as the all-perfect being. Or, to use the terminology of St. Anselm of Canterbury, these features describe that being than which no greater can be conceived.

> What art thou, then, Lord God, than whom nothing greater can be conceived? But what art thou, except that which, as the highest of all beings, alone exists through itself, and creates all other things from nothing? For, whatever is not this is less than a thing which can be conceived of. But this cannot be conceived of thee. What good therefore does the supreme God lack. . . . Therefore, thou art just, truthful, and blessed, and whatever it is better to be than not to be (Proslogium, chapter 5).

There are, no doubt, many other features of the Judao-Christian God. He is conceived of as the creator of the universe, the revealer to mankind of his divine will, the performer of miracles, etc. But we shall be focusing in on the features mentioned above, all of which help comprise the idea of God as the all-perfect being.

Why do Jews and Christians have this conception of God? Why weren't they satisfied with the Greek conception of many finite corporeal gods? Part of the answer has to do with a variety of historical and sociological factors that influenced the early Jews and Christians. But I think that we can also see at least two religious reasons, reasons that are still valid today, for preferring this conception of God. One has to do with man's relation to God and the other has to do with the religious idea of salvation. In order, once more, to appreciate these points, let us look at the contrast with Zeus.

The ancient Greeks had what might be called a trading relationship with Zeus. Zeus wanted certain things from man (e.g., sacrifices) and man wanted certain things from Zeus (e.g., fertile fields). Man gave to Zeus what Zeus wanted in the hope and expectation that Zeus would give man what man wanted. It is this view of the man-God relationship that Plato attacked in the following passage from his dialogue

Euthyphro. (In reading this passage, remember that Plato is expressing his own ideas through the character Socrates.)

> *Socrates:* Then piety, Euthyphro, is an art which gods and men have of doing business with one another?
>
> *Euthyphro:* That is an expression which you may use, if you like.
>
> *Socrates:* But I have no particular liking for anything but the truth. I wish, however, that you would tell me what benefit accrues to the gods from our gifts. There is no doubt about what they give to us; for there is no good thing which they do not give; but how we can give any good thing to them in return is far from being equally clear. If they give everything and we give nothing, that must be an affair of business in which we have very greatly the advantage of them.

This trading view of the man-God relation is still held by some people today. (There are others who hold, as a variation of it, what could be called an "insurance-policy" view of the man-God relation: there may not be any God, but in case there is, give him what he wants once or twice a year). But most religious people want a different man-God relation, a relation in which man treats God as an ideal to be adored, worshipped, and emulated. Zeus is obviously not the sort of God for such religious people. Indeed, as one reflects upon it, it seems that the most appropriate view for such people is the Judao-Christian conception of Jehovah.

We turn then to salvation. As one looks around the world, one has the impression of a world in which injustice often prevails, in which the good often suffer while the evil flourish. Innocence is often rewarded with tragedy. This impression is very disturbing, and man has developed a variety of ways of handling it. Often man will accept this picture as reality and try to find the psychological mechanisms for living with it. A very different approach, claiming that this impression of the world is misleading, sees justice as ultimately winning out. The good and the innocent will be rewarded while the evil and guilty will suffer. This second approach naturally raises many questions, the most important of which concern the precise way in which things will be set right. It is just at this point that the religious believer introduces God. The Jew or Christian believes that God will, in the fullness of time, bring about this rectification both for the individual and the universe. In this way, the Judao-Christian religious message is an optimistic one. Zeus is obviously not the right sort of God to play the role of divine rectifier. He is too limited a being to do so. What is needed is a powerful wise God who is morally perfect. And so we arrive at the Judao-Christian conception of

Jehovah. The only question that remains to be considered is whether such a being exists.

5.2 THE ARGUMENTS FOR DIVINE EXISTENCE

Many philosophers have tried to prove that God exists. And they have done so even though they already believe that God exists. They have done so for two reasons, to convince the nonbeliever and to reinforce their own beliefs. Even the strongest believer sometimes has doubts, and there is something psychologically very satisfying in the knowledge that one's beliefs can be backed up by rational proofs.

Most of these philosophical arguments are nothing more than elaborations and improvements of the intuitive arguments that ordinary religious believers put forward when defending their faith. This is not surprising, for it is just these intuitive considerations that guided the philosophers in question long before they had become philosophers. So let us begin by listing the intuitive arguments of the ordinary man of faith.

    1.   There must be a God; otherwise, how did the Universe come into existence? What else could be its cause?

    2.   As we study the world, we discover that things work in remarkable ways. Consider, as just one example, the ways in which the various structures and systems of the human body work together. Could such an intricate, well-ordered system have come about by accident? To say it could would be like saying that the wind could accidentally blow together lots of pieces of metal to form a well-designed watch. It is surely much more plausible to say that the universe contains these intricate well-designed systems because they were designed by the creator of the universe, God. This argument (the intuitive version of the teleological argument) was forcefully set out by David Hume in his *Dialogues Concerning Natural Religion* (although there it was for the purpose of attacking the argument):

> Look round the world: Contemplate the world and every part of it: You will find it to be nothing but one great machine, subdivided into an infinite number of lesser machines. . . . All of these various machines, and even their most minute parts, are adjusted to each other with an accuracy which ravishes into admiration all men who have ever contemplated them. The curious adapting of means to ends, throughout all nature, resembles exactly, though it much exceeds, the productions of human contrivance—of human design, thought, wisdom, and intelligence. Since therefore the effects resemble each other, we are led to infer, by all the rules of analogy,

that the causes also resemble, and that the Author of Nature is somewhat similar to the mind of man, though possessed of much larger faculties, proportioned to the grandeur of the work which he has executed.

3. Many religious people have actually experienced the presence of God, whether in visions or in mystical experiences. So God must exist. We know that God exists in the same way that we know of the existence of other things that many people experience.

4. At times throughout the course of history, God has brought about results he wants in human affairs by performing miracles. These miracles cannot be due to natural causes, since they violate the laws of nature. So their occurence, which can only be due to God's intervention, proves that God exists.

5. God is the source of all morality; without him, there would be no validity to morality. Moreover, without God and religion, life would be meaningless and without purpose. But morality is valid and life does have meaning and purpose, so God must exist.

At first glance, these arguments are impressive. Taken together, they seem to present a powerful case for believing in the existence of God. But initial impressions can mislead us, so let us look more carefully at the philosophical versions of these arguments.

The first—formally called the cosmological argument—we find in the writings of St. Thomas Aquinas:

> Everything that is moved is moved by another. That some things are in motion—for example, the sun—is evident from sense. Therefore, it is moved by something else that moves it. This mover is itself either moved or not moved. If it is not, we have reached our conclusion—namely, that we must posit some unmoved mover. This we call God. If it is moved, it is moved by another mover. Now, it is not possible to proceed to infinity. Hence, we must posit some prime unmoved mover. (*Summa Contra Gentiles*, I, 13.)

As we look over the argument, we see that this is the crux of it: There are things in the world and they are in motion. Their motion, like all motion, requires a cause, and this cause requires still another cause. This chain of causes cannot go on forever, so there must be a first unmoved cause, God.

The argument, however, rests upon a variety of unproved assumptions. To begin with, it assumes that every motion must have a cause, i.e., that there cannot be uncaused events. It also assumes that there could not have been an infinite series of causes—a series *without* a beginning— that preceeded the event in question (the motion of the sun). Because of these assumptions, most philosophers have rejected this version of the cosmological argument. They have also rejected it because they have not seen any justification for concluding that God is the first unmoved mover. Why couldn't it be, for example, mere matter?

At least one philosopher, Samuel Clarke, has claimed that the basic idea behind the cosmological argument is valid even if St. Thomas's way of presenting it runs into difficulties. Clarke was a follower of Isaac Newton and he realized that Newton's work in science implied an infinitely large universe. This suggested that St. Thomas was wrong in assuming that it couldn't also be infinitely old, with an infinite causal series in it. So Clarke wanted to find a version of the cosmological argument that didn't employ Thomas's questionable assumption.

Clarke thought we should turn our attention from the individual object or event to the whole universe. Let us suppose, said Clarke, that every individual object or event can be explained by some earlier object or event. Let us suppose there is an infinite series of causes with no beginning. This still leaves something unexplained. What is the cause of the whole infinite universe? In order to find that cause, we must look outside the universe to God. To quote Clarke:

> I shall not argue against it [atheism] from the supposed impossibility of infinite succession, barely and absolutely considered in itself . . . if we consider such an infinite progression, as one entire endless series of dependent beings; 'tis plain this whole series of beings can have no cause from without, of its existence; because in it are supposed to be included all things that are or ever were in the universe: and 'tis plain it can have no reason within itself, of its existence; because no one being in this infinite succession is supposed to be self-existent or necessary.˙ . . . An infinite succession therefore of merely dependent beings, without any original independent cause, is a series of beings, that has neither necessity nor cause, nor any reason at all of its existence, neither within itself nor from without. (Demonstration of the Being and Attributes of God, Part II.)

Clarke's argument has another advantage over St. Thomas's. St. Thomas, as we mentioned, had no way of showing that his first cause is actually God rather than some object or objects in the universe. Clarke's argument doesn't face this difficulty. In looking for the cause of the whole universe, Clarke feels we have to refer to something outside of it.

Nevertheless, Clarke's argument also runs into trouble. Like St. Thomas, he assumes that everything must have a cause. But, perhaps this is false, perhaps the universe is uncaused. Moreover, he assumes without any clear justification that the whole universe must have a cause over and above the causes of its individual parts. Paul Edwards, in a famous passage, has explained why philosophers are dubious about this assumption.

> The demand to find the cause of the series as a whole rests on the erroneous assumption that the series is something over and above the members of which it is composed. . . . But reflection shows this to be an error. If we have explained the individual members there is nothing additional left to be explained. Supposing I see a group of five Eskimos standing on the corner of Sixth Avenue and 50th Street and I wish to explain why the group came to New York. Investigation reveals the following stories:
>
> Eskimo No. 1 did not enjoy the extreme cold in the polar region and decided to move to a warmer climate. No. 2 is the husband of Eskimo No. 1. He loves her dearly and did not wish to live without her. No. 3 is the son of Eskimos 1 and 2. He is too small and too weak to oppose his parents. No. 4 saw an advertisement in the *New York Times* to appear on television. No. 5 is a private detective engaged by the Pinkerton Agency to keep an eye on Eskimo No. 4.
>
> Let us assume that we have now explained in the case of each of the five Eskimos why he or she is in New York. Somebody then asks: "All right, but what about the group as a whole; why it it in New York?" This would plainly be an absurd question. . . . It is just as absurd to ask for the cause of the series as a whole as distinct from asking for the causes of individual members. ("The Cosmological Argument," *The Rationalist Annual*, 1959.)

We can conclude then that the cosmological argument fails because of its unproven assumptions.

Let's turn to the second argument, which is known at the teleological argument. This argument claims that we must posit the existence of God to explain the well-ordered systems of the universe, clearly assuming that these systems could not have come about through natural causes. But this assumption has been seriously challenged by the discoveries of modern science. Let us see how this has happened in two cases.

At one time, defenders of the teleological argument would refer to our solar system (the sun, the planets, the comets, etc.) as a stable, well-ordered system that could only have come about through the activity of a great designer. Unfortunately. since the time of Kant and Laplace (the end of the eighteenth century), scientists have explained how purely *natural* forces, operating without any guidance from an intelligent being, could produce just such a system. A similar point has been made about the well-ordered systems found in the organic world. One of the consequences of Darwin's Theory of Evolution, after all, is that these well-ordered organic systems could have come about solely through the operation of mutations and natural selection. These scientific advances have, in short, presented a nonreligious explanation for the well-ordered systems in the universe and have therefore undercut the teleological argument.

It is important to keep two points in mind: (1) Nothing that we have said shows that God didn't plan and bring about these systems, perhaps by use of the very forces that science has discovered. All we have claimed is that science shows how such systems *could* have come about without God and why they cannot therefore be used to prove his existence. (2) We have here an extremely important source of the conflict between science and religion, for this is an instance of science challenging the rational foundations of the belief in the existence of God.

This second point is worth pausing over. Normally, when people talk about the conflict between science and religion, they have in mind a conflict between some specific scientific result, on the one hand, and some specific biblical passage or religious teaching, on the other. Such conflicts have been around for a long time. When the Copernican Theory was first proposed, there were many who objected to its claim that the earth moves around the sun. They insisted it was the sun that moved, since the Bible describes, as a *miraculous* event, how the sun stood still in the days of Joshua. Again, when Darwin's theory of Evolution was first put forward, many claimed that it simply couldn't be correct: it contradicted the account of creation presented in the Book of Genesis.

These are not serious conflicts. Religious people usually avoid them by reinterpreting the particular passage symbolically so it no longer conflicts with scientific findings. Thus, the religious person can say that the Book of Genesis is meant to be a myth which teaches certain themes (that the universe depends for its existence upon God, that man is the culmination of creation, and so forth) rather than a literal account of how creation actually took place. Not all religious people have been willing to do this; there are some who take these passages literally. This helps explain the ongoing fight in several states about the teaching of Darwin's theories in the public schools. Still, the option of reinterpretation provides a possible solution to some of these conflicts between science and religion. But when science comes along and explains the order and harmony of the universe without referring to God, this is a much more serious, although indirect, conflict between science and religion. We have here an instance of science undercutting a rational foundation for religious belief.

The third argument listed above, the argument from religious experiences, holds that we know about God through mankind's direct experience of him. This approach to religious knowledge is especially popular today. Clearly, there is a preference today for experiential knowledge over knowledge based upon reason. Many of our contemporaries hold the view that you really know something only if you (or at least someone) can directly experience it. Reinforcing this tendency is a widespread acquaintance with unusual psychic experiences through the use of drugs. So let us look at this argument very carefully.

There are two types of religious experiences, visionary experiences and mystical experiences. A visionary experience is a sensory experience; it affects one through the normal senses. But the normal senses perceive an unusual object, one that the religious person views as a manifestation of God. Thus, when Moses heard the voice from the burning bush, he was having a visionary experience. He was hearing a voice coming from a most unusual place and he identified it as the voice of God. Mystical experiences are very different. They are totally nonsensory. As a result, they are so different from our ordinary experiences that mystics feel that they are indescribable. Despite that fact, mystics have tried to give us at least a hint of what such experiences are like. Let me quote one such description:

> Irresistibly it took possession of my mind and will, lasted what seemed an eternity, and disappeared in a series of rapid sensations. One reason why I disliked this kind of trance was that I could not describe it to myself. I cannot even now find words to render it intelligible. It consisted in a gradual but swiftly progressive obliteration of space, time, sensation, and the multitudinous factors of experience which seem to qualify what we are pleased to call our self. In proportion as these conditions of ordinary consciousness were subtracted, the sense of an underlying or essential consciousness acquired intensity. At last nothing remained but a pure, absolute, abstract self. The universe became without form and void of content. But self persisted, formidable in its vivid keenness, feeling the most poignant doubts about reality, ready, as it seemed, to find existence break as breaks a bubble round about it. (quoted in William James's *Variety of Religious Experiences*, Lectures 16 and 17).

Mystics insist that they learn deep truths from these experiences. The basic truth learned, according to most mystics, is that all differentiation is an illusion and that the ultimate reality is the unity of the universe. Religious mystics go on to identify this unity with God.

Now, even if we grant, as we undoubtedly should, that religious people have had these experiences, certain questions arise. How can we tell whether or not the experiences are delusions. Are these people really experiencing anything in reality, and, if they are experiencing something, what is it that they are experiencing? In particular, are they experiencing God, and if so, the God of which religion?

Two points must be noted here. The first has to do with the relation between religious experiences and drugs. In recent years, there has been much discussion about this relationship. Many have reported having religious mystical experiences after taking such drugs as LSD. This is not really a new phenomenon. William James, at the beginning of our century, called attention to the use of nitrous oxide (laughing gas) as a source of religious experiences. And there are many religious traditions which have used drugs for such purposes over the centuries. The important philosophical question is as to the relevance of these facts to the validity of such experiences. There are, no doubt, those who feel that religious experiences are illusory just because they can be induced by the use of drugs. But this hardly follows; indeed, for all we know, these drugs may be a source of special knowledge. James himself seems to have had this attitude:

> One conclusion was forced upon my mind at that time, and my impression of its truth has ever since remained unshaken. It is that our normal waking consciousness, rational consciousness as we call it, is but one special type of consciousness, whilst all about it, parted from it by the filmiest of screens, there lie potential forms of consciousness entirely different. We may go through life without suspecting their existence; but apply the requisite stimulus, and at a touch they are there in all their completeness, definitive types of mentality which probably somewhere have their field of application and adaptation. (*ibid.*)

The second point to be noted is that individuals have tended to identify the God they experience in these states with the God of their religion. And there are, no doubt, those who feel that this too discredits religious experiences. But again, this does not follow. For all we know, there may be a common religious truth that all these people are experiencing but which they describe in the different symbols of their different religions.

We have seen that some of the standard reasons for dismissing religious experiences are not satisfactory. Still, the religious person has hardly shown that these experiences are not illusions. We cannot therefore appeal to them as a way of proving the existence of God. The question of what is being experienced in religious experiences remains open.

In considering the argument from religious experiences, we conceded that such experiences had occurred. The only question was whether this showed that God existed. In the case of our next argument, the argument from miracles, many philosophers would have us challenge the very occurrence of the event in question. They remind us that a miracle is not merely an unusual event; it is an event that violates the very laws of nature. They therefore feel that it is more plausible to suppose that the event did not occur (and that those who report it are mistaken or lying) than to suppose that it did. This argument was presented most forcefully by David Hume:

> A miracle is a violation of the laws of nature; and as a firm and unalterable experience has established these laws, the proof against a miracle, from the very nature of the fact, is as entire as any argument from experience can possibly be imagined. . . . There must, therefore, be a uniform experience against every miraculous event, otherwise the event would not merit that appellation. And as a uniform experience amounts to a proof, there is here a direct and full proof, from the nature of the fact, against the existence of any miracle. . . . The plain consequence is (and it is a general maxim worthy of our attention) that no testimony is sufficient to establish a miracle unless the testimony be of such a kind that its falsehood would be more miraculous than the fact which it endeavors to establish. (*Inquiry Concerning Human Understanding*, section 10)

Now, even the very faithful are skeptical about *some* purported miracles, but their skepticism is usually based upon the weakness of the evidence for a *particular* miracle. Hume, on the other hand, doubts that we can know that any miracle has occurred. He feels that the evidence for the occurrence of a miracle can *never* (or just about never) be strong enough. And whether or not Hume is right in his far-reaching general claim, he certainly reminds us of the strength of evidence we should require before we accept the occurrence of the purported miracle.

Let us imagine a case in which there is so much evidence for the purported miracle that we rightfully believe that it has occurred. Could the occurrence of that event be used to prove that God exists? It could, but only if we could establish that the event truly was a miracle in the sense that it could *only* be caused by God. But how could we establish that? How could we rule out the possibility that it was only an extraordinary occurrence due to an unusual natural cause?

We have here another case in which the increasing power of science to explain the world has cast doubt upon the validity of religious arguments. As more and more unusual events are explained scientifically, it becomes harder and harder to be sure that some purported miracle is truly a miracle. Even when science cannot explain the event today, we must still concede that it may explain it tomorrow. And when we remember all the times in the past when purported miracles were later explained scientifically, we can hardly be confident in saying of any event that it is a miracle whose occurrence establishes the existence of God.

We turn finally to the last argument, which has been called the argument from value. In the next chapter we will discuss its claim that the validity of morality and the meaningfulness of life depends on the existence of God. All we have to note now is that God's existence would not follow even if that claim were true. All that can be inferred from that claim is: *either* God exists *or* morality is invalid and life is meaningless. Religious philosophers often seem to forget about the latter possibility.

We have seen that the normal, intuition-based arguments for the existence of God fail. This does not mean that God does not exist. There may be other valid proofs, or he might exist without that existence being provable. We must not suppose that only what we can prove exists does exist. And indeed, faith in God is the belief in his existence without proof. We shall eventually consider the validity of such faith, but before doing so, we must examine the atheist's arguments *against* God's existence.

5.3 THE ARGUMENTS AGAINST DIVINE EXISTENCE

Let us begin by listing many of the familiar arguments offered against religious beliefs. Having done so, we will then examine each of them carefully.

1. An examination of history shows that religious beliefs have too often stood in the way of human progress. Many scientific advances had to fight for acceptance against religious obscurantism. The Church's condemnation and imprisonment of Galileo for teaching the "heretical" ideas of Copernicus is only one example of this widespread phenomenon. Similarly, religious teachings have stood in the way of social and political progress and have been used to defend tyranny and injustice. As one example, consider the religious idea of the divine right of kings. So, if mankind is to make further progress, it must reject these religious beliefs (including the belief in God). Thus, Bertrand Russell writes:

> You find as you look around the world that every single bit of progress in humane feeling, every improvement in the criminal law, every step toward the diminution of war, every step toward better treatment of the colored races, or every mitigation of slavery, every moral progress that there has been in the world, has been consistently opposed by the organized churches in the world. I say quite deliberately that the Christian religion, as organized in its churches, has been and still is the principal enemy of moral progress in the world. ("Why I Am Not a Christian")

2. People believe in God merely because such belief satisfies their psychological needs. To quote Sigmund Freud:

> In the course of time the first observations of law and order in

> natural phenomena are made, and therewith the forces of nature lose their human traits. But men's helplessness remains, and with it their father-longing and the gods. The gods retain their threefold task: They must exorcise the terrors of nature, they must reconcile one to the cruelty of fate, particularly as shown in death, and they must make amends for the sufferings and privations that the communal life of culture has imposed on man. (*The Future of an Illusion,* chapter 3)

Once we realize that religious beliefs have this kind of psychological origin, shouldn't we reject them as mere illusions to be transcended by the rational person?

3. In light of all the evil that exists in the world, how can one believe in the existence of God? This belief is especially hard to maintain because evil is often distributed in such a way that the good and the bad suffer equally, or, what is even worse, the good suffer while the bad flourish. How can all of this be reconciled with the existence of God? In his novel, *Night,* Elie Wiesel describes the force with which this argument strikes even the devout believer when he confronts the brute reality of evil.

> I know. One has no right to say things like that. I know. Man is too small, too humble and inconsiderable to seek to understand the mysterious ways of God. But what can I do? I'm not a sage, one of the elect, nor a saint. I'm just an ordinary creature of flesh and blood. I've got eyes, too, and I can see what they're doing here [in a concentration camp]. Where is the Divine Mercy? Where is God? How can I believe, how could anyone believe, in this merciful God?

The first of these arguments, the claim that religious beliefs should be rejected because they stand in the way of human progress, has many problems. To begin with, there have been many cases in which religious ideas have been used to aid progress, both intellectual and social. As just one example, consider the important religious influence on the thinking of the abolitionists. A more balanced picture would show these positive uses of religious beliefs; the picture presented by people like Russell is remarkably one-sided. Secondly, all of this historical evidence is only relevant to the question of how these religious beliefs have been *used* by religious believers; it does not necessarily apply to the question of the intrinsic *nature* of these beliefs. Even if it were true—and we maintain that it is not—that religious beliefs have usually been used in a reactionary fashion, this would not show that these beliefs are intrinsically reactionary, it might only be the case that religious people have misused these beliefs in a reactionary way. Finally, all of this is irrelevant to the question of the truth and falsity of these religious beliefs. Even if religious beliefs were intrinsically reactionary it would not follow that they must therefore be false.

Very similar problems arise for the second of these arguments, the argument that religious beliefs should be rejected in light of their psychological origin. To begin with, many psychologists would quarrel with this account of the psychology of religious belief. But even if Freud were right, how would this show that religious beliefs (especially the belief in God) are false? True beliefs can be held for all kinds of psychological reasons. Hence, the psychological origin of religious beliefs seems irrelevant to their truth.

We turn now to the third main argument against the existence of God, the argument from evil. This is a serious argument, and even devout believers concede that it poses a fundamental challenge to their faith. The first point to note about this argument is that it poses a challenge only to belief in the Judao-Christian conception of God. In order to see this, consider the following, very bad, argument against the existence of Zeus:

a. there is evil in the world

b. if Zeus existed, there would be no evil in the world

c. therefore, Zeus does not exist

This argument is very bad because there is no reason to believe *b*. Zeus himself often acts unjustly, so he may even be the direct cause of the evil. Moreover, he is neither all-knowing nor all-powerful. So he may not know how to get rid of the evil or he may not be able to get rid of it. In short, even if Zeus existed, there would be many explanations for the world's evil. None of this will work for Jehovah. He is all-good, so he would want there to be no evil. He is all-knowing, so he would know how to avoid the evil. And he is all-powerful, so he could do what is required to avoid the evil. Therefore, why is there evil in the world? Doesn't its existence show that Jehovah does not exist?

A second thing about this argument from evil is that it does not begin from the mere presence of some evil in the world. It begins with a full picture of the presence of evil in the world. It is a dramatic fact that a large part of the world lives in a state of constant misery and suffering due to hunger, disease, etc. Moreover, this evil is distributed unequally. Some people suffer a lot more than others. But the evil is far from being distributed according to people's merits. As one example of this, consider those children who are born with severe illnesses or into conditions of severe poverty and deprivation. One can hardly say that these infants deserve their suffering. It is important to keep all of these points about evil in mind. As we shall see, many attempts to explain away evil fail just because they cannot do justice to these points.

In short, then, this argument against the existence of Jehovah runs as follows:

A. There is a great deal of evil in the world, and this evil is unequally and unfairly distributed

B. because he is supposed to be all-good, all-powerful, and all-knowing, none of this evil would exist if Jehovah existed.

C. therefore, Jehovah does not exist

We turn to the various ways in which religious people try to meet this argument. Some of them challenge the very existence of evil or the other facts about evil referred to in A. Most of them challenge B: they attempt to explain *why* God has allowed all of this evil to exist (such an explanation is called a *theodicy*). Let us begin by examining the challenges to A.

Some have claimed that all the supposed evil in the world is an illusion, one brought about by a lack of faith. They have also claimed that this illusion of evil can be eliminated by a strengthening of faith. (Such people often go so far as to refuse medical treatment). In any case, they argue that there is no evil to challenge the existence of God. This approach faces several obvious problems. The suffering and evil that we experience seems just as real as the good that we experience. So to claim that the evil is an illusion, while the good is real, is highly dubious. Consider, for example, pain and suffering that seems to be due to disease. Even if we grant, for the sake of argument, that the disease is just an illusion, the pain and suffering is still real. So the whole theory just doesn't make any sense in the case of some types of evil.

There is another view that evil is merely an absence of good and that there is nothing existent in the world which is evil. But certain types of evil (e.g., diseases) seem to involve the presence of something positive even if other types of evil (e.g., starvation) might be viewed as mere absences of a particular good. More important, even if all evil were merely the absence of good, our problem still wouldn't be solved. We would still have to explain why God didn't permit the good to be present. As a student once wrote on an exam, this solution acquits God of the creation of evil, a sin of commission, by convicting him of the failure to create the good, a sin of omission.

We turn then to the attempts to challenge *B* by explaining why an all-perfect God would allow there to be evil in the world. Let us begin by listing a number of the traditional theodocies.

1. *The contrast theodicy.* A perfect world would be a world which we wouldn't recognize and appreciate, because we only recognize and appreciate something like good if we also experience its opposite evil. This is why God had to put some evil in the world.

2. *The purpose theodicy.* A life that is all pleasure and no challenge, a life in which we have no wrongs and imperfections to overcome, would be a life without meaning and purpose. So God created the world with evil in it in order to give human life meaning and purpose.

3. *The moral quality theodicy.* One of the greatest goods we possess are our moral qualities of courage, mercy, and compassion. But these qualities arise and develop out of our confrontation with evil and wrongs. So in order to allow us these prized moral qualities, God had to create a world in which evil exists.

4. *The punishment and warning theodicy.* Evil is God's tool for punishing the guilty and warning those who are tempted to sin. So evil is a tool of justice in the universe.

5. *The free-will theodicy.* God wanted to give us the gift of freedom, the ability to choose how we will behave. But once human beings are given that freedom they can and often do act wrongly. Evil in the world is due to the abuse of human freedom.

These theodocies all attempt to explain evil without sacrificing any part of the Judao-Christian conception of God. In this way, they differ from the position of those who would solve the problem of evil by limiting God. John McTaggart put this latter position as follows:

> It seems to me that when believers in God save his goodness by saying that he is not really omnipotent, they are taking the best course open to them, since both the personality and goodness of God present much fewer difficulties if he is not conceived as omnipotent. (*Some Dogmas of Religion*)

Though the holders of our theodocies would surely not accept the consequences that McTaggart describes, it is clear that limiting God's power would solve the problem of the existence of evil.

> . . . the efforts of a non-omnipotent God in favor of good may, for anything that has yet been shown, be doomed to almost total defeat.

> It is not a very cheerful creed, unless it can be supplemented by some other dogmas which can assure us of God's eventual victory. But it is less depressing and less revolting than the belief that the destinies of the universe are at the mercy of a being who, with the resources of omnipotence at his disposal, decided to make a universe no better than this. (*ibid.*)

Another thing to note about all of our theodocies is that they share a common form. They all identify a certain kind of good and then claim that the world must contain some evil if that good is to exist. And they finish by saying that the evil that exists in the world is explained and justified by its being needed for this good. (This common structure explains why it is often said that the defenders of theodocies are committed to the view that this is the best of all possible worlds.) But is the good that they identify of such great value as to make up for, and justify, all of the evil that exists in the world? And if it isn't, then the problem still remains as to why God allowed all the evil to exist. Also, one might well challenge the claim that evil must really be present in order for good to be realized. But why couldn't God, who is all-powerful, structure the world so that the evil would not be necessary. For example, why couldn't he create us in such a way that we could recognize and appreciate good without experiencing the contrasting evil? But most important is the fact that none of these theodocies really explains the great extent of evil and its unfair distribution. The first three for example, fail to explain why we need so much evil in order to appreciate the good, give us a purpose in life, and develop moral qualities. The punishment and warning theodicy fails to explain why the innocent often suffer and why evil is not distributed according to merit. And the free-will theodicy fails to explain the evil not due to human actions (disease, natural disasters, etc.).

Some religious philosophers have tried to respond to these challenges, but many others have felt that such an attempt is unlikely to succeed. They have, instead, adopted a different approach. They agree with the basic idea behind all theodocies—that the evil in the world is necessary for some great purpose that God has in mind. But, unlike the traditional theodocies, they do not attempt to say what this great purpose is. Instead, they argue that the divine purpose is a mystery, one that lies beyond the capacity of human understanding. This idea is found in the Book of Job. And at the end of the book, the voice from the whirlwind tells Job:

> Who is this that darkens counsel by words without knowledge? Gird up your loins like a man, I will question you and you will declare to me.

> Where were you when I laid the foundations of the earth? Tell me
> if you have such understanding.

Is this approach satisfactory? Two opposing arguments seem plausible. One might argue, on the one hand, that it is extremely unlikely that there is some great, but unfathomable, good served by all this evil. This last theodicy could therefore be called an unlikely, "last-ditch" approach. But, on the other hand, is there reason to suppose that the good served by all this evil would be recognizable by our limited human minds, with our limited view of the universe?

Which side is right? The dispute seems to hinge upon whether or not we should be able to perceive what that greater good is which is served by the evil in the universe. And I do not see how we are to decide this question. The argument from evil, therefore, has not conclusively proven that God does *not* exist, and whether it has made his existence *implausible* is a question that we cannot determine. And so we turn to a discussion of faith, the kind of belief held when there is no proof either way.

5.4 FAITH

As we turn to the question of faith, it is important to remember that, as far as we can see, the existence of God is neither provable nor disprovable. Three options seem therefore open to us: (1) to believe in the existence of God even though his existence has not been proven (to have *theistic faith*); (2) to believe in the nonexistence of God even though his nonexistence has not been proven (to have *atheistic faith*); (3) or to hold no beliefs at all on this question (to be an *agnostic*).

Which of these options is best for a reasonable person? At the end of the nineteenth century, two great American thinkers, William Clifford and William James debated this question, and since the quality of their debate has not been surpassed, we shall end this chapter by considering their arguments.

Cliflord's view was that any faith, on any issue, is immoral. According to him, the moral person believes only when there is sufficient evidence for his belief; when there isn't sufficient evidence, the moral person remains in doubt. This, said Clifford, is the only way to avoid superstition and naive credulity, the two great enemies of human progress.

> Every time we let ourselves believe for unworthy reasons, we
> weaken our powers of self-control, of doubting, of judically and
> fairly weighing evidence. We all suffer severely enough from the
> maintenance and support of false beliefs and the fatally wrong

THE EXISTENCE OF GOD 119

> actions which they lead to, and the evil born when one such belief is entertained is great and wide. But a greater and wider evil arises when the credulous character is maintained and supported, when a habit of believing for unworthy reasons is fostered and made permanent. . . . if I let myself believe anything on insufficient evidence, there may be no great harm done by the mere belief. . . . But I cannot help doing this great wrong to Man, that I make myself credulous. The danger to society is not merely that it should believe wrong things, though that is great enough; but that it should become credulous and lose the habit of testing things and inquiring into them; for then it must sink back into savagery. ("The Ethic of Belief")

In short, then, Clifford offered a moral argument for agnosticism on any issue for which there isn't sufficient evidence.

James agreed with Clifford's view in most cases. But he claimed that some cases are special. There are some cases, he said, in which faith is both permissible and reasonable. Now one should always be wary of claims that certain cases are special; it is always possible that the claim is just "special pleading," asserting an exception without justification. So we have to examine carefully James's description of his special cases and his argument for treating them as an exception to our normal rules.

James said that faith is justifiable only when we face a situation where our choice or option is, in James's terms, forced, lively, and momentous. A forced option is when, if we try to remain in doubt, we wind up behaving as though we held one of the beliefs in question. A lively option is when it is psychologically possible for us to believe either of two beliefs. A momentous option is when a great deal depends upon which of the two beliefs we hold. In such cases, James said, faith is reasonable. In the case of religious belief, James argued that:

> Religion offers itself as a momentous option. We are supposed to gain, even now, by our belief, and to lose by our non-belief, a certain vital good. Secondly, religion is a forced option, so far as that goes. We cannot escape the issue by remaining skeptical and waiting for more light, because, although we do avoid error in that way if religion be untrue, we lose the good, if it be true, just as certainly as if we positively chose to disbelieve. It is as if a man should hesitate indefinitely to ask a certain woman to marry him because he was not perfectly sure that she would prove an angel after he brought her home. Would he not cut himself off from that particular angel-possibility as decisively as if he went and married someone else? . . . To preach skepticism to us as a duty until "sufficient evidence" for religion be found, is tantamount therefore to telling us, when in

presence of the religious hypothesis, that to yield to our fear of its being error is wiser and better than to yield to our hope that it may be true. ("The Will to Believe")

James's defense of belief in the existence of God rests heavily upon his realizing that this belief is not merely an intellectual belief, it is one that has a great impact upon the way in which one lives (we shall be discussing this impact in the next chapter). It is this feature of religious belief that makes the question of the existence of God a forced option. Now there are many who would consider that all such practical matters should be disregarded in weighing the rationality of a belief. James rejected that view. For him, since there was a close connection between belief and practice, it was legitimate to think of the practical implications of belief and agnosticism in deciding whether the one or the other was the rational stance.

James's defense of faith is impressive. But it is important to keep in mind (though it is not clear that James himself saw this) that his defense is a defense of both theistic and atheistic faith (just as Clifford's attack is an attack on both of these faiths). We can conclude, therefore, that faith of either type is a permissible and reasonable response to the question, "Does God exist"?

6

The Implications of Religious Belief

In chapter 5, we discussed a variety of intellectual arguments for and against the existence of God. In doing so, we treated the belief in the existence of God as an intellectual matter. But that leaves out a whole aspect of belief. Those who believe that God exists also believe, in most cases, that that belief has profound implications for human life. In this chapter, we shall balance things out by considering the nature of these implications.

Some of these implications are ethical. Many religious people feel that their beliefs have radically shaped their morality. There are some who make the more extreme claim that no moral belief makes any sense if it is not backed up by religious belief. We will consider these two claims in the first two sections of this chapter.

Other implications of religious belief have to do with the meaning and purpose of life. Though these notions are not completely clear, I think we can all intuitively feel the difference between certain types of lives; some seem full of meaning and others seem meaningless. Religious people have claimed that the meaning and purpose of their lives derive mainly from their religious beliefs. And some have made the more extreme claim that no life has meaning without this religious dimension. We will consider both the weaker and the stronger versions of these claims in the third section of this chapter.

Religious believers also feel that their beliefs lead them to adopt a wide variety of religious practices or rituals, ranging all the way from prayer to restrictions on such things as diet and manner of dress. We shall, in the final section of this chapter, consider these claims as well.

6.1 DOES MORALITY NEED RELIGION?

Let us begin with the strongest claim about the implications of religion for morality, the claim that no morality can make any sense if it is not backed up by religious beliefs. Such a claim, as it stands, is nebulous. What is needed is some fuller version of it. Looking to religious writings, we find three very different versions of this claim.

1. *The motivational claim.* People need a reason for being moral. Morality often calls upon us to make great sacrifices, so it is just not true that being moral is in our self-interest. And it is not clear what other reasons we could possibly have for making these sacrifices. Religion, then, is the only source for such reasons. If, after all, there is a God who will judge our actions and reward and punish us accordingly, we have a reason for doing what is right. This reason is sufficient to outweigh any earthly sacrifice we must make.

2. *The epistemological claim.* It's all very good to want to do what is right, but we still have to figure out what is right and what is wrong. How are we human beings supposed to do that? Different people hold widely different moral views. And their different viewpoints are often supported by persuasive arguments. The only way out of this impass is to appeal to divine revelation, the true source of moral knowledge.

3. *The ontological claim.* What makes one action right and another wrong? Some say a given action is just an action, and is not instrinsically right or wrong. But, if this is true, what then is the source of an action's value? It is the will of God. An action is right because God wants us to do it while an action is wrong because God wants us not to do it. The will of God is then the only source for these very basic moral distinctions.

It is important to understand the differences between these three claims. One of them, the ontological claim, attempts to draw the very basic distinction between the moral and the immoral. It grounds that distinction upon the will of God, and claims that there is no other basis for it. The epistemological claim doesn't go that far. All that it says is that our knowledge about that distinction depends upon divine revelation. The motivational claim is neutral about both the basis of that distinction and the basis of our *knowledge* about that distinction. It merely says that the desire for divine reward and the fear of divine punishment are the real motives for behaving morally.

THE IMPLICATIONS OF RELIGIOUS BELIEF

Let us begin with the motivational claim. This claim partially explains the presence in many religious systems of a belief in some form of personal survival (whether it be the immortality of the soul, the resurrection of the body, or something else). Since it doesn't seem that the divine reward or punishment takes place in *this* life, these religions have to postulate another form of existence in which this divine judgment is to be carried out. But, the motivational claim is not committed to some particular picture of how that divine judgment takes place. It is not committed, say, to any traditional view of heavenly bliss or eternal hellfire. All that it is committed to is a belief in some form of divine reward and punishment sufficient to motivate moral behavior. And, it should be said, many religious thinkers have put forward very elevated and noble pictures of the process of divine judgment.

> The good that the righteous seek is life in the world to come. . . . the punishment that the wicked receive is that they do not receive this life, but are cut off and die. . . . wise men have told us that this world to come contains no bodily pleasure; instead, the righteous take pleasure from their contemplation of the divine presence. (Maimonides, *Laws of Repentance,* chapter 8)

It might be appropriate to note, at this point, the extent to which these beliefs—in survival and divine punishment and reward—have fallen into disfavor in recent years, even among religious people. To some extent, this is due to the uneasiness that people feel about believing in an immaterial soul that is supposed to survive the destruction of the body. Whether this uneasiness is justified is a question we will be considering in the next chapter when we talk about the nature of man. At any rate, people seem to find such beliefs as the belief in eternal salvation or damnation either intellectually or ethically unacceptable. This leads them (without any real justification) to reject the whole doctrine of survival and divine reward and punishment.

It seems to me that this outright rejection is greatly in error. The belief in survival and divine reward and punishment plays a fundamental role in many religious conceptions of ethics. And, as we see in later sections of this chapter, it plays a fundamental role in many religious conceptions of the meaning of life. It is fundamental to the religious claim that justice and right ultimately prevail. Religious people would do better, I should like to suggest, to purge these beliefs of their objectionable elements rather than to do away with them entirely. Doing away with them entirely leaves tremendous gaps in the religious conception of man and his place in the universe.

Returning to the motivational claim, however, there are a number of difficulties that we must note. We have already seen (in chapter 2) that there are a variety of motives for moral behavior that rest neither upon self-interest nor upon divine reward and punishment. So the motivational claim is simply wrong when it asserts that religion is the *only* source of an adequate motive for behaving morally. More important, perhaps, is that there is something both morally and religiously unsatisfactory about the motivational claim, at least as it is usually put. If the moral person behaves morally for selfish motives, to gain a divine reward, his action is no better than the giving of a donation to gain honor and praise. Actions done from such motives merit no reward. A person deserves no credit for performing such actions. It is for this reason that Antigonus of Soko said:

> Do not serve God in the manner of a slave who serves a master to receive his reward; rather, serve Him in the manner of a slave who serves his master with no anticipation of a reward. (*Avot,* chapter 1)

This objection doesn't apply to certain other religious notions as to why one should behave morally. For example, religious people often present the following picture: We make sacrifices to satisfy the desires and wishes of those whom we love. Parents do this for their children, for example, and lovers for each other. We don't even do this for the pleasure of seeing the happiness of those whom we love. In cases of true love, it is done purely for the sake of one's beloved. Now the same thing holds for those who love God. Knowing that God desires that we do what is right, they try to satisfy his desire out of their love for him. To quote Bahya ibn Pakudah:

> Then the cup of love for God is overflowing, and the individual thinks only of God and he unifies his heart to love Him and to dedicate his heart to Him and to depend upon Him, and he has no concern but for the service of God and he thinks of nothing else and he does nothing except for what the Divine Will desires him to do. ("Divine Love" in *Duties of the Heart*)

It is important to remember that this view about love of God only provides us with an additional religious motive for behaving morally. It in no way proves that morality *presupposes* religious beliefs, for it in no way rules out the other, nonreligious, motives that we discussed in chapter 2.

We turn then to the epistemological claim, the claim that God is the only source of moral knowledge. Now, there is a crucial difference between knowledge and mere belief. Obviously, there are a great many people who have no religious beliefs but who do have moral beliefs.

THE IMPLICATIONS OF RELIGIOUS BELIEF

It is very likely then that their moral beliefs are not based upon revelation. So what the epistemological claim must be saying is that such atheistic moral beliefs are mere beliefs, and not knowledge. They are mere beliefs because they are not based upon the sole source of moral knowledge, divine revelation.

The epistemological claim therefore really comes down to the following two claims: (1) divine revelation is a source of moral knowledge and (2) while there are many sources of moral belief, there are no other sources of moral knowledge.

It is very hard for us to evaluate these two claims at this point in the book. This is because we have not yet talked about the distinction between mere belief and true knowledge, nor about the possible sources of knowledge in general and moral knowledge in particular. (We shall examine these subjects in chapter 10.) But I think that we can at least see in a preliminary way that there are serious difficulties with both of the epistemological claims.

Let us begin with claim (1). Clearly, if we know that a certain purported divine revelation R really is a divine revelation, then we can use R as a source of moral knowledge. What could be a better source of moral knowledge than the words of a totally trustworthy deity? But could we ever be sure that R really is a divine revelation? Remember, there are many competing purported revelations; each religious movement has its own. So unless we can *prove* that R truly is a divine revelation, we won't *know* that it is. At most, we might believe that it is. But if we don't know that it is a divine revelation, R is at most a source of moral belief, not moral knowledge. So claim (1) is in trouble unless its defenders are able to prove that some purported divine revelation is authentic.

How might one go about trying to establish that? Religious people have traditionally tried two approaches, the external approach and the internal approach. The first argues that miracles associated with some particular revelation establish it as a divine revelation. The latter argues that the character of the revelation itself can be used to establish it as a divine revelation.

We find instances of the external approach in the Bible. When God orders Moses into Egypt, Moses asks God for a sign to show the children of Israel. In other words, he wants God to give him a miracle to perform which will establish God's order as a divine revelation. The external approach faces serious difficulties, however. As we saw in chapter 5, it is not clear that we could ever establish that something is a miracle. And, failing that, we could hardly use the miraculous character of the event in question to establish the authenticity of a revelation.

What about the internal approach, then? Religious people argue that the lofty character of a revelation is testimony that it derives from

God. This approach can be of no use to us here, for it leads to a circularity. What we are attempting to find out is whether a set of beliefs about values and morals that are not known to be true can be raised to the status of knowledge through an appeal to divine revelation. But if we then turn around and authenticate that divine revelation by appealing to the very values it preaches—which are undoubtedly an important part of its intrinsic quality—we will indeed be arguing in a circle and getting nowhere.

It would appear then that claim (1) won't do. Claim (2) is a very different matter. In order to prove that it is wrong, we would have to show that there is some other source of moral knowledge besides divine revelation. Any attempt to do so now would certainly be premature, for we have yet to develop a basic theory of knowledge itself. Let us merely note, for now, that claim (2) has, on the whole, been rejected by moral theologians. They have wanted to distinguish between the moral and religious truths that can be established by human reason and those that can be established only through divine revelation. To quote St. Thomas:

> All of the moral precepts belong to the law of nature, but not all in the same way. For there are some things which the natural reason of every man . . . judges to be done or not to be done. And there are certain things which, after a more careful consideration, wise men judge to be obligatory. . . . And there are some things to judge of which human reason needs Divine instruction. (*Summa Theologica,* Part I of Second Part, Question 100, Article 1)

Such a distinction challenges, of course, the truth of claim (2), for it presupposes other sources of moral knowledge for at least some moral truths.

We turn finally to the ontological claim, the claim that what God wants us to do determines morality. Generally suspicious of this claim, philosophers and theologians have felt that the will of God cannot provide the distinction between right and wrong. One objection they have made has to do with the reasons God wills as he does and another has to do with the nature of the willer.

The first of these objections was originally presented by Plato in the *Euthyphro.* In that dialogue, Euthyphro is trying to explain to Socrates what holiness is, and he puts forward the thesis that to be holy is to be loved by the gods. In other words, the moral quality of holiness is based upon the gods' attitudes and desires. Socrates puts forward the following objection to this claim:

> *Socrates:* Then what are we to say about the holy, Euthyphro? According to your argument, is it not loved by all the gods?

Euthyphro: Yes

Socrates: Because it is holy, or for some other reason?

Euthyphro: No, it is for that reason.

Socrates: And so it is because it is holy that it is loved; it is not holy because it is loved.

What Socrates is pointing out is that the attitudes of God, his loving something or his wanting us to do it, must be based upon the intrinsic quality of the thing in question. The attitudes of God cannot be the *source* of that intrinsic quality. The ontological claim has things backward.

Why did Socrates believe that God's attitude toward something— our behavior, for example—must be based upon the thing's intrinsic quality? It is not difficult, I think, to reconstruct the thoughts that led Socrates to this conclusion: God must have some reason for wanting us to do the action in question, some reason for loving the thing in question. If he didn't, then he would be arbitrary and capricious. That certainly doesn't fit our picture of the deity. Indeed, given our conception of God, there could be no other reason than the intrinsic quality of the action or thing.

This argument clearly rests upon the presupposition that the will of God is not an arbitrary will. Even if we don't know God's reasons—and there is no reason for thinking that we should—he has them anyway. This picture of God's will is widely held. But it should be noted that there is another theological tradition which has it that God's very arbitrariness shows his majesty and power. To quote Jonathan Edwards:

> It is meet that God should order all these things according to his own pleasure. By reason of his greatness and glory, by which he is infinitely above all, his is worthy to be sovereign, and that his pleasure should in all things take place.

Naturally, writers in this tradition would not be moved by the Socratic argument. They would not see any reason to grant that the holy is loved by all the gods "because it is holy."

The second objection philosophers have made to the ontological claim has to do with whether or not the will of anything, even God, could be the basis for moral distinctions. Suppose, the argument goes, someone wants us to do something and commands us to do it. Now, if the person is important enough or powerful enough, that may provide us with good reason for performing the action. But it doesn't make the action right. If we love the person, that may make us want to do the action. But again it doesn't make the action right. Why then, asks the argument, does it make a difference that the willer is God? How can the will of God make an action right?

One might say that this argument is mistaken because God is different: his will is always right, so he always wills that we do what is right. But this won't do, for to say this is to recognize that the ontological claim is in error. If we have to say that we obey God's will because it is always right, we have admitted that rightness and wrongness are grounded on something other than the will of God. To quote Kai Nielsen:

> No information about the nature of reality, the state of the world, or knowledge that there is a God and that He issues commands, will by itself tell us what is good or what we ought to do. The statement 'God wills x' is not a moral pronouncement. Before we know whether we ought to do x, we must know that what God wills is good. And in order to know that what God wills is good, we would have to judge independently that it is good. That something is good is not entailed by God's willing it, for otherwise it would be rhetorical to ask 'Is what God wills good?' But it is not rhetorical to ask that question. 'God wills x' or 'God commands x' is not equivalent to 'x is good' in the same way as 'x is a male parent' is equivalent to 'x is a father'. 'God wills it, but is it good?' is not a senseless or self-answering question like 'Fred is a male parent, but is he a father?' The moral agent must independently decide that whatever God wills or commands is good. ("Religion, Morality, and Bertrand Russell," *The Amherst Reivew* (1959))

Most philosophers have been convinced by the two lines of argument that we have discussed. Thus, they have rejected the ontological claim, our last attempt to ground morality upon the will of God.

6.2 CAN RELIGION MAKE A DIFFERENCE TO MORALITY?

In thinking about the relation between morality and religion, one must distinguish between two types of claim: claims that say there can be no morality unless certain religious beliefs are true and claims that say religion can make a difference in the sphere of morality. What we saw in section 6.1 was that claims of the former type are false. Religion is not needed as the basis for morality. But this does not mean that claims of the latter type are false. Religion may still have a contribution to make to morality.

Actually, we have already seen two contributions that it can make. While we may have nonreligious motives as well, the love of God may

THE IMPLICATIONS OF RELIGIOUS BELIEF

provide an additional motive for behaving morally. And while we may have nonreligious sources for our moral beliefs, religious teachings can at least serve as an additional source of such beliefs. In this section, we will be looking for additional contributions that religion can make to morality. In particular, we will be looking for moral beliefs whose truth may rest upon the truth of religious beliefs.

Let me begin with a simple example of such a contribution. There is a philosophical tradition about the right to private property that runs as follows: At one time, the natural resources of the earth (land, minerals, etc.) had no owner; everyone was free to use them. But when people did use them, and added their labor to these resources, they produced from them a new resource which they had a legitimate right to. This process of mixing one's labor with the natural resources is the origin of the right to private property. If the laborer does not come to own the property, his labor would not have been his own. But, of course, it was. So those who would take the property away from him or would prevent him from using it as he wishes are violating one of his basic rights. If he is to have his rights, he must be able to use the property he has worked on to promote his own interests. As John Locke wrote:

> Though the earth and all inferior creatures be common to all men, yet every man has a property in his own person. The labor of his body and the work of his hands, we may say, are properly his. Whatsoever, then, he removes out of the state that Nature hath provided and left it in, he hath mixed his labor with it, and joined it to something that is his own and thereby makes it his property. ("Second Treatiste," chapter 5)

There are a number of nonreligious ways of attacking this ethical tradition, and philosophers are in disagreement about its validity. But there is also a religious attack. The tradition presupposes the existence of unowned resources of which man can become the absolute owner. But, says this religious attack, the true owner of the whole universe is God, its creator. Man can at best be God's steward over these natural resources. At best he can be allowed to use them in accordance with God's plans (for example, using them for the general good and not merely for the good of the particular individual). So, this is an example of religion contributing to morality. The idea that God is the creator and ultimate owner of the universe alters the moral views one holds about the rights of owners of private property.

This idea of God as the creator and master of the universe has been extended to include man as a part of God's domain. As a result, it has been used by some philosophers for an argument against the morality of suicide. Thus, Socrates offered the following explanation as to why he would be acting wrongly if he took his own life:

> If one of your own possessions, an ox or an ass, for example, took the liberty of putting himself out of the way . . . would you not be angry with him? . . . Then, if we look at the matter thus, there may be reason in saying that a man should wait, and not take his own life, until God summons him. (*Phaedo*)

It is very hard to see, from a nonreligious perspective, why there should be a moral objection to suicide. No doubt, there are many cases in which the suicide may be foolish, but that is an objection to the wisdom of the act and not to its morality. No doubt, there are other cases in which the person who commits suicide is running away from his obligations, and for that reason is acting wrongly. But that is not a basis for a general moral objection to suicide (unless, as seems implausible, there are *always* such obligations). Many nonreligious moralists have concluded that, lacking special obligations, we always have the right to take our own lives. In that way, we are absolute masters over our lives.

What Socrates was pointing out was that the moral situation is very different if we accept the idea of God as the master of the universe and everything in it. For then, even if the individual wants to die, he does not have the right to commit suicide. In doing so, he is depriving God, his master, of a servant. This, said Socrates, constitutes the moral objection to suicide.

But two additional points should be noted about the religious attitude towards suicide. First of all, not all religious systems adopt this attitude towards suicide. Some find suicide permissible, either because they reject at least this part of the idea that God is the master of all men or because they believe that God has given his servants permission to make such decisions about their lives. Secondly, even some traditions that disapprove of suicide in general believe that suicide is permissible in some cases. One such case might be that of a person who commits suicide rather than face being compelled to do some very evil act. Thus, in a great many religious traditions, it would even be thought to be a meritorious act to commit suicide rather than face being tortured into other, worse, acts. For example, a person might be considered virtuous if he commits suicide rather than revealing under torture secrets that would lead to the destruction of many innocent people. Can these exceptions be reconciled with the argument against suicide that we have been considering? It seems to me that they can. After all, the crucial objection to our destroying ourselves is that we have no right to do so without the permission of our master, God. The religious person might well feel

THE IMPLICATIONS OF RELIGIOUS BELIEF 131

that these are cases in which we have God's permission to destroy ourselves.

Let us see where we stand now. We have seen that the religious doctrine of God as creator and master of the universe can make a difference to the moral beliefs that we hold. Naturally, there are many other religious claims that might effect our moral beliefs, and the reader might well want to identify them and think about their implications. It is sufficient for our purposes to conclude that religious beliefs can play an important role in moral systems, even though there are purely secular moralities that require no religious grounding.

6.3 RELIGION AND THE MEANING OF LIFE

We often distinguish between meaningful and meaningless activities. We sometimes go further than that, and distinguish between meaningful and meaningless lives. Albert Schweitzer, we say, led a very meaningful life, but others waste their lives in meaningless pursuits. Yet, when we try to explain these distinctions, we find it is very hard to do so. In this section, we will attempt to develop one conception of the meaningful life. And in the light of that conception, we will discuss the contributions that religion might make to the meaning of life.

A first suggestion that might be offered is that a meaningful activity is one that leads to an appropriate goal. The goal, then, provides a justification for performing that activity. Thus, "hanging around" and doing nothing is thought to be a meaningless activity, precisely because it fails to lead us in the direction of some real goals. On the other hand, spending years in training so that we can learn a profession which we would find enjoyable and satisfying is a meaningful activity. Here there is an identifiable goal and purpose towards which the action is directed.

This way of drawing the distinction between meaningful and meaningless activities is based upon the distinction, in the realm of actions, between the means and the end, or goal. Actions themselves are means; their results are goals. If the action leads to some worthwhile goal, it is meaningful; otherwise, it is a meaningless action.

This account of the distinction won't do for two reasons. To begin with, suppose that you work at something for a very long period of time. But suppose the goal that you obtain on the basis of that work is very trivial, something that you don't really care about after all. Then, although your action does lead to some goal, we would probably want to think of it as a meaningless action. The result is not commensurate with the effort that you have put in, and this leads to a kind of meaninglessness. Secondly, there seem to be some actions that are meaningful in and of themselves. They do not find their meaning in being a means to some goal. Thus, a pleasant day of sailing, a good game of tennis, etc., are meaningful actions, but not because they lead to the attainment of some goal beyond themselves.

A better suggestion about meaningful activities, then, could be summarized as follows:

1. There are some things that are desirable in and of themselves. We shall call them ends.

2. Some actions are ends. The performance of these actions is meaningful.

3. Other actions are not ends. These actions are meaningless unless they result in the attainment of ends that are commensurate to the effort involved in performing them.

Plato, in the *Republic,* raises the following question about virtuous actions:

> . . . do you agree that there is a kind of good which we would choose to possess, not from desire for its aftereffects, but welcoming it for its own sake? As, for example, joy and such pleasures as are harmless and nothing results from them afterward save to have and to hold the enjoyment.
>
> I recognize that kind, said I.
>
> And again a kind that we love both for its own sake and for its consequences, such as understanding, sight, and health? For these I presume we welcome for both reasons.
>
> Yes, I said.
>
> And can you discern a third form of good under which fall exercise and being healed when sick and the art of healing and the making of money generally? For of them we would say that they are laborious and painful yet beneficial, and for their own sake we would not accept them, but only for the rewards and other benefits that accrue from them.
>
> Why yes, I said, I must admit this third class also. But what of it?
>
> In which of these classes do you place justice? he said.

In our terminology, the question that was raised at the end was whether just actions, virtuous actions, are meaningful.

This account is, of course, very schematic. In particular, it has to be filled out with an account of what makes certain things desirable, what makes them ends, and with an account of when consequences are

THE IMPLICATIONS OF RELIGIOUS BELIEF

commensurate with the efforts expended. But, schematic as it is, it will do for our purposes. Using it, we shall now turn to the distinction between meaningful and meaningless lives.

There are two very different ways of seeing the connection between meaningful lives and meaningful actions. These two models could be summarized as follows:

1. A meaningful life is one in which meaningful actions predominate.

2. A meaningful life is one in which most of our actions are directed towards one commensurate goal (and we can call that goal the meaning of the life in question).

There are, obviously, very significant differences between these two. The former finds the meaning of life in the performance of a wide variety of meaningful actions, actions that are not necessarily related to each other or to some one basic goal. The latter insists that while individual actions can be meaningful in this way, life itself acquires meaning only when it is directed towards some one goal as a totality.

It is reasonably clear that one can develop a nonreligious conception of the meaningful life if one adopts the first model. After all, there are many things (pleasant experiences, satisfactory interpersonal relationships, the gaining of understanding, a sense of helping others, etc.) that we find valuable and desirable. Since we have many opportunities to perform actions that either embody or lead to these ends, we can have lives that are full of meaningful actions. To say this is, of course, not to say that any life can be given meaning this easily. There are some lives—lives full of pain and suffering, lives of harsh servitude, lives which are very confined and tedious—which would be very hard to infuse with meaning in this way. (It is in the context of such a life that the question of the appropriateness of suicide—as an act affirming the meaninglessness of life—becomes particularly appropriate.) On the whole, however, we can say that the secular life can be meaningful in the pattern described by our first model.

Religious thinkers, who claim that life is given a special meaning, or perhaps its only meaning, through religion, normally have in mind the second model. For them, religion provides us with the all-embracing, commensurate goal which serves as the meaning of life. What would such a life be like? The following selections from St. Thomas give us an idea.

> From what has been said it is clear that the last end of all things is to become like God. Now that which has properly the nature of an end is the good. Therefore, properly speaking, things tend to become like God inasmuch as He is good. . . . Now, seeing that

all creatures, even those that are devoid of reason, are directed to God as their last end, and that all reach this end insofar as they have some share of a likeness to Him, the intellectual creature attains to Him in a special way, namely, through its proper operation, by understanding Him. Consequently this must be the end of the intellectual creature, namely, to understand God. . . . Seeing, then, that man's ultimate happiness does not consist in that knowledge of God whereby He is known by all or many in a vague kind of opinion, nor again in that knowledge of God whereby He is known in the speculative sciences through demonstration, nor by that knowledge whereby He is known through faith, as we proved above, and seeing that it is not possible in this life to arrive at a higher knowledge of God in His essence . . . and since we must place our ultimate happiness in some kind of knowledge of God, as we have shown:—it is impossible for man's happiness to be in this life. (*Summa Contra Gentiles*, III)

Interestingly enough, and this is common to much religious thought, the meaning of life—the end to which we aspire and for which we do everything else—is placed in something that lies outside the natural span of our life.

Why do religious people tend toward the second model? I suspect that their idea is that any one goal that is to serve as the meaning of life must be a very great goal. This goal must be commensurate with all of the struggles and tribulations of life. Hence, it is only some religious goal, with its dimension of eternity, that can serve. There are nonreligious thinkers who have agreed with this evaluation. But, unwilling to accept its religious conclusions, they have set out a very different conception of the process by which life obtains meaning. Thus, Camus wrote:

The gods had condemned Sisyphus to ceaselessly rolling a rock to the top of a mountain, whence the stone would fall back of its own weight. They had thought with some reason that there is no more dreadful punishment than futile and hopeless labor. . . . You have already grasped that Sisyphus is the absurd hero. He *is*, as much through his passions as through his torture. His scorn of the gods, his hatred of death, and his passion for life won him that unspeakable penalty in which the whole being is exerted toward accomplishing nothing. This is the price that must be paid for the passions of this earth. Nothing is told us about Sisyphus in the underworld. Myths are made for the imagination to breathe life into them. As for this myth, one sees merely the whole effort of a body straining to raise the huge stone, to roll it and push it up a slope a hundred times over; one sees the face screwed up, the cheek tight against the stone, the shoulder bracing the clay-covered mass, the foot wedging it, the fresh start with arms outstretched, the wholly human security of two earth-clotted hands. At the very end of his long effort measured by skyless space and time without depth, the purpose is achieved. Then Sisyphus watches the stone rush down in a few moments toward that lower world whence he will have to push it up again toward the summit. He goes back down to the plain.

It is during that return, that pause, that Sisyphus interests me. A face that toils so close to stones is already stone itself! I see that man going back down with a heavy yet measured step toward the torment of which he will never know the end. That hour like a breathing space which returns as surely as his suffering, that is the hour of consciousness. At each of those moments when he leaves the heights and gradually sinks toward the lairs of the gods, he is superior to his fate. He is stronger than his rock.

If this myth is tragic, that is because its hero is conscious. Where would his torture be, indeed, if at every step the hope of succeeding upheld him? The workman of today works every day in his life at the same tasks, and this fate is no less absurd. But it is tragic only at the rare moments when it becomes conscious. Sisyphus, proletarian of the gods, powerless and rebellious, knows the whole extent of his wretched condition: it is what he thinks of during his descent. The lucidity that was to constitute his torture at the same time crowns his victory. There is no fate that cannot be surmounted by scorn. (*Myth of Sisyphus*)

A less dramatic, but perhaps sounder, approach would be to reject the second model entirely, and to return to the first approach to the meaningful life. But, the point we are making is that there is this special religious conception of the meaning of life.

6.4 RELIGION AND RITUAL

Almost all religious believers engage in rituals. Some kinds of ritual, most notably prayer, are very widespread. Others, for example, dietary restrictions, are less so and occur in only some religions. And, of course, even when several religions share a given type of ritual activity, the details are likely to differ. So ritual activities are both central to the religious life and important in distinguishing one religious life from another. They are another way in which religion makes a difference. In this final section of the chapter, we will consider a variety of questions about such activities including: (1) What makes an activity a ritual activity? (2)

What is the purpose of these activities? And (3) Are these activities compatible with the theological conception of God?

Let's begin with definitions. The following have been offered:

1. A ritual activity is one believed to be commanded by God.

2. A ritual activity is one believed to be commanded by God and for which there is no rational basis.

3. A ritual activity is one which is engaged in because the practitioner holds certain religious beliefs.

4. A ritual activity is one believed to be binding only upon a given religious community.

5. A ritual activity is one performed in the service of God.

6. A ritual activity is one performed to worship God.

Definition 1 is obviously defective. To begin with, the religious believer often believes that God commands him to perform a great many moral actions, so this definition fails to distinguish the moral action from the ritualistic. Moreover, definition 1 commits religious believers to the belief that all rituals are divinely commanded, and there are many religious thinkers (the "more liberal theologians") who would not be willing to accept this commitment. Such thinkers believe in rituals which are not divinely ordained. Definition 2 is meant to deal with the first of these problems. It distinguishes the moral from the ritualistic on the grounds that the former has a rational basis while the latter does not. But this won't do. As we see below, much of the theology of ritual is devoted to developing and explaining rational bases for at least some rituals. Moreover, definition 2 still leaves the believed committed to the claim that all rituals must be divinely ordained.

Definition 3 seems better on both accounts. Even if some ritual activities have a rational basis, they still involve religious aspects, so they would still be rituals according to definition 3. Moreover, according to definition 3, rituals don't have to be divinely ordained. Nevertheless, definition 3 is unsatisfactory because of certain results we found in section 6.3. We saw there that some moral beliefs and practices (e.g., stewardship over property) are engaged in because of religious beliefs (e.g., the mastership of God). So 3 fails to distinguish rituals from moral practices. This leads us to definition 4, which is based upon the idea that rituals are particular to certain communities—while morals are presumably universal. The trouble is that neither rituals nor moral

THE IMPLICATIONS OF RELIGIOUS BELIEF

practices are universally followed, though the believers in both—at least in many religions—feel that they should be. So 4 also fails to distinguish moral practices from rituals. Definition 5, again, fails to make this distinction, for religious people believe that all of their actions, both moral and ritual, are to be performed in the service of God. And the same trouble arises for definition 6.

The truth of the matter is that within a religious community, the distinction between the moral and the ritual has little significance, and within the framework of religious belief, there is little basis for a theoretical distinction between the two. It is all a matter of worshiping God by obeying his commands. There are important distinctions—the distinction between what is rationally based and what is not, the distinction between what is meant to be universal and what is meant for only some people, etc. But none of these are equivalent to the distinction between the moral and the ritual. From the outside, of course, it looks very different. Outside observers often will identify as rituals those actions performed by members of a religious community that are not performed by others. This won't do as a firm distinction, of course, because such actions often include as well many moral as opposed to ritual actions. In short, then, it is much easier to point to clear-cut examples of rituals (e.g., prayer) than to give any clear account of what a ritual is.

Be that is it may, religious people are convinced that the performance of rituals is of great importance. To the religious mind, the explanation of this is very simple. In performing rituals, man gives God that which he desires and needs. In return he receives the blessing and aid of God. Since receiving that is so vital to success in life, the performance of rituals is crucial. But this notion amounts to what we have called (in section 5.1) a "trading view" of the relation between man and God. So religious thinkers have had to search for an alternative theory of ritual, one that is more compatible with an elevated conception of the deity. The main thrust of their alternative approach has been the claim that these rituals mold and educate our feelings and thoughts. Thus, in a passage typical to this tradition, Saadiah ben Joseph offered the following account of the biblical laws of cleanliness and uncleanliness:

> Some of the benefits are that man is thereby led to think humbly of his flesh, that it enhances to him the value of prayer by virtue of his being cut off therefrom for a while during the period of defilement, that it endears to him the Temple which he was prevented from entering in the state of impurity, and finally that it causes him to dedicate his heart to the fear of God. (*Book of Beliefs and Opinions*)

Clearly, such an approach is theologically vastly superior to the trading approach. But it raises a fundamental problem for religious traditionalism. For most religions have a traditional set of rituals, many of which are—at least at first glance—very foreign to our time and our situation. Now it is one thing to argue for keeping them on the grounds that God in some way *requires* their performance. But if their whole purpose lies in the *effect* they have on us, then wouldn't it perhaps be better to substitute some more contemporary form of ritual?

These considerations are not, however, the only relevant ones. We should recognize that the celebration of certain traditional rituals is essential to the preservation of the identity of a religious community. The substitution of contemporary rituals might serve to weaken that identity and continuity. It is this consideration that leads many religious communities to retain their traditional rituals but to try to find contemporary meanings for them. This is a delicate process, and the results are mixed.

Though we cannot pursue these problems any further, we recognize that the sensitive religious mind will confront them. It is only through such a confrontation that an adequate theory of ritual can be developed.

7

Man and His Place in Nature

In this chapter and the next, our focus will be more "down to earth." At least, our concerns now will be with understanding the nature of human beings and the ways in which they resemble and differ from other things in the material world.

Our first question, the one with which we shall be concerned in this chapter, is normally called the mind-body problem. This is the question of the relation between the mental and the physical. I think, however, that this question and its significance can best be understood if we approach if from two perspectives, the perspective of the confrontation with death and the perspective of the place of man in nature.

At a certain point in the existence of every human being the body stops functioning. We call that the moment of death. Since some parts of the body can continue to function long after other parts of the body have ceased functioning, the exact moment of death is not clear. There have been cases, for example, in which a person's brain stopped functioning but in which that person's heart continued to function for a relatively long period. In such cases, it is actually not clear whether the person is alive or dead. Be that as it may, we consider that when the body's main systems have all stopped functioning, the person clearly is dead.

What is the significance of death? Some obviously feel that death is the end of human existence. According to them, we simply cease to exist when our body stops functioning. Death, in this view, is not another aspect of existence; it is the end of existence. This view of death is usually based upon the following conception of a human being: a human being is a functioning body. This conception is a *materialist* one. So long as the material body continues to function, the human being exists. When it stops functioning, the human being no longer exists.

This approach brings with it a number of fundamental questions: Is the cessation of existence always bad, or is it sometimes a good thing? Does it add meaning to our life (we can, after all, view the fact that we have only a limited existence as providing us with a reason for using our time in meaningful activities)? Or does it subtract from the meaningfulness of human existence (how can any activities have significance when our ultimate fate is nonexistence, no matter what we have accomplished)?

There is another way of viewing death: death is merely the end of one part of human existence, the embodied part. After we die, we continue to exist in a disembodied fashion, without a functioning body and independent of our "dead" body. This view of death is usually based upon the following conception of a human being. A human being is composed of two separate entities, a material body and a nonmaterial soul. When we die, the nonmaterial part continues to exist after the body no longer functions. This is the *dualist* position, and it constitutes an alternative to the materialist conception of human beings.

Consider the perspective, now, of man's place in nature. There are clearly ways in which human beings resemble inanimate objects like rocks and tables. Like them, we are located at particular places at given times; we have a definite weight, shape, and size; and we are composed out of atoms and are therefore subject to a whole variety of physical and chemical laws. Far from being totally removed from the physical world surrounding us, we are a definite part of it. At the same time, however, there are important ways in which we differ from rocks and tables. To begin with, we are capable of taking in nutrition—absorbing certain foreign objects, i.e., foods, and modifying them and making them part of us. Secondly, we are capable of locomotion, of moving from one place to another. Rocks and tables can be moved by forces impinging upon them; we are capable of self-initiated motion. Thirdly, we are capable of having sensations, such as pain and pleasure, and of perceiving the world about us. Fourthly, we are capable of having a wide variety of emotions—love, fear, envy, hope, etc. And, finally, we are capable of carrying through a variety of intellectual processes, both theoretical and practical. In all of these ways, human beings are not just another part of the natural world that surrounds us. The duality of our nature is expressed by P. F. Strawson when he says:

> The concept of a person is to be understood as the concept of a type of entity such that both predicates ascribing states of consciousness and predicates ascribing corporeal characteristics, a physical situation etc. are equally applicable to an individual entity of that type. (*Individuals*, p. 104)

It should be noted, though Strawson does not, that human beings are not unique in this way. Some animals, for example, seem capable of engaging in some form of all of these activities. And plants are capable of engaging in at least the first and perhaps more. This is important to note, for it is directly connected to a variety of moral issues.

Consider, for example, the killing of animals for food. Most people find this morally unobjectionable, although they would certainly have grave objections to doing the same thing to human beings. But can this distinction be maintained given what we have just noted? What are the characteristics of human beings that justify this distinction? And if there are none, how else could it be justified? A similar point can be made about the moral issues surrounding abortion. By the end of the first trimester after conception (and probably even before then), the fetus is capable of engaging in at least some form of each of these activities. And yet, many feel that it is permissible to take fetal life in circumstances under which they would not be prepared to take other forms of human life. Again, what are the differences that justify this moral distinction?

This point can also be put as follows. Strawson has called our attention to one fundamental feature of persons. These moral issues raise the question as to whether there are other fundamental features of persons. If there are not, we may have to rethink certain issues, for example, those having to do with the rights of fetuses and animals. Having made this point, however, let us return our main focus to the features that Strawson has noted.

There have been, in the history of western thought, two basic approaches to the duality of human nature. One, our dualist approach, takes this duality very seriously. According to this, those of our qualities which are comparable to physical objects are really qualities of our body, while those of our qualities and activities that are restricted to us are qualities of our soul. The other approach, our materialist approach, insists that a human being is nothing more than a body which is so structured and organized that it is capable of engaging in all of these special activities.

In this chapter, we will examine these two approaches and see their strengths and weaknesses. We will also discuss their implications for a variety of other issues.

7.1 MIND-BODY DUALISM

The dualist position advances the following claims about human beings:

1. They are composed out of two entities, a body which is a physical object located in space, and a soul which is nonphysical and not located in space.

2. It is the soul that thinks, feels emotions, has perceptions, and makes decisions.

3. The soul and the body interact, so that the thoughts and decisions of the soul cause the body to move and act in certain ways, while the physical stimuli impinging upon the body cause certain perceptions in the soul.

4. The purely physical characteristics of human beings are characteristics of the body.

We find a well-known presentation of this view in the writings of René Descartes:

> All that we experience as being in us, and that to observation may exist in wholly inanimate bodies, must be attributed to our body alone; and, on the other hand, all that which is in us and which we cannot in any way conceive as possibly pertaining to a body, must be attributed to our soul. Thus because we have no conception of the body as thinking in any way, we have reason to believe that every kind of thought which exists in us belongs to the soul. . . . Those [thoughts] which we relate to the things which are without us, to wit the objects of our senses, are caused, at least when our opinion is not false, by these objects which, exciting certain movements in the organs of the external senses, excite them also in the brain by the intermission of the nerves, which cause the soul to perceive them. . . . The whole action of the soul consists in this, that solely because it desires something, it causes the little gland [in the body] to which it is closely united to move in the way requisite to produce the effect which relates to this desire. (*Passions of the Soul,* Part I)

Some dualists have gone even further. They have claimed that a human being is really just a soul, that the body is simply a physical object to which the soul is attached. They have sometimes even claimed that the body is best compared to a prison or a trap for the soul. The desires and perceptions that it causes in the soul interfere with the proper activities of the soul, so the best thing for us to do is to ignore them (especially, the desires) as much as possible. This extreme dualism, which is very widely spread in certain religious writings, was expressed by Socrates in Plato's *Phaedo*:

> And purification, as we saw sometime ago in our discussion, consists in separating the soul as much as possible from the body, and accustoming it to withdraw from all contact with the body and concentrate itself by itself, and to have its dwelling, so far as it can, both now and in the future, alone by itself, freed from the shackles of the body.

Not all dualists, however, have held these additional views, and we shall put them aside to concentrate on the more central themes of dualism that are outlined above.

Why are people dualists? We have already seen a number of factors that explain the attractiveness of dualism. Dualism clearly offers a straightforward explanation of certain undeniable dualities in human nature. In particular, it tells why human beings, physical themselves, are capable of performing a wide variety of activities that cannot be performed by ordinary physical objects. According to the dualist explanation, human beings can perform these activities only because they have a soul as well as a body, for these activities are activities of the soul.

This factor immediately raises the question of whether animals also have souls. After all, they are also capable of performing many activities that cannot be performed by ordinary physical objects. This issue was hotly debated in the seventeenth and eighteenth centuries. At that time, there were dualists who were fully prepared to accept the view that animals have souls (a view which had been held, in a different way, by Aristotle and many medieval thinkers). In a reply to Descartes, Antoine Arnauld wrote:

> It seems incredible that there is any way by which, *without any intervention of the soul*, it can come to pass that the light reflected from the body of a wolf into the eyes of a sheep should excite into motion the minute fibres of the optic nerves and by the penetration of this movement to the brain, discharge the animal spirits into the nerves in the manner requisite to make the sheep run off. (*Objections to Descartes's Meditations*, IV, 1)

However, most thinkers at the time, like Descartes, felt that the activities of animals could be completely explained by special facts about their bodies. Naturally, this raised the question as to whether the same thing couldn't be said about human beings. Perhaps our special capacities are explainable by the special and complex structure of our bodies.

This leads us to another point. The fact that human beings perform activities which ordinary objects do not is obviously going to fail as an argument for dualism unless the dualist can show that the materialist explanation is inadequate. We shall consider this important question in the sections 7.2 and 7.3.

A second factor which attracts people to dualism is that it leaves open the possibility of survival after death. One fact that we are all aware of—though many of us try to avoid thinking about it—is that we will die. Each of us knows that his body will to a large extent be destroyed in a relatively short period after death. Is that the end of us, or do we continue to exist anyway? This is the question of personal survival. Dualism suggests that we may, for there is a major part of us, the soul, that might survive the destruction of the body. (Believers in psychic phenomena, in fact, often feel that it offers evidence for dualism.)

Regarding this factor we should note, to begin with, that a dualist need not be committed to belief in personal survival. Dualism itself is neutral on that issue. All that can legitimately be said is that dualism leaves open the possibility that a major part of us will survive the destruction of the body after death. Secondly, the fact that dualism leaves open this possibility is not an argument for its truth. For that, we would have to know that we actually do survive our death. All that can be said is that this factor is responsible for much of the popularity of dualism.

Traditional materialism offers two sorts of objections to dualism. One (the interaction objection) is directed towards the claims of the dualist, and the other (the other-minds objection) is concerned with the question of knowledge and the implications of dualism in this realm. Let us look at each of these objections and at the responses that dualists have made to them.

The interaction objection. This objection addresses itself to claim 3 of dualism, the claim that the body and the soul interact. It is not surprising that the dualist makes this claim, for it certainly appears as if our thoughts and feelings influence our actions, and as if physical stimuli influence our perceptions and thoughts. But this objection asks how this interaction can take place if the dualist is right about the soul and body being of such different natures? As David Hume put it:

> Is there any principle in all nature more mysterious than the union of soul with body, by which a supposed spiritual substance acquires

such an influence over a material one that the most refined thought is able to actuate the grossest matter? Were we empowered by a secret wish to remove mountains or control the planets in their orbit, this extensive authority would not be more extraordinary, nor more beyond our comprehension. (*Inquiry Concerning Human Understanding*, section 7.)

The basic strategy for meeting this objection has traditionally been put as follows. We clearly need to concede that there is a relation between the mental and the physical. After all, our thoughts and feelings are clearly related to the bodily motions which follow them in time. And the physical stimuli impinging upon our sensory organs are clearly related to the perceptions and thoughts which follow them in time. There is no reason, however, to concede that the relation in question is a causal relation. And if we can find some other account of the relation, the interaction problem will be solved. But what is that other relation?

It is the relation of *correlation*. Our subsequent bodily motions are correlated with earlier thoughts and feelings but the latter do not cause the former. The physical stimuli impinging upon our sensory organs are correlated with subsequent perceptions and thoughts, but they do not cause them. Another question arises here, however, for what is the cause of these correlations? Why, for example, are our decisions to act in certain ways normally correlated with our subsequently acting that way if the former do not cause the latter? In response to these obvious and overwhelming objections, the seventeenth and eighteenth century dualists invoked the deity. They did so, however, in two different ways. Some, like Malebranche, held a view called *occasionalism*. This said that the correlation is maintained by the constant intervention of God. Others, like Leibniz, felt there was a *pre-established harmony*, that is, that the correlation was established for all time by God when he created the universe. One can get a sense of the nature of this dispute by reading the following passage from a letter of Leibniz:

> I say that God created the universe in such a way that the soul and the body, each acting according to its laws, agree in their phenomena. You think, M., that this coincides with the hypothesis of occasional causes. . . . My opinion is different. . . . Everything happens to each substance in consequence of the first state which God gave to it in creating it, and putting aside extraordinary interventions the originary agreement consists only in the conservation of the substance itself conformably to its preceding state and to the changes which it carries in itself. (*Letter to Arnauld*, April 30, 1687)

Despite their ingeniousness, these theories of correlation have been rejected by most dualists. They have felt that the use of God in this sort of way is a form of intellectual cheating; one cannot just invoke him as a solution to any unresolved problem. Moreover, this whole approach may be based on a nonexistent distinction because it is not clear that there is a difference between the causal relation and the correlation invoked as a substitute.

In recent years, dualists have claimed that the whole interaction problem is a pseudoproblem based upon the unwarranted and mistaken assumption that two substances must be sufficiently like each other to interact causally. With what justification, they have asked, can we rule out the possibility of two substances interacting just because they are different? Jerome Schaffer puts this argument for dismissing the interaction problem as follows:

> Cause and effect are where we find them, and it would be in violation of the principles of scientific reasoning if we rejected some apparent causal connections on the a priori ground that the events were 'too different' to be causally connected.

The other-minds objection. This objection cannot be dismissed that easily. It begins by observing that, according to dualism, the soul is a nonphysical object which has no spatial location. It cannot, then, be perceived by external senses. Now, as a matter of fact, dualists feel that we have a power of introspection, an ability to perceive what is going on in our own souls. In this way, we are able to immediately know that we have a soul and which thoughts and emotions it has and which decisions it makes. But what about the soul (the mind) of others? How can we know that they have one? And even if we can, how do we know what is going on in it? Doesn't dualism really commit us to a terrible ignorance about other people? And isn't it therefore in error?

Dualism, then, must deal with this problem of how we can know about the minds of others. How do we know that someone else is in pain? How do we know when someone else loves us (or doesn't)? How can we find out what anyone believes? These can be practical as well as philosophical problems, and the truth of the matter is that we often don't know. But, in many cases, we can figure out what other people think or feel. How do we do that? Presumably, we figure it out on the basis of their behavior. For example, if we see someone writhing on the ground we infer on the basis of their behavior that they are in pain. Again, we conclude that someone loves us on the basis of the way that person behaves toward us.

It is just this that gives rise to problems for the dualist. According to the dualist, pain is a sensation that we feel in our soul. How then can we infer that it is occurring in someone else's soul when all that we can observe is the writhing of that person's body? According to the dualist, love is an emotion that takes place in our soul. How then can we infer that it is occurring in someone else's soul when all that we can observe are certain ways of behaving? In short, the dualist has to explain how we can infer what is going on in the soul when all that we can observe is the behavior of the body.

Obviously, dualists will insist that that inference is legitimate. But they have to offer an explanation of its legitimacy. There are two major dualist accounts, the *analogy-account* and the *explanation-account*.

According to the analogy-account, we first learn about the connection between what goes on in the soul and how bodies behave by observing it in our own case. We see, for example, the way that the love in our soul leads us to behave in certain ways. Then, we infer that other people behave analogously. They must be feeling love when they behave similarly towards us. John Stuart Mill wrote:

> I conclude that other human beings have feelings like me, because, first, they have bodies like me, which I know, in my own case, to be the antecedent condition of feelings; and because, secondly, they exhibit the acts, and other outward signs, which in my own case, I know by experience to be caused by feelings. (*Examination of Sir William Hamilton's Philosophy*, chapter 12)

This account seems incomplete. What is the justification for assuming that other people behaved analogously? If we know only about the connection between the mental and the physical from our own case, how can we be sure that the same connection holds for other people? Perhaps, for example, they feel a different emotion and not love? Perhaps they don't feel any emotion at all? Somehow, the analogy of our own case seems too weak a foundation for the whole of our knowledge about other minds. It would be different, of course, if we could at least sometimes directly check to see that other people have analogous feelings and thoughts. But we never can. Herbert Feigl has written:

> The philosophical trouble with inferring another person's mental states consists in the impossibility of an independent, direct check-up. There seems to be no criterion, in the sense of necessary and sufficient conditions, which would enable one person to convince himself conclusively of the actual occurrence of mental states on the part of the other person. The analogical argument concerning other minds thus differs fundamentally from the ordinary type of analogical inference. In the ordinary cases *direct* evidence can be obtained for the truth of the conclusion. If we reason, for example, from the many similarities between two human bodies and the

presence of a brain in one of them, to the presence of a brain in the other, the conclusion by itself is clearly open to direct (surgical) examination. In any case, it is safe to say that the conclusion here may be verified with the same degree of certainty that attaches to the premises of the analogical argument. But if person A, on the basis of the regular concomitance of his own mental states with certain aspects of his behavior (or ultimately with his brain processes) infers similar mental states as concomitant with the other person's, i.e., B's, behavior (or brain processes), then he cannot by any known or even conceivable procedure convince himself of the truth of his conclusion—certainly not in the manner he can know the truth of the premises of his analogical argument. ("Other Minds and the Egocentric Predicament," *Journal of Philosophy*, 1958)

Not all philosophers find this objection to the analogical approach conclusive. There are philosophers who claim that there is no significance to the fact that I cannot directly check whether someone else has feelings and thoughts. The analogy is valid so long as there are no features distinguishing us that might provide the basis for my having thoughts and feelings while you don't. A. J. Ayer, for one, claimed this.

The analogy between two persons is never perfect: this follows simply from the fact that they are two different persons. Neither can one suppose it to be perfect; for to suppose it perfect would be to merge the two persons into one. At the same time, it may be very extensive, and it can always be conceived as being more extensive than it is. Now when one ascribes some inner experience, some thought or feeling, to another, the rational ground for this ascription consists in one's knowing him to possess some further properties. The assumption is that there is a uniform connection between the possession of these properties and the undergoing of an experience of the sort in question. I infer that my friend is in pain, because of the condition of his tooth, because of his nervous system, because of his wincing, and so forth; and the connection of these properties with a feeling of pain is one that I can, in principle, test, one that I may in fact have tested in my own experience. But, it may be objected, the connection may not hold good in his case. How can you tell? But if it does not hold good in his case, this must be because of some other property that he possesses, the addition of which creates a counter-example to the rule. It would not hold good, for instance, if the additional property were that of his having been hypnotized to feel no pain. But with regard to any further property that he possesses it is conceivable at least that I should test the rule so as to find out whether the addition of this property does make a difference. Sometimes I can carry out the test directly by myself acquiring the properties concerned. Of course there are many properties that I cannot acquire. If I happen, for example, to have been born on a Thursday, I cannot directly test the hypothesis that people who were born on a Wednesday do not in these circumstances feel pain. But I have no reason to suppose that this is a relevant factor, and good indirect evidence that it is not. And, if our argument is correct, there will be no properties that I am in principle debarred from testing, however many there may be that I cannot test in fact. But even if my friend has no properties which make him an exception to the rule about feeling pain, may he not still be an exception just as being the person that he is? And in that case how can the rest of us ever know whether or not he really does feel pain? But the answer to this is that nothing is described by his being the person that he is except the possession of certain properties. If, *per impossibile*, we could test for all the properties that he possesses, and found that they did not produce a counter-example to our general hypothesis about the conditions in which pain is felt, our knowledge would be in this respect as good as his: there would be nothing further left for us to discover.

To sum up, it is necessarily true that, being the person that I am, I am not also someone else. It is necessarily true that I could not conceivably satisfy all the descriptions that some other person satisfies and still remain a distinct person. And if this is made the requirement for my really knowing what he thinks or feels, then it is necessarily true that this is something that I can never really know. On the other hand, with regard to any given property, which I may or may not myself in fact possess, there seems to be no logical reason why I should not test the degree of its connection with some other properties: and what I am asserting when I ascribe an experience to some other person is just that the property of having it is co-instantiated with certain others. The inference is not from my experience as such to his experience as such, but from the fact that certain properties have been found to be conjoined in various contexts to the conclusion that in a further context the conjunction will still hold. This is a normal type of inductive argument; and I cannot see that it is in any degree invalidated by the fact that, however far one is able to extend the positive analogy, it always remains within the compass of one's own experience. ("Our Knowledge of Other Minds," *Theoria*, 1953)

Despite this attempt to defend the analogy-account, many philosophers have concluded that it would be preferable to find a different, more satisfactory account. They have proposed the explanation-account of our knowledge of other minds.

In order to understand the explanation-account, we should understand the basis for inferences made from what has been observed to what has not been observed. Suppose, for example, that you are a detective trying to figure out who the murderer is. You collect a number of observations (the clues) and you infer from them something that you have not observed (that x is the murderer). What is the justification for such an inference? Well, suppose that the clues are that the butler's fingerprints were found on the murder weapon, that the missing $10,000 was found in his Swiss bank account, etc. The conclusion that is inferred, that the butler is the murderer, is justified because it seems to be the best explanation of the clues. If the butler didn't kill the victim, what are his fingerprints doing on the murder weapon, what is the money doing in his Swiss bank account, etc.? And if there is a better explanation, if these questions can be answered, then the inference is not justified.

This seems to be a very common pattern of inferences from the observed to the unobserved. Consider, as a more substantial example, the inferences that lead scientists to accept the theory that all material objects are composed of atoms. No one has seen these atoms that are supposed to make up all matter, and yet we all believe that they exist. Why? Well, the atomic theory of matter does, in fact, seem to be the best explanation of a whole variety of observed phenomena (e.g., the ways in which chemical elements combine to form compounds). It is this that justifies the inference to its truth.

According to the explanation-account, then, the very same type of inference underlies our knowledge of the thoughts and feelings of other people. When we see someone's body writhing, we infer that he is in pain because his being in pain is the best account of why his body is moving in the ways that it is moving. When we see a man behaving in certain ways towards a woman, we infer that he loves her because his being in love is the best explanation of his behavior. In general, we believe in the thoughts and feelings of others because that belief is the best explanation of their behavior. To quote H. H. Price:

> But the argument is not only analogical. The hypothesis which it seeks to establish may also be considered in another way. It provides a simple explanation of an otherwise mysterious set of occurrences [intelligent speech acts]. . . . If there is another mind which uses the same symbols as I do and combines them according to the same principles, and if this mind has produced these noises in the course of an act of spontaneous thinking: then I can account for the occurrence of these noises. ("Our Evidence for the Existence of Other Minds," *Philosophy*, 1938)

We have seen then that the dualists have ways of responding both to the interaction objection and the other-minds objection. Nevertheless, there are many philosophers who would prefer a materialist account of human beings. Some of them do so because they do not find that the dualists have satisfactorily explained away their problems. But others have a different reason, one that needs to be explored more fully.

There are many different conceptions of the nature and function of philosophy. One of these conceptions is particularly important for understanding this last basis for a materialist approach. According to this conception, the purpose of philosophy is to present a comprehensive way of thinking about the nature of the world. In other words, this conception would ask philosophy to present a unified picture of the nature of things. Arguing from such a conception of philosophy, some philosophers have concluded that dualism is unacceptable. One such philosopher, J. J. C. Smart, presented that argument in the following fashion:

> Presumably a comprehensive way of thought would be one that brought all intellectual disciplines into a harmonious relationship with one another. It may turn out that there are some realms of discourse, such as theology, which cannot be brought into a harmonious relationship with the various sciences. Any attempt to do so would result in violence to logic or to scientific facts, or may involve arbitrariness and implausibility. (Consider, for example, the implausibility of a theory which asserts that the mechanistic account of evolution by natural selection and mutation is broadly true, but that there is a special discontinuity in the case of man, to whom was superadded an immortal soul.) If this is so, such anomalous branches of discourse will have to be rejected and will not form part of the reconstruction of our total conceptual scheme. (*Philosophy and Scientific Realism*, chapter 1)

In order to properly evaluate this argument, we must first review the sorts of scientific facts that Smart and philosophers like him feel are important in putting forward a unified view of man. There are two main sets of such facts, those having to do with the origin of life and those having to do with the origin of man.

The question of the origin of life has perplexed mankind for a long time. There is, of course, the religious view that life was created by God in a special act of creation. But could one offer a nonreligious account of the origin of life? Pasteur, of course, in a series of famous experiments, had attacked the old view that living organisms can be generated spontaneously from inorganic matter. As a result, important nineteenth century scientists like Lord Kelvin and Helmholtz concluded that life on earth must have been transmitted to the earth from other places in the universe. This view, is of course extremely implausible, since the conditions in outer space (extreme cold, intense radiation, etc.) make it highly unlikley that any living things could survive the trip.

As a matter of fact, the great Russian scientist, A. I. Oparin, was the first to put forward a reasonable, scientific account of the origin of life. On Oparin's view, life emerged from the nonliving as intense radiation caused the formation of more and more complex organic compounds until the simplest living things appeared. In his fundamental work, *The Origin of Life* (first published in Russian in 1936), Oparin worked out the main outlines of this process and showed how the whole process was chemically possible.

Suppose then that we have a world in which there are simple living organisms. How does that serve as the foundation for explaining the origin of the more complex organisms that we encounter in the world today? To answer this question, scientifically minded philosophers turn to the theory of evolution (which was first put forward in the nineteenth century by Charles Darwin and developed extensively since then).

Briefly, this theory contains two elements. One is devoted to explaining the way in which new forms of life emerge from earlier forms. The other explains the mechanisms by which these new forms persevere once they have developed. In the modern theory of evolution, the process of mutation is used to explain the origin of the new forms while that of natural selection is used to explain the perseverance of certain new forms (the ones that are favorably adapted to the ecological niche in which they first emerge).

But how is all of this related to the dispute between materialism and dualism? Smart and others would presumably argue as follows: In trying to put forward a unified picture of man, we must take into account these factors about the origin of man. Looking at scientific theories, we see an earth which at one time contained only inorganic chemical elements. Over a long period of time, organic compounds developed, eventually of such complexity that we can justifiably talk of them as being alive. Then, through the process of evolution, even more complex forms of life emerged. Finally, man appears. At what point in this whole process did the soul appear? Phrased, perhaps, in a more sophisticated way, doesn't a materialistic conception of man fit more naturally into this process than a dualistic conception? And if so, doesn't that provide us with at least some reason for adopting materialism?

Those who offer this argument do not think of it as a conclusive refutation of dualism. It is good that they do not because (1) while the evidence for this account of the origin of man is quite strong, it would certainly be incorrect to call it absolutely conclusive, and (2) the dualist can claim that his thesis is, nevertheless, compatible with this scientific view of the origin of man. (Religious dualists have sometimes said, for example, that God united the soul with the body only when a certain complexity of life had been achieved). Nevertheless, these considerations certainly are sufficient to make us look more closely at materialism, and we turn therefore to a consideration of the various versions of materialism.

There are two major forms of materialism, *behaviorism* and the *brain-state theory*. We shall look at each of them in turn.

7.2 BEHAVIORISM

The crucial things that make us different from the material objects that surround us are our abilities to perceive, to feel, to think, etc. The dualist feels that these activities are activities of the soul and that a human being differs from a material object just because he has a soul. The behaviorist, as a materialist, denies that there is a soul. Instead, says the behaviorist, these activities are nothing more than the body behaving in certain ways.

Let us look at a few examples to get better idea of what the behaviorists are aiming at. Suppose that Matilda loves John. According to the dualist, that love is an emotion in Matilda's soul, an emotion that leads her to behave towards John in certain ways. She may, for example, be led by it to take the same courses in school that he is taking. According to the behaviorist, however, her love is nothing more than that behavior. Suppose that Harry believes that it is going to rain today. According to the dualist, that belief occurs in Harry's soul and leads Harry to behave in certain ways (for example, he may take an umbrella with him). According to the behaviorist, Harry's belief is nothing more than his behavior in doing whatever things he does which relates to the weather.

In short, the behaviorist thinks that human beings are different merely because their bodies are so structured that they are capable of behaving in certain special ways. We are not special because of the possession of a soul. To quote A. J. Ayer:

> The distinction between a conscious man and an unconscious machine resolves itself into a distinction between different types of perceptible behavior. . . . When I assert that an object is conscious, I am asserting no more than that it would, in response to any conceivable test, exhibit the empirical manifestations of consciousness. I am not making a metaphysical postulate concerning the occurrence of events which I could not, even in principle, observe. (*Language, Truth, and Logic*, chapter 7)

It is important to keep in mind the differences between the thesis of behaviorism that we are considering and the behaviorist methodology that is found in much contemporary experimental psychology. Many psychologists have proposed that their investigations should center on readily observable human behavior and not on the unobservable thoughts, feelings, and emotions that may or may not lie behind this behavior. They claim that only in this way will psychology become an objective science. This theme was found already in that classic manifesto of this approach, John Watson's *Behaviorism*:

> The behaviorist asks: Why don't we make what we can observe the real field of psychology? Let us limit ourselves to things that can be observed, and formulate laws concerning only these things. Now what can we observe? We can observe behavior—what the organism does or says. And let us point out at once: that saying is doing—that is, behaving. Speaking overtly or to ourselves (thinking) is just as objective a type of behavior as baseball. . . . As a result of this major assumption that there is such a thing as consciousness and that we can analyze it by introspection, we find as many analyses as there are individual psychologists. There is no way of experimentally attacking and solving psychological problems and standardizing methods.

We are not concerned here with the question of whether or not this is a good methodology for psychological research (there are many who feel that it is not). All that we want to note is that even if it is, it offers no support for the behaviorist thesis that we are considering. Even if psychologists do better by studying behavior rather than thoughts, feelings and emotions, this in no way indicates that these mental events are nothing more than behavior.

Why do some philosophers advocate behaviorism? Partially, as with most materialists, they do so because they feel that the dualist cannot adequately resolve all of his problems (especially the other-minds problem). And they are partially led to behaviorism by reflecting upon the ways in which we do learn about the mental life of other people. After all, we do advance claims about their mental life by observing their behavior, and doesn't this at least suggest (though, admittedly, it does not prove) that their mental life is really nothing more than their behavior? These seem, in any case, to be the main considerations that lead philosophers to advocate behaviorism.

Behavioristic analyses have less difficulty with cases where the thoughts or feelings or emotions are immediately expressed in behavior. The behaviorist can then identify them with the behavior. But what about those cases in which, for example, we have a certain belief or feel a certain emotion but don't act upon it? Aren't those cases in which a mental event occurs without there being some corresponding behavior, and don't those cases show that the mental cannot be reduced to bodily behavior. In order to respond to this objection, behaviorists have distinguished *behavior* from the *disposition to behavior*. And they have claimed that the mental is identical with bodily behavior or dispositions to bodily behavior. So even if the person doesn't act on the belief or the emotion, he still has the disposition to do so, and the mental events in question are to be identified with that disposition. As Gilbert Ryle has written:

> I have already had occasion to argue that a number of the words which we commonly use to describe and explain people's behaviour signify dispositions and not episodes. To say that a person knows something, or aspires to be something, is not to say that he is at a particlar moment in the process of doing or undergoing anything, but that he is able to do certain things, when the need arises, or that he is prone to do and feel certain things in situations of certain sorts.
>
> This is, in itself, hardly more than a dull fact (almost) of ordinary grammar. The verbs 'know', 'possess' and 'aspire' do not behave like the verbs 'run', 'wake up' or 'tingle'; we cannot say 'he knew so and so for two minutes, then stopped and started again after a breather', 'he gradually aspired to be a bishop', or 'he is now engaged in possessing a bicycle'. Nor is it a peculiarity of people that we describe them in dispositional terms. We use such terms just as much for describing animals, insects, crystals and atoms. We are constantly wanting to talk about what can be relied on to happen as well as to talk about what is actually happening; we are constantly wanting to give explanations of incidents as well as to report them; and we are constantly wanting to tell how things can be managed as well as to tell what is now going on in them. Moreover, merely to classify a word as signifying a disposition is not yet to say much more about it than to say that it is not used for an episode. There are lots of different kinds of dispositional words. Hobbies are not the same sort of thing as habits, and both are different from skills, from mannerisms, from fashions, from phobias and from trades. Nest-building is a different sort of property from being feathered, and being a conductor of electricity is a different sort of property from being elastic.
>
> There is, however, a special point in drawing attention to the fact that many of the cardinal concepts in terms of which we describe specifically human behaviour are dispositional concepts, since the vogue of the para-mechanical legend has led many people to ignore the ways in which these concepts actually behave and to construe them instead as items in the descriptions of occult causes and effects. Sentences embodying these dispositional words have been interpreted as being categorical reports of particular but unwitnessable

matters of fact instead of being testable, open hypothetical and what I shall call 'semi-hypothetical' statements. The old error of treating the term 'Force' as denoting an occult force-exerting agency has been given up in the physical sciences, but its relatives survive in many theories of mind and are perhaps only moribund in biology. (*Concept of Mind*, chapter 5)

→ dying

Even with this modification, behaviorism faces a number of difficulties that are sufficient to have led most philosophers to reject it. They can be summarized as follows:

1. The behaviorist cannot do justice to our knowledge of our own mental life. In the case of others, we do have to observe their behavior before we can know what they think or feel. In our own case, however, we are able to introspect (to experience directly) at least some of our thoughts and feelings without having to observe our bodily behavior. It would seem therefore that at least in our own case, thoughts and feelings cannot be reduced to bodily behavior.

2. The behaviorist wants to identify mental events with bodily behavior or dispositions to behave in certain ways. But which bodily behavior? Consider, for example, the emotion of love. Which behavior is that emotion to be identified with? Remember, human beings behave in an immense variety of different ways when they feel love. The best then that the behaviorist can do is to identify love with some variety of forms of behavior—to say that to be in love is to behave in this way, or that way, or the other way. Even this, however, is unsatisfactory, because it always seems as though his list will be incomplete, as though there will be still other ways in which love can be expressed. And the same thing seems to hold for most other complicated thoughts and emotions. So it is very unlikely that the behaviorist will be able to offer satisfactory behaviorist analyses of mental events.

3. Most important, the behaviorist cannot do justice to one fundamental aspect of the relation between the mental and bodily behavior. Normally, we explain bodily behavior by reference to the mental. We say, for example, that a person behaves in certain ways because he is in love or because he believes that he is being pursued by his enemies. If, however, the behaviorist is right and there is only bodily behavior, what can be posulated to explain it?

Sophisticated behaviorists, like B. F. Skinner, are well aware of these objections. The following passage gives one some sense of how Skinner would respond to them:

> The statement that behaviorists deny the existence of feelings, sensations, ideas, and other features of mental life needs a good deal of clarification. Methodological behaviorism and some versions of logical positivism ruled private events out of bounds because there

could be no public agreement about their validity. Introspection could not be accepted as a scientific practice, and the psychology of people like Wilhelm Wundt and Edward B. Titchener was attacked accordingly. Radical behaviorism, however, takes a different line. It does not deny the possibility of self-observation or self-knowledge or its possible usefulness, but it questions the nature of what is felt or observed and hence known. It restores introspection but not what philosophers and introspective psychologists had believed they were "specting," and it raises the question of how much of one's body one can actually observe.

Mentalism kept attention away from the external antecedent events which might have explained behavior, by seeming to supply an alternative explanation. Methodological behaviorism did just the reverse: by dealing exclusively with external antecedent events it turned attention away from self-observation and self-knowledge. Radical behaviorism restores some kind of balance. It does not insist upon truth by agreement and can therefore consider events taking place in the private word within the skin. It does not call these events unobservable, and it does not dismiss them as subjective. It simply questions the nature of the object observed and the reliability of the observations.

The position can be stated as follows: what is felt or introspectively observed is not some nonphysical world of consciousness, mind, or mental life but the observer's own body. This does not mean . . . that introspection is a kind of physiological research, nor does it mean (and this is the heart of the argument) that what are felt or introspectively observed are the causes of behavior. An organism behaves as it does because of its current structure, but most of this is out of reach of introspection. At the moment we must content ourselves, as the methodological behaviorist insists, with a person's genetic and environmental histories. What are introspectively observed are certain collateral products of those histories. (*About Behaviorism*, chapter 2)

Philosophers have, for the most part, not found these responses adequate, and they have therefore rejected behaviorism. To reject behaviorism is not, however, to reject all versions of materialism. We shall, in the last section of this chapter, examine a different version of materialism, one that is not open to the objections faced by behaviorism.

7.3 THE BRAIN-STATE THEORY

Perhaps the best way to introduce this second version of materialism is to return for a moment to the dualist's understanding of the interaction between the soul and the body. Suppose that you see someone that you want to avoid and that you therefore turn into a side street. What, according to dualism, happens when you spot that person? Certain light rays impinge upon your sensory organs, causing a reaction in the nerves that lead to your brain. This, in turn, causes the occurrence of certain brain states. They then cause, according to the dualist, your soul to see the person. This, in turn, causes in your soul a decision to walk down the side street. This decision causes the occurrence of another brain state, which causes a reaction in the nerves leading to the right muscles, which, finally, causes your muscles to contract so that your body moves into that side street. Graphically, what happens is:

$$\text{stimuli} \to \begin{array}{c}\text{nerve}\\ \text{message}\end{array} \to \text{brain state } A \xrightarrow{\uparrow} \begin{array}{c}\text{perception} \to \text{decision}\end{array} \xrightarrow{\downarrow} \text{brain state } B \to \begin{array}{c}\text{nerve}\\ \text{message}\end{array} \to \begin{array}{c}\text{muscular}\\ \text{contractions}\end{array}$$

This decision could obviously be simplified by eliminating the two events in the soul and by treating brain state A as the cause of brain state B. Now, this is precisely what is proposed by this second type of materialism. According to it, human beings are different from other physical objects because of our brain and nervous system, and not because of the possession of a soul.

Another way of think of this theory is as follows. We saw in section 7.2 that one of the difficulties with behaviorism is its inability to explain the cause of behavior. The dualist, of course, treats mental events occurring in the soul as the causes of our behavior. In doing so, however, he also has to refer to brain states and nerve messages. Why then, asks these materialists, can't we simplify our explanation of human behavior by eliminating the soul and treating these brain states as the cause of our behavior. To quote J. J. C. Smart:

> It seems to me that science is increasingly giving us a viewpoint whereby organisms are able to be seen as physiochemical mechanisms: it seems that even the behavior of man himself will one day be explicable in mechanistic terms. There does seem to be, so far as science is concerned, nothing in the world but increasingly complex arrangements of physical constituents. All except for one place: in consciousness . . . sensations, states of consciousness, do seem to be the one sort of thing left outside the physicalist picture, and for various reasons I just cannot believe that this can be so. That everything should be explicable in terms of physics . . . except the occurrence of sensations seems to me to be frankly unbelievable. ("Sensations and Brain Processes," *Philosophical Review*, 1959)

There are two versions of this type of materialism (which we shall call, for obvious reasons, the brain-state theory). The first believes in the existence of mental states such as perceptions, thoughts, feelings, and emotions. According to it, however, they are not things that occur in some nonmaterial soul. They are simple states of our brain. As Smart puts it:

> When a person says "I have an after-image" he is making a genuine report and when he says "I have a pain" he is doing more than "replace brain behavior" . . . I am not sure, however, that to admit this is to admit that there are non-physical correlates of brain processes. Why should not sensations just be brain processes of a certain sort? . . . All it claims is that insofar as a sensation statement is a report of something, that something is in fact a brain process. Sensations are nothing over and above brain processes. (*ibid.*)

The second version looks at things differently. It concedes that, if they existed, these mental events would be occurrences in some nonbodily soul. It therefore claims that these mental events do not exist, and that all that exists to cause our behavior are brain states. We mistakenly believe that the mental events exist because we have confused them with brain states. This way of presenting the brain-state theory was put forward by Richard Rorty.

> The Identity Theorist's claim is that sensations may be to the future progress of psycho-physiology as demons are to modern science. Just as we now want to deny that there are demons, future science may want to deny that there are sensations. . . . To this question [what was I reporting when I said I felt a pain], the science of the future may reply, "You were reporting the occurrence of a certain brain-process, and it would make life simpler for us if you would, in the future, say 'my c-fibers are firing' instead of saying 'I'm in pain'." ("Mind-Body Identity, Privacy, and Categories," *Review of Metaphysics*, 1965)

The development of this second version of materialism out of the first version is an interesting historical phenomenon, and it sheds much light on the philosophical problems involved. In the mid-1950s, the psychologist U. T. Place and the philosopher J. J. C. Smart began advocating the first of these versions of the brain-state theory, the view that mental events in general (and sensations in particular) should be identified with the occurrence of certain brain states. Their view was that, just as astronomers had come to discover that the morning star is identical with (i.e., is numerically the same object as) the evening star, so modern scientists had come to discover that mental events are identical with the occurrence of brain states.

Many philosophers immediately objected to this identification. Their objections were based upon the following basic principle in the logic of identity:

if A is identical with B, then every property (characteristic) of A must also be a property (characteristic) of B

The rationale for this principle is fairly obvious. If, after all, A and B are the same object (the identical object), then there is only one object involved, and how can it both have and fail to have some property.

So, given this principle, it is easy to raise various objections to Smart's thesis. After all, there seem to be many characteristics of mental events that are not characteristics of brain states, and vice versa. Thus, while sensations can be red or yellow, brain states are not, and while brain states can be definitely located in the portion of the brain in which they occur, sensations do not seem to be located at all. Therefore, concluded many philosophers, Smart must be wrong. As James Cornman put it:

> The central conceptual problem for the Identity Theory arises, I believe, from the fact that mental phenomena seem to have properties inappropriate to physical phenomena, and physical phenomena seem to have properties inappropriate to mental phenomena. ("The Identity of Mind and Body," *Journal of Philosophy*, 1962)

It is just these considerations that led Richard Rorty to put forward the second version of the brain-state theory:

> The obvious objection to the identity theory is that "identical" either means a relation such that
>
> $$(x)(y)[(x = y) \supset (F)(Fx \equiv Fy)]$$
>
> (the relation of "strict identity") or it does not. If it does, then we find ourselves forced into saying truthfully that physical processes such as brain processes are dim or fading or nagging or false, and that mental phenomena such as after-images are publicly observable or physical or spatially located or swift, and thus using meaningless expressions, for we may say that the above expressions are meaningless in the sense that they commit a category mistake; i.e., in forming these expressions we have predicated predicates, appropriate to one logical category, of expressions that belong to a different logical category. This is surely a conceptual mistake.
>
> But if by "identical" the Identity Theory does *not* mean a relation of strict identity, then what relation *is* intended? How does it differ

from the mere relation of "correlation" which, it is admitted on all sides, might without confusion be said to hold between sensations and brain-processes? . . . From the point of view of this second form of the theory, it is a mistake to assume that "X's are nothing but Y's" entails "All attributes meaningfully predictable of X's are meaningfully predicated of Y's," for this assumption would forbid us ever to express the results of scientific inquiry in terms of (in Cornman's useful phrase) "cross-category identity." It would seem that the verb in such statements as "Zeus's thunderbolts are discharges of static electricity" and "Demoniacal possession is a form of hallucinatory psychosis" is the "is" of identity, yet it can hardly express *strict* identity. The disappearance form of the Identity Theory suggests that we view such statements as elliptical for e.g., "What people used to call 'demoniacal possession' is a form of hallucinatory psychosis," where the relation in question *is* strict identity.

Although there is this subtle difference between these two ways of expressing the brain-state theory, Rorty's approach agrees with the following basic points that Smart was trying to make:

1. A human being is special because it is composed of a body with a special brain and nerve system.

2. Occurrences in this brain and nerve system, and not in some nonbodily soul, cause our bodily behavior.

On the basis of our examination of materialism, I think that we may, at least tentatively, conclude that it is possible to develop a version of materialism that presents us with a viable alternative to dualism and that offers us the possibility of putting forward a unified picture of man and his place in the universe.

8

Responsibility for Our Actions

There are a number of contexts in which the question of human responsibility arises. In some of these contexts, what is at stake is the assignment of liability for something undesirable. If, for example, there has been an automobile accident with extensive damages, we want to know who is liable for paying for those damages. In other contexts, what is at stake is the assignment of rewards for something desirable. If, for example, a "first-rate job" has been done with great efficiency and speed, we want to know who should be rewarded for this. In these contexts, there are really two issues that have to be resolved. The first is finding whose actions have led to the desirable or undesirable consequences. The second is whether, on the basis of those actions, that person should be held liable or should be rewarded. Both questions raise interesting philosophical issues, and these are what we will be concerned with in the rest of this chapter.

Two preliminary points: In considering these issues, we will have to deal with such difficult concepts as knowledge, intention, and freedom. These concepts are intimately related to those special aspects of human nature that we discussed in chapter 7. So this chapter will in many ways supplement that discussion. Also, these questions are of great importance to certain parts of the law (e.g., the law of torts and criminal law) as well as to philosophy. Hence, much of the material we will be discussing is drawn from legal literature.

8.1 ACTS AND THEIR EFFECTS

We have noted that the first question that arises in assessing liability or rewardability (to coin a term) is the question: whose action led to the consequences? Here, two points must be kept in mind:

1. There are cases where no one person caused the consequences in question. The best that can be said is that the actions of several people jointly produced those consequences. For example, suppose that I am a passenger in a taxi which goes through a red light and crashes into another automobile which was speeding through the intersection. Suppose, moreover, that if that second automobile had not been speeding, it could have stopped in time and there would have been no accident. In such a case, it seems that the taxi driver's passing the red light together *with* the speeding of the other driver caused the accident and the subsequent damages to me. Several interesting questions occur: (a) We cannot, in the case just described, pick out which damages are due to which actions. But are there cases where we can divide up the damages so that some are caused by one person's actions and the rest are caused by the other person's actions. (b) In cases like ours, can we meaningfully talk about one action being more of a cause of the damages than the other action? Can we talk about degrees of causation?

2. There are cases in which it is a person's failure to act, rather than his action, that causes the desirable or undesirable consequences. Thus, if parents fail to feed their children (something they are both morally and legally obligated to do) and the children die, the parents' failure clearly causes the death of the children and they are liable for that death. There are, however, more difficult cases of omissions about which philosophers and jurists have disagreed. Chief Justice Carpenter summarized the Anglo-American legal position in the following passage:

> Suppose A, standing close by a railroad, sees a two-year-old babe on the track and a car approaching. He can easily rescue the child with entire safety to himself and the instincts of humanity require him to do so. If he does not, he may, perhaps justly be styled a ruthless savage and a moral monster; but he is not liable in damages for the child's injury, or indictable under the statute for its death.

Carpenter's opinion leaves the situation somewhat unclear. Is it the case that A's failure to act does not cause the child's death? Or rather is it the case that it does but A is still not liable? The following standard defense of this legal position makes it seem as though it is the former claim that is intended.

An infant starved to death in Chicago. Its parents did not supply it with the food necessary to sustain life. No one in the block fed it. No one in Chicago fed it. There were more than two hundred million people in the United States who did not feed it, not to mention the inhabitants of other lands. Obviously it would be absurd to say that everyone caused the death of the infant because no one fed it. (*Perkins on Criminal Law,* p. 594)

On the other hand, there are many who would feel that at least in the railroad case, and perhaps even in the Chicago case, the omissions in question are causes of the deaths in question and the people who failed to act should be liable for those deaths.

Leaving aside these more complicated cases, we return to the simple case of one person whose action causes certain consequences. What does it mean to say that the action caused those consequences? It surely means, in part, that the action preceded those consequences. But that is not enough to make it their cause. What else is required? There is a standard answer, the *sine qua non* (without which not) rule, that says that an action X causes a consequence Y just when the occurrence of X is *necessary* for the occurrence of Y—in other words, just when Y would not have occurred if X had not occurred previously. Let us look at a simple automobile accident case to see what this definition comes to.

Suppose a person drives past a stop sign and crashes into a car that had no chance to stop to avoid the accident. Then the passing of the stop sign caused the accident because the accident would not have occurred if the stop sign had not been passed. The passing of the stop sign was necessary for the occurrence of the accident.

Although this is a very popular theory, there are a number of grave difficulties with it:

1. Suppose that we consider the following actual case of an "overcaused" accident. A and B were both riding motorcycles and they passed C's horse, one on either side. They so frightened the horse by their excessive noise, smoke, and speed that it ran away and injured C. It is clear, moreover, that the accident would have occurred even if only one of them had passed C's horse. Now, in such a case, the action of A caused the accident and the action of B caused the accident. Each, by itself, is a cause of the consequence. (In this way, the case is unlike our earlier case of the reckless cab driver and the speeding motorist; where the accident is caused only by the combination of both of their actions; neither action by itself is a cause.) Unfortunately, the *sine qua non* theory rejects this analysis. According to it, neither the action of A nor the action of B caused the accident. A's driving by the horse didn't cause the accident since it would have occurred even if A hadn't

driven by (B's doing so would have been enough) and B's driving by didn't cause the accident since it would have occurred even if B hadn't driven by (A's doing so would have been enough). Neither of their actions are necessary for the occurrence of the accident, yet both are causes. Hence, we must suspect that the *sine qua non* theory is in error.

2. The *sine qua non* theory leads to the absurd consequence that all accidents are caused by the births of the parties involved. After all, for any given accident, it would not have occurred if the parties involved were not born; their births are necessary for the occurrence of the accident. In order to avoid this conclusion, legal writers have claimed that we have to distinguish *causes* (necessary conditions) from *proximate* (or immediate) *causes*, and that liability is based only upon the latter. The difficulties of drawing such a distinction are brought out in the following well-known passage:

> The right to recover damages rests on additional considerations. The plaintiff's rights must be injured, and this injury must be caused by the negligence. We build a dam, but are negligent as to its foundations. Breaking, it injures property down stream. We are not liable if all this happened because of some reason other than the insecure foundation. But when injuries do result from our unlawful act we are liable for the consequences. It does not matter that they are unusual, unexpected, unforeseen, and unforeseeable. But there is one limitation. The damages must be so connected with the negligence that the latter may be said to be the proximate cause of the former.
>
> These two words have never been given an inclusive definition. What is a cause in a legal sense, still more, what is a proximate cause, depends in each case upon many considerations, as does the existence of negligence itself. Any philosophical doctrine of causation does not help us. A boy throws a stone into a pond. The ripples spread. The water level rises. The history of that pond is altered to all eternity. It will be altered by other causes also. Yet it will be forever the restraint of all causes combined. Each one will have an influence. How great only omniscience can say. You may speak of a chain, or if you please, a net. An analogy is of little aid. Each cause brings about future events. Without each the future would not be the same. Each is proximate in the sense it is essential. But that is not what we mean by the word. Nor on the other hand do we mean sole cause. There is no such thing.
>
> Should analogy be thought helpful, however, I prefer that of a stream. The spring, starting on its journey, is joined by tributary after tributary. The river, reaching the ocean, comes from a hundred sources. No man may say whence any drop of water is derived.

Yet for a time distinction may be possible. Into the clear creek, brown swamp water flows from the left. Later, from the right comes water stained by its clay bed. The three may remain for a space, sharply divided. But at last, inevitably no trace of separation remains. They are so commingled that all distinction is lost.

As we have said, we cannot trace the effect of an act to the end, if end there is. Again, however, we may trace it part of the way. A murder at Serajevo may be the necessary antecedent to an assassination in London twenty years hence. An overturned lantern may burn all Chicago. We may follow the fire from the shed to the last building. We rightly say the fire started by the lantern caused its destruction.

A cause, but not the proximate cause. What we do mean by the word "proximate" is that because of convenience, of public policy, of a rough sense of justice, the law arbitrarily declines to trace a series of events beyond a certain point. This is not logic. It is practical politics. Take our rule as to fires. Sparks from my burning haystack set on fire my house and my neighbor's. I may recover from a negligent railroad. He may not. Yet the wrongful act as directly harmed the one as the other. We may regret that the line was drawn just where it was, but drawn somewhere it had to be. We said the act of the railroad was not the proximate cause of our neighbor's fire. Cause it surely was. The words we used were simply indicative of our notions of public policy. Other courts think differently. But somewhere they reach the point where they cannot say the stream comes from any one source. (Palsgraff v. Long Island Railroad Co.)

We turn therefore to a different view, the view that an action X causes some consequences Y just in case the occurrence of X is *sufficient* for the occurrence of Y. In our motorcycle case, for example, the action of A caused the accident because A's action was sufficient for the occurrence of the accident. Similarly, the action of B caused the accident because B's action was sufficient for the occurrence of the accident. So this theory can deal with the case of the overcaused accident. Moreover, according to this theory, the birth of the parties involved in the accident is, properly, never the cause of the accidents because it is never sufficient for their occurrence. (If nothing else, the parties might have died before the accident.) This view is summarized (and also modified in a way that will be discussed in a moment) in the following claim by H. L. A. Hart and A. M. Honore:

> In ordinary life and in the law we treat, e.g., the death of a human being as an effect sometimes of poisoning (plus other conditions),

sometimes of starvation (plus other conditions); similarly for common sense, heat may be the effect of friction, chemical change, or percussion (in each case together with other conditions). This being so, we can only say of one such complex set of conditions that it is sufficient, according to our general laws, to produce the effect, not that it is necessary, according to these laws. . . .

There is one very important complication and modification of this theory that must be noted. We said just a moment ago that A's passing the horse on his motorcycle caused the accident because it was sufficient for the occurrence of the action. But is this really true? Suppose there was someone present to grab the horse when it started to run away. The accident would not have occurred. Or suppose that C was such a good rider that he could have stayed on the horse. Again, the accident would not have occurred. Or suppose that . . . The long and short of the matter is that A's action is sufficient only in a given context. Strictly speaking, all that we should say is that A's passing the horse on his motorcycle in that context caused the accident. More generally, all that we can really say is that the occurrence of an action X in a given context caused the occurrence of some consequences Y, for it is in that context that the occurrence of X is sufficient for the occurrence of Y. All of this raises a fundamental problem for assigning liability and rewardability: why is an action X picked out from all the other circumstances (the so-called context, which may include the actions of other people) so that its performer is held liable or rewardable?

This question is just one instance of a general philosophical problem about causality. Suppose that we adopt the view that X is the cause of Y when X is sufficient for the occurrence of Y. Considerations of the type we have just gone through would quickly lead us to recognize that, in general, X is sufficient for the occurrence of Y only in a certain context. On what basis, in general, do we pick X out of the context and treat it specially?

R. G. Collingwood, at one point, raised just this problem and put forward the thesis that the crucial distinction between cause and context is based upon our abilities to control things. Roughly speaking, the causes are those conditions which we can produce or prevent.

> A "cause" in sense II never means something which is able by itself to produce the "effect." When in this sense we say that x causes y, we are never talking about x by itself. We are always talking about x in combination with other things which we do not specify; these being called *conditions sine quibus non*. For example, damp will not cause books to go mouldy unless there are mould-spores about.

> The relation between the cause and these "conditions," as I shall call them, has often been misunderstood, for example, by Mill. Mill defines the cause of an event as its invariable antecedent. . . . If so, the event should follow given the cause and nothing else. If certain conditions are necessary, over and above the cause, in order that the event should follow . . . then surely the *true* cause is not what we have just called the cause but this *plus* the said conditions. Mill concludes that the true cause is the sum of a set of conditions, and that what people ordinarily call the cause is one of these, arbitrarily selected and, by a mere misuse of language, dignified with a name that properly belongs only to the whole set.
>
> Closer inspection would have shown Mill that this "selection" is by no means arbitrary. It is made according to a definite principle. If my car "conks out" on a hill and I wonder what the cause is, I shall not consider my problem solved by a passer-by who tells me that the top of a hill is further away from the earth's center than its bottom, and that consequently more power is needed to take a car uphill than to take her along the level. All this is quite true; what the passer-by has described is one of the conditions which, together, form the "true cause" of my car's stopping; and as he has "arbitrarily selected" one of these and called it the cause, he has done just what Mill says we always do. But now suppose an A.A. man comes along opens the bonnet, holds up a loose high-tension lead, and says "look here, sir, you're running on three cylinders." My problem is now solved. I know the cause of the stoppage. It is *the* cause, just because it has not been "arbitrarily selected"; it has been correctly identified as the thing that I can put right, after which the car will go properly. If had I been a person who could flatten out hills by stamping on them, the passer-by would have been right to call my attention to the hill as the cause of the stoppage; not because the hill is a hill, but because I can flatten it out. ("On the So Called Idea of Causation," *Proceedings of the Aristotelean Society*, 1938)

Many philosophers feel that this account is incorrect, and that a different (and perhaps more complex) account is needed. Thus Hart and Honore write:

> The line between cause and mere condition is in fact drawn by common sense on principles which vary in a subtle and complex way, both with the type of causal question at issue and the circumstances in which causal questions arise. Any general account of these principles is therefore always in danger of over-simplifying them. Some philosophers have succumbed to this temptation. Col-

RESPONSIBILITY FOR OUR ACTIONS

lingwood, who notices much that Hume and Mill neglected, treats the question 'What is the cause of an event?' as if it was always equivalent to 'How can we produce or prevent this?' On his view the cause is always the event or state of things which we can produce or prevent in order to produce or prevent the effect. This is to identify all cases with the fundamental type of case considered above; whereas in fact often only *analogies* with the fundamental type can be found. Such a view would make it improper to speak of knowing, for example, the cause of cancer if we could not use our knowledge to prevent it. Perhaps the only general observation of value is that in distinguishing between causes and conditions two contrasts are of prime importance. These are the contrasts between what is abnormal and what is normal in relation to any given thing or subject-matter, and between a free deliberate human action and all other conditions. (*Causation in the Law*, chapter 2)

While this suggestion seems promising, it needs much further development. So, at least for the moment, the development of an adequate theory of causality is not complete.

8.2 LIABILITY

There was a time when the question of liability (which we will be focusing on from now on) was easy to settle. For, at one time, a person was held liable for all of the consequences of his actions. No excuses were accepted. A person could not say that my actions lead to those consequences but I shouldn't be held liable for them. This is no longer true. We now believe that there are many excuses or reasons why someone should not be held liable for the consequences of his actions. These include the following (notice that it may make a difference to the force of the excuse if we are considering punishment or having to pay compensation):

1. the performer of the action is a minor

2. the performer of the action is mentally incompetent or diseased

3. the performer of the action didn't know what he was doing or what the consequences are that result from such an action

4. the performer of the action didn't intend to perform that action or didn't intend those consequences to occur

5. the performer of the action was compelled to perform it

What has brought about this change? To some degree, it is due to a feeling that there is no point to holding such people liable, to punishing them or making them pay compensation, because this will not prevent the occurrence of similar actions. We find this theme in the writings of Jeremy Bentham:

> All punishment is mischief: all punishment in itself is evil. Upon the principle of utility, if it ought at all to be admitted, it ought only to be admitted in as far as it promises to exclude some greater evil. It is plain, therefore, that in the following cases punishment ought not to be inflicted: . . . II. Where it must be inefficacious. These are . . . 3 where the penal provision, though it were conveyed to a man's notice, could produce no effect on him, with respect to the preventing him from engaging in any act of the sort in question. Such is the case, I in extreme infancy, II in insanity, III in intoxication . . . 4. where the penal provision could not have this effect, with the individual act he is about to engage in: to wit, because he knows not that it is of the number of those to which the penal provision relates. This may happen, I. in the case of unintentionality II. in the case of unconsciousness. (*The Principles of Morals and Legislation*, chapter 13)

But there is also a feeling that these excuses must be allowed if we are to be fair and just. To quote Hart:

> It [the principle of justice involved] incorporates the idea that each individual person is to be protected against the claim of the rest for the highest possible measure of security, happiness, or welfare which could be got at his expense by condemning him for a breach of the rules and punishing him. For this a moral licence is required in the form of a proof that the person punished broke the law by an action which was an outcome of his free choice, and the recognition of excuses is the most we can do to ensure that the terms of the licence are observed. (*Punishment and Responsibility*, chapter 1)

In this section, we will consider some of the many philosophical problems that arise in connection with these excuses. Let us begin with excuse (4), that the performer of the action didn't intend the action or the consequences. It is this excuse that explains why a doctor would not be held liable in the following case: Suppose that you are treating a patient for a minor illness and that you give him the standard medicine. Neither you nor anyone else knows that there are a few people (and this patient is one of them) in whom this medicine produces a terrible reaction. As a result of your giving him the medicine, the patient suffers much pain. Nevertheless, because that consequence was unintended, you are not liable for it.

Notice, by the way, that our feelings about this would be very different if that reaction to the medicine were known to be quite common and if you failed to check whether the patient would suffer that reaction. Then, although you certainly didn't intend that the patient suffer, your behavior was at least negligent and you should and would be held liable to pay compensation. And suppose you point your gun at someone and pull the trigger without checking to see if the gun is loaded. Then even if you didn't intend the person any harm (perhaps because you believed that the gun was not loaded), your behavior in not checking to see if the gun was loaded was negligent and reckless, and you are liable for the harm you caused and you would be punished.

Philosophers and moralists have been very interested in this notion of intending an action or a consequence. What is it to intend something? Is it anything more than merely foreseeing its occurrence? The legal disputes about this question are summarized in the following analysis by Herbert Morris:

> Legal theorists traditionally attempt to elucidate the concept of intention in terms of two other concepts: desire for, or expectation of, certain foreseen consequences. There has always been disagreement over which of the two is essentially related to intention. Some theorists take the line that . . . whether or not a person expects a certain consequence to follow from his act is irrelevant. If he desires the consequence to follow from his act, he intends the consequence. If it in fact follows, it is intentional. . . . if one shoots at a person who is a great distance away, desiring (wishing?) to kill that person but believing success highly improbable, in this view of intention one intends to kill a person. . . . Theorists who adopt this view of intention introduce a distinction between desiring something "as a means" and desiring something "as an end". . . . . Another approach rejects this analysis. What is essential is an expectation that a consequence will follow one's act; *desire* is irrelevant. . . . If a person does not expect to kill another, as in the long-shot case, he does not intend to kill. (*Freedom and Responsibility*, pp. 158-59)

Both of these approaches suggest a certain model of intentional actions and intended consequences. According to this model an intentional action or an intended consequence is one that is preceeded by the occurrence of a certain mental event, namely an *intention*. All that these views disagree about is the nature of that event. One view holds that it is a *desire* to perform that action or to produce that consequence.

The other view holds that it is an *expectation* that one will perform that action or produce that consequence.

This whole model of intentions has been challenged by certain philosophers. They feel that the occurrence of these mental events is not what is central to intending and intentional actions. Thus, in criticizing the desire-view of intentional actions, G. E. M. Anscombe wrote:

> Now one might think that when the question "Why?" is answered by giving the intention with which a person acts. . . . this is also a case of a mental cause. For couldn't it be recast in the form: "Because I wanted . . ." or "Out of a desire that . . ."? If a feeling of desire for an apple affects me and I get up and go to a cupboard where I think there are some, I might answer the question what led to this action by mentioning the desire as having made me . . . etc. But it is not in all cases that "I did so and so in order to . . ." can be backed up by "I felt a desire that . . ." I may, e.g., simply hear a knock on the door and go downstairs to open it *without experiencing any desire*. ("Intention," *P.A.S.*, 1956–57)

While there is a widespread feeling that neither desire nor expectation adequately explains intentionality, it is not clear what model should be substituted.

In recent years, there has been a growing feeling that, at least in some areas of the law, an agent should not be excused even if he didn't intend the consequence and even if his action wasn't negligent. In a number of areas, the law holds one responsible for one's actions and their consequences, and excuse (4) cannot be raised. Such laws are called laws of *strict liability*. What has led to this development? Didn't we see just a short while ago that there are a number of good reasons for accepting excuses in general and excuse (4) in particular?

The arguments for laws of strict liability vary for the different contexts in which such laws are proposed. I would like to focus on one set of arguments that might be employed to defend such laws in the context of certain dangerous activities. Bentham, you will remember, had argued for the excuse of unintended consequences on the grounds that there is nothing to be gained from holding the person liable in such cases. But Richard Wasserstrom has persuasively argued that this is not so:

> There seem to be at least two respects in which strict liability statutes might have a greater deterrent effect than "usual" criminal statutes. In the first place, it might be the case that a person engaged in a certain kind of activity would be more careful precisely

because he knew that this kind of activity was governed by a strict liability statute. ... In the second place ... a person who did not regard himself as capable of conducting an enterprise in such a way so as to not produce the deleterious consequences presented by the statute might well refuse to engage in that activity at all. ("Strict Liability in the Criminal Law," *Stanford Law Review*, 1959-60)

On the other hand, considerations of justice of the type mentioned by Hart might seem to argue against such laws. If there was no fault in his doing what he did, why should the person be held liable?

It is interesting that our attitude toward such laws is probably different when the liability involved leads to criminal punishment rather than merely to an obligation to pay for the damages one has caused. Perhaps the considerations of justice are more pressing in the former case than in the latter case.

We have, so far, been considering some of the issues that arise in connection with excuse (4). Let us now look at some of the issues that arise in connection with excuse (5), the excuse of compulsion. It is this excuse that would explain why a person is not held liable in the following case: Suppose that you are parked in front of a bank and some robbers run out with their loot, jump into your car, and threaten to kill you unless you drive them to safety. You do so. Although your action leads to their escaping with the loot, you are not punished for helping them because you were compelled to do so.

In cases of compulsion, the agent is threatened by someone (or at least believes that he is) and it is this threat that leads him to perform the action for whose consequences he is not held liable. There are other cases in which the agent performs an action to avoid disastrous consequences, but which do not involve any threats. In some of these cases, the agent is also not liable for his action and its consequences. Such cases are said to involve the excuse of necessity.

It is interesting to note that the law is much more generous with the excuse of compulsion than with the excuse of necessity. The starving Jean Valjean (in Victor Hugo's *Les Miserables*) is held liable for stealing the loaf of bread; he cannot plead necessity based upon his hunger. But if he had stolen the loaf of bread on orders from someone who threatened to hurt him, he would not have been held liable because he could then have pleaded the excuse of compulsion. The justification for this distinction is not immediately evident.

One of the most difficult problems involved in defining the excuse of compulsion is that of distinguishing cases in which the person was compelled to do what he did from cases in which he did what he did to gain some reward. (In the latter case, the individual is not excused.) Suppose, for example, that a drug pusher tells an addict that he can have drugs only if he aids in a robbery. Was the addict compelled to aid in the crime or was he merely promised a reward for helping? It might be thought that the addict could not have been compelled because he still had a choice; he could have refused to help. But the same thing is true about the driver who helped the thieves get away. He also had a choice; he also could have refused to help. Obviously, then, having a choice is compatible with being compelled. So the question of how to analyze the case of the addict remains unsettled.

Drug addiction raises, of course, an even more fundamental question about liability. Suppose that an addict steals to raise the money he needs to pay for drugs. Should he be held liable for this action? This case, unlike the first addict case, is clearly not a standard case of compulsion. Here, there is certainly no one present who is threatening the addict. Still, there are those who feel that the addict should not be held liable because he is compelled by his internal need for the drug. Naturally, the adoption of the view that we can be compelled by internal needs would complicate even further the analysis of compulsion, but that doesn't mean that we shouldn't consider this claim seriously.

There is one additional set of issues that must be considered in connection with the excuse of compulsion. Clearly, not every threat will excuse every action. If, in time of war, the enemy threatens to burn down your house unless you aid their cause and turn traitor against your country, that threat will not excuse your treasonable actions if you collaborate. But a threat like that would certainly excuse your committing a relatively minor offense. It seems to be a matter of weighing the threat against the harm your action will cause. A rule along this line is found in the laws of Hawaii: "No one shall be able to justify himself against a charge of his doing an injury to another, by showing the threat of imminent danger of an equal or less injury to himself."

The difficult question arises when it is your life that is threatened unless you take the life of someone else. Actually, there are two questions that arise in such cases: (1) Are you justified in taking the life of the other person to save your life? Can we think of this as a justifiable act of self-defense or shall we conclude that such an act is not justified because that other person is innocent? (2) Even if it would be wrong to take the other person's life, is your action excused because of the compulsion involved? The Anglo-American legal tradition answers both of these questions negatively:

> The common law does not recognize any compulsion, even the threat of innocent death, as sufficient to excuse the intentional kill-

RESPONSIBILITY FOR OUR ACTIONS

> ing of an innocent and unoffending person. . . . In the words of Blackstone "he ought rather to die himself than escape by the murder of an innocent." No sound analogy can be drawn from the self-defense case because such defense does not involve the killing of an innocent person. As Hale points out, while one acting under threat of instant death has no excuse if he kills an innocent victim to save his own life, he may be excused for killing the threatener. (*Perkins on Criminal Law*, p. 951)

Maimonides, on the other hand, felt that the two questions should be answered differently:

> If someone threatens to kill you unless you violate one of the laws of the Torah, you should violate that law. . . . That is so in all cases except for idolatry, adultery, and murder. For these three sins, if your life is threatened, you should let yourself be killed and not violate the law. . . . Nevertheless, because you were compelled, you should not be punished corporeally and you should certainly not be killed even if you killed someone, because only one who acts voluntarily can be so punished. (*Laws of the Foundation of the Tora*, chapter 5)

In this section, we have only briefly analyzed some of the major questions that arise in connection with a few excuses. There are many other questions that arise in connection with these excuses, and still others that arise in connection with the other excuses we mentioned. Though we are not able to carry it further here, the whole theory of excuses is clearly worth further exploration.

8.3 PUNISHMENT AND FREEDOM

In some cases in which a person is held liable for his actions, all that he is required to do is to pay the victim compensation for the damages he has caused. In other cases, the person held liable will be punished by society for performing the action in question. This distinction is related to several other distinctions: (1) In the first case, it is the victim who brings the liable party to court, while in the second, society brings that party to court. (2) In the first case, the victim can waive his right to collect—either by consenting to the act at the time it is performed or by not bringing suit at a later time. In the second case, the feelings of the victim, at either time, are (at least theoretically) irrelevant. It is an interesting question (though one we cannot explore here) as to what distinguishes the two types of cases. Why do we treat them so differently?

In this final section of the chapter, we will explore the second type of case, which raises the issues surrounding punishment as a social institution.

Why do we punish people? One theory, the so-called *retributive* theory, says that the purpose of punishment is to do justice. It says that the very act of punishing a person who deserves it is a good thing.

> Punishment is punishment, only where it is deserved. We pay the penalty, because we owe it, and for no other reason; and if punishment is inflicted for any other reason whatever than because it is merited by wrong, it is a gross immorality, a crying injustice, an abominable crime, and not what it pretends to be. . . . punishment is justice; justice implies the giving what is due. (F. H. Bradley, *Ethical Studies*)

The other major theory, the so-called *teleological* theory, says that punishment is a necessary evil. It is required to deter the criminal and others from further wrongdoing. The punishment may also serve to reform the criminal.

> Social life would not be possible without the constant subordination of the claims of individuals to the like claim of a greater number of individuals; and there may be occasions when in punishing a criminal we have to think more of the good of society generally than of the individual who is punished. No doubt it is a duty to think also of the good of the individual so far as that can be done consistently with justice to other individuals; it is obviously the duty of the state to endeavour to make its punishments as far as possible reformatory as well as deterrent and educational to others. (Hastings Rashdall, *Theory of Good and Evil*, vol. 1)

Granting then, at least for the moment, that there are adequate justifications for punishing people, what should be the nature and extent of that punishment? Should it consist of fines or of imprisonment? How great a fine? How long a term of imprisonment? Is capital punishment ever justified? These are the obvious questions that any theory of punishment must consider.

From the perspective of the teleological theory, punishment is always an evil. But it is necessary to accomplish the social goods of deterrence and reform. This fundamental assumption provides the basis of an attempt to answer the questions just listed from the teleological perspective. Jeremy Bentham, one of the most important advocates of this theory of punishment, once wrote a list of rules to be used in determining the appropriate extent of punishment. Among the most important of these were the following:

Rule 1. The value of the punishment must not be less in any case than what is sufficient to outweigh that of the profit of the offence.

Rule 2. The greater the mischief of the offence, the greater is the expense, which it may be worth while to be at, in the way of punishment.

Rule 5. The punishment ought in no case to be more than what is necessary to bring it into conformity with the rules here given.

Rule 7. To enable the value of the punishment to outweigh that of the profit of the offence, it must be increased, in point of magnitude, in proportion as it falls short in point of certainty.

Rule 8. Punishment must be further increased in point of magnitude, in proportion as it falls short in point of proximity.

Rule 9. Where the act is conclusively indicative of a habit, such an increase must be given to the punishment as may enable it to outweigh the profit not only of the individual offence, but of such other like offences as are likely to have been committed with impunity by the same offender.

These last rules are particularly important. Many criminologists have noted that a lesser penalty can be more effective as a deterrent if it is quickly and universally applied than a more stringent penalty that is often not applied and is applied only after a long delay. Those who advocate stricter crime control might do better to advocate more money for the administration of justice rather than heavier penalties.

What about capital punishment? From the perspective of the teleological theory, the crucial question is not whether the death penalty is a deterrent but rather whether it is a superior deterrent than alternatives like life imprisonment. After all, Bentham's Rule 5 tells us that we should use the stronger penalty (capital punishment) only if the weaker penalty (life imprisonment) would not work equally well.

Those who have studied the problem of capital punishment from the teleological perspective have generally concluded that it cannot be justified. The crux of their argument is that the statistical evidence fails to show any improvement in deterrence when capital punishment laws are passed. We find this argument summarized in the following passage by Thorsten Sellin:

When we think of deterrence, restraint or prevention—these terms are used interchangeably—we usually think of the effect which a punishment has (1) on the future conduct of the person punished and (2) on the future conduct of others. Some writers distinguish these two effects by calling the one individual and the other general prevention. In the case of the executed death penalty individual prevention is, of course, completely effective. This is the one executed punishment in connection with which general prevention alone can be studied. . . . It seems reasonable to assume that if the death penalty exercises a deterrent or preventive effect on prospective murderers, the following propositions would be true: (a) Murders should be less frequent in states that have the death penalty than in those that have abolished it, other factors being equal. Comparisons of this nature must be made among states that are as alike as possible in all other respects—character of population, social and economic condition, etc.—in order not to introduce factors known to influence murder rates in a serious manner but present in only one of these states.

(b) Murders should increase when the death penalty is abolished and should decline when it is restored.

(c) The deterrent effect should be greatest and should therefore affect murder rates most powerfully in those communities where the crime occurred and its consequences are most strongly brought home to the population.

(d) Law enforcement officers would be safer from murderous attacks in states that have the death penalty than in those without it.

.   .   .   .   .   .

The data examined reveal that
1. The *level* of the homicide death rates varies in different groups of states. It is lowest in the New England areas and in the northern states of the middle west and lies somewhat higher in Michigan, Indiana and Ohio.

2. With each group of states having similar social and economic conditions and populations, it is impossible to distinguish the abolition state from others.

3. The *trends* of the homicide death rates of comparable states with or without the death penalty are similar.

The inevitable conclusion is that executions have no discernible effect on homicide death rates which, as we have seen, are regarded as adequate indicators of capital murder rates. (*The Death Penalty*)

We have so far examined the questions of the nature and extent of punishment from the perspective of the teleological theory. These questions look very different, of course, from the perspective of the retributive theory of punishment.

Immanuel Kant, one of the great defenders of the retributive theory, put its answer to these questions as follows:

> What kind and what degree of punishment does public legal justice adopt as its principle and standard? None other than the principle of equality (illustrated by the pointer on the scales of justice), that is, the principle of not treating one side more favorably than the other. Accordingly, any undeserved evil that you inflict on someone else among the people is one that you do to yourself. If you vilify him, you vilify yourself; if you steal from him, you steal from yourself; if you kill him, you kill yourself. Only the Law of retribution (*jus talionis*) can determine exactly the kind and degree of punishment; it must be well understood, however, that this determination [must be made] in the chambers of a court of justice (and in not your private judgment). All other standards fluctuate back and forth and, because extraneous considerations are mixed with them, they cannot be compatible with the principle of pure and strict legal justice. (*Metaphysical Elements of Justice*)

In a later passage, Kant goes on to explain how this theory would work and how it could serve to justify capital punishment:

> But what is meant by the statement: "If you steal from him, you steal from yourself"? Inasmuch as someone steals, he makes the ownership of everyone else insecure, and hence he robs himself (in accordance with the Law of retribution) of the security of any possible ownership. He has nothing and can also acquire nothing, but he still wants to live, and this is not possible unless others provide him with nourishment. But, because the state will not support him gratis, he must let the state have his labor at any kind of work it may wish to use him for (convict labor), and so he becomes a slave, either for a certain period of time or indefinitely, as the case may be.
>
> If, however, he has committed a murder, he must die. In this case, there is no substitute that will satisfy the requirements of legal justice. There is no sameness of kind between death and remaining alive even under the most miserable conditions, and consequently there is also no equality between the crime and the retribution unless the criminal is judicially condemned and put to death. But

the death of the criminal must be kept entirely free of any maltreatment that would make an abomination of the humanity residing in the person suffering it. Even if a civil society were to dissolve itself by common agreement of all its members (for example, if the people inhabiting an island decided to separate and disperse themselves around the world), the last murderer remaining in prison must first be executed, so that everyone will duly receive what his actions are worth and so that the bloodguilt thereof will not be fixed on the people because they failed to insist on carrying out the punishment; for if they fail to do so, they may be regarded as accomplices in this public violation of legal justice. (*ibid.*)

Objections can be raised against both defenses of punishment. The teleological theory clearly rests upon strong assumptions about the extent to which punishment serves to deter people from committing crimes and about the possibility of reform. But it is sometimes said that these assumptions are totally wrong. It is claimed that the extent of recidivism shows that punishment as an institution for deterrence and reform has failed miserably. So strong a claim for this seems wrong. Consider, for example, the fact that the rates of serious automobile accidents went down considerably (especially in the main drinking hours) after the passing of the British Road Safety Act of 1967. This law imposed a heavy fine on those who drive after even a moderate amount of drinking. Nevertheless, even a balanced attitude finds serious fault with many aspects of punishment according to the teleological theory:

> There is every reason to believe that detection and punishment have a deterrent effect in the majority of cases as compared with the alternative of no detection and punishment. . . . But, of course, to deal with the effects of actual punishment under the aspect of deterrence alone, is a too narrow perspective. The punishment may change the offender for better or worse, quite apart from its deterrent or nondeterrent effects. The situation is very different for the various penalties. As far as the fine is concerned there will not be much other effect than a more or less pronounced deterrence. Much the same is the case with the short prison sentence. . . . The case is different and more complex with long-term imprisonment. The prison staff tries to train and reform the offender in order to release him from the prison as a better man than he was on his arrival. Both the day to day experience of the prison staff and sociological prison research shows how the influence of fellow inmates often works in the opposite direction. The prisoner may leave prison as a worse man than when he entered, more deeply entrenched in a criminal culture, more hostile to society and its values, and less fit to meet the problems of

life in a free society. (Johannes Andenaes, "Does Punishment Deter Crime," *Criminal Law Quarterly*, 1968)

There is a second, and perhaps even more important, objection to the teleological theory. It claims, after all, that punishing the guilty is an evil. This is the way in which it differs from the retributive theory that feels that it is intrinsically good that the guilty suffer. The teleological theory claims, however, that this evil can be justified because of the social benefit to others. But isn't punishment, therefore, an objectionable institution by virtue of this very fact that it mistreats some to benefit others, and that it involves using the criminal as a means to benefit of others. To quote Kant:

> Juridical punishment can never be administered merely as a means for promoting another good, either with regard to the criminal himself or to civil society, but must in all cases be imposed only because the individual on whom it is inflicted has committed a crime. For one man ought never to be dealt with merely as a means subservient to the purpose of another. . . . Against such treatment his inborn personality has a right to protect him. *(Metaphysical Elements of Justice)*

On the other hand, defenders of the teleological theory believe that the whole retributive theory rests upon vengeance and not upon any theory of justice. To quote Plato:

> No one punishes the evil-doer under the notion, or for the reason, that he has done wrong,—only the unreasonable fury of a beast acts in that manner. But he who desires to inflict rational punishment does not retaliate for a past wrong that cannot be undone; he has regard to the future, and is desirous that the man who is punished, and he who sees him punished, may be deterred from doing wrong again. (*Protagoras*, 324)

We have so far examined two justifications of the institution of punishment and the objections that are normally raised against them. But there is still a further objection to be considered. This objection, made from the point of view of *determinism*, claims that no one ought to be held liable or be punished for his actions, because no one has a choice about his actions.

Let us define determinism as the thesis that all human actions are caused. There are many philosophers and scientists who have been determinists. Some of those who have been determinists have been so on philosophical grounds. They feel that all events (including human actions) must be caused. The concept of an uncaused event, they feel, is in one way or another incoherent. But most who have been determinists have been so on scientific or quasi-scientific grounds. David Hume, for example, argued that our ordinary everyday knowledge of psychology revealed to us that human actions are predictable and caused.

> Hence, likewise, the benefit of that experience acquired by long life and a variety of business and company, in order to instruct us in the principles of human nature and regulate our future conduct as well as speculation. By means of this guide we mount up to the knowledge of men's inclinations and motives from their actions, expressions, and even gestures, and again descend to the interpretation of their actions from our knowledge of their motives and inclinations. The general observations, treasured up by a course of experience, give us the clue of human nature and teach us to unravel all its intricacies. . . . We must not, however, expect that this uniformity of human actions should be carried to such a length as that all men, in the same circumstances, will always act precisely in the same manner, without making any allowance for the diversity of characters, prejudices, and opinions. Such a uniformity, in every particular, is found in no part of nature. On the contrary, from observing the variety of conduct in different men we are enabled to form a greater variety of maxims which still suppose a degree of uniformity and regularity. . . . The philosopher, if he be consistent, must apply the same reasonings to the actions and volitions of intelligent agents. The most irregular and unexpected resolutions of men may frequently be accounted for by those who know every particular circumstance of their character and situation. . . . Thus it appears not only that the conjunction between motives and voluntary actions is as regular and uniform as that between the cause and effect in any part of nature, but also that this regular conjunction has been universally acknowledged among mankind and has never been the subject of dispute either in philosophy or common life. *(An Inquiry Concerning Human Understanding)*

Other determinists, like B. F. Skinner, feel that the truth of determinism only emerges as a result of modern psychological investigations. Skinner presents his views in the following passage:

> Two features of autonomous man are particularly troublesome. In the traditional view, a person is free. He is autonomous in the sense that his behavior is uncaused. He can therefore be held responsible for what he does and justly punished if he offends. That view, together with its associated practices, must be re-examined when a scientific analysis reveals unsuspected controlling relations between behavior and environment. . . . Many anthropologists, sociologists,

and psychologists have used their expert knowledge to prove that man is free, purposeful, and responsible. Freud was a determinist—on faith, if not on the evidence—but many Freudians have no hesitation in assuring their patients that they are free to choose among different courses of action and are in the long run the architects of their own destinies.

This escape route is slowly closed as new evidences of the predictability of human behavior are discovered. Personal exemption from a complete determinism is revoked as a scientific analysis progresses, particularly in accounting for the behavior of the individual. *(Beyond Freedom and Dignity)*

We will not now attempt to resolve the question of whether or not determinism is true. What we shall consider instead is the following question: if determinism were true, would it follow that no one should be punished, or is there some justification for punishing people for their actions even if those actions were caused?

Many adherents of the teleological theory of punishment maintain that their justification of punishment would persist even if determinism were true. After all, they argue, the threat of punishment can still deter potential criminals even if determinism were true because that threat of punishment becomes a determining factor. Punishment, from the perspective of the teleological theory, seems therefore to be perfectly compatible with determinism. To quote P. H. Nowell-Smith:

> To say that a man could have acted otherwise is to say that he might have been the sort of person who would have acted otherwise; and to attribute his acting as he did to his moral character, as opposed to some amoral defect, is to say that his action was due to one of the characteristics that can be altered by means of rewards and punishments.

It is not necessary to undertake an elaborate analysis of the other examples used. If a man kills someone because he is physically compelled to do so, he will not be prevented from doing so again in similar circumstances by the knowledge that the action will be severely punished. But if his action is due to his own decision, this knowledge may cause him to decide otherwise in future. In the same way the basis for the distinction between the kleptomaniac and the thief is that the latter is held to have decided to steal. Here the cause in both cases lies within the agent and the distinction of internal and external causation did not help us. The fact that one commits a voluntary action and the other does not is important, but by itself it does not account for the differential treatment of the two men. Why are men who steal as a result of a decision said to be worthy of punishment, while those who steal from some other cause are not? The reason is that we believe that the fear of punishment will affect the future behaviour of the thief but not that of the kleptomaniac. If a man steals because he has decided to do so, we can prevent his doing so again by causing him to decide otherwise. If he expects to be punished, then in addition to the motive that tends to make him steal there will be a powerful motive tending to make him refrain. Now the fear of punishment has no such influence on the kleptomaniac; on the other hand, psychoanalysis, by removing the subconscious cause of his tendency to steal, may achieve the desired result. Nor is this merely an interesting but unimportant distinction between kleptomaniacs and thieves: it is the very basis for the distinction. ("Free Will and Moral Responsibility," *Mind*, 1948)

The English novelist, Samuel Butler, described a society in which people were punished for being ill but "medically" treated for committing a crime:

This is what I gathered. That in that country if a man falls into ill health, or catches any disorder, or fails bodily in any way before he is seventy years old, he is tried before a jury of his countrymen and if convicted is held up to public scorn and sentenced more or less severely as the case may be. There are subdivisions of illness into crimes and misdemeanors as with offenses amongst ourselves—a man being punished very heavily for serious illness, while failure of eyes or hearing in one over sixty-five, who has had good health hitherto, is dealt with by fine only, or imprisonment in default of payment. But if a man forges a check, or sets his house on fire, or robs with violence from the person, or does any other such things as are criminal in our own country, he is either taken to a hospital and most carefully tended at the public expense, or if he is in good circumstances, he lets it be known to all his friends that he is suffering from a severe fit of immorality, just as we do when we are ill, and they come and visit him with great solicitude, and inquire with interest how it all came about, what symptoms first showed themselves, and so forth,—questions which he will answer with perfect unreserve; for bad conduct, though considered no less deplorable than illness with ourselves, and as unquestionably indicating something seriously wrong with the individual who misbehaves, is nevertheless held to be the result of either pre-natal or post-natal misfortune. (*Erewhon*)

One of the points that Butler was trying to make, presumably, was that if people's crimes are caused, it seems more appropriate to treat them as we treat the ill, rather than punish them. Nowell-Smith's theory offers an explanation of this difference. Punishing the ill will not deter others from becoming ill, but punishing those who commit crimes will deter potential criminals. If this is so, we have all the reason that is needed from the teleological perspective for punishing criminals.

The question that remains to be considered is whether or not retributive punishment is compatible with determinism. It is often felt that it cannot be. After all, according to the retributive theory, punishment is justified because it is the just treatment of those who deserve it. But if our actions are caused, we had to do them, and we should no more be held liable for them than should the person whose action is compelled.

There is a standard philosophical answer to this question which claims that freedom does not necessarily presuppose uncaused actions. What is required for us to be free (and liable) is that we do what we want to do, or that we are not compelled to act.

> Freedom means the opposite of compulsion; a man is free if he does not act under compulsion, and he is compelled or unfree when he is hindered from without in the realization of his natural desires. Hence he is unfree when he is locked up, or chained, or when someone forces him at the point of a gun to do what otherwise he would not do. This is quite clear, and everyone will admit . . . that a man will be considered quite free . . . if no such external compulsion is exerted upon him. (Moritz Schlick, *The Problems of Ethics*, p. 150)

Determinism, this answer goes on to claim, does not mean that our actions are compelled. According to most reasonable versions of determinism, the chain of causes that determines our actions usually operates *through* our desires and decisions. It does not take place through some external force. So we usually do what we want to do and are usually not compelled into acting. Therefore, this answer concludes, determinism is compatible with freedom and does not undercut, even from the retributive perspective, the validity of punishment.

This distinction, between the compelled act and the merely caused act, seems relatively clear when we are merely considering examples of external compulsion. But we do also have a notion of internal compulsion. The kleptomaniac, we say, is not free and ought not to be punished even though there is no external compulsion present. But how are we to distinguish cases of pure causality from cases of compulsion if we have to admit into our theory internal compulsion?

Suppose, however, that we agreed that this distinction could be made. Suppose we could distinguish between cases of compulsion (even internal compulsion) and cases of mere causation. Would this solve our problems? Mightn't it be argued, with much justification, that we ought not be punished, merely because we did what we wanted to do, if our very desires were caused by factors beyond our control. To quote John Hospers:

> Schlick's analysis is indeed clarifying and helpful to those who have fallen victim to the confusions he exposes—and this probably includes most persons in their philosophical growing-pains. But *is* this the end of the matter? Is it true that all acts, though caused, are free as long as they are not compelled in the sense which he specifies? May it not be that, while the identification of "free" with "uncompelled" is acceptable, the area of compelled acts is vastly greater than he or most other philosophers have ever suspected? (Moore is more cautious in this respect than Schlick; while for Moore an act is free if it is voluntary in the sense specified above, he thinks there may be another sense in which human beings, and human acts, are not free at all.) We remember statements about human beings being pawns of their early environment, victims of conditions beyond their control, the result of causal influences stemming from their parents, and the like, and we ponder and ask, "Still, are we really free?" Is there not something in what generations of sages have said about man being fettered? Is there not perhaps something too facile, too sleight-of-hand, in Schlick's cutting of the Gordian knot? . . . Though not everyone has criminotic tendencies, everyone has been molded by influences which in large measure at least determine his present behavior; he is literally the product of these influences, stemming from periods prior to his "years of discretion," giving him a host of character traits that he cannot change now even if he would. So obviously does what a man is depend upon how a man comes to be, that it is small wonder that philosophers and sages have considered man far indeed from being the master of his fate. It is not as if man's will were standing high and serene above the flux of events that have molded him; it is itself caught up in this flux, itself carried along on the current. An act is free when it is determined by the man's character, say moralists; but what if the most decisive aspects of his character were already irrevocably acquired before he could do anything to mold them? What if even the degree of will power available to him in shaping his habits and disciplining himself now to overcome the influence of his early environment is a factor over which he has no control? What are we to say of this kind of "freedom"? Is it not rather like the freedom of the machine to stamp labels on cans when it has been devised for just that purpose? Some machines can do so more efficiently than others, but only because they have been better constructed. ("Free Will and Psychoanalysis," *Philosophy and Phenomenological Research*, 1950)

It would seem reasonable, therefore, to tentatively conclude that punishment can be justified, even if determinism is true, providing that one holds a teleological theory of punishment. If, however, one holds a retributive theory of punishment, the truth of determinism would seem to lead one to the conclusion that punishment cannot be justified.

9

Truth

In the last two chapters, we discussed some of those aspects of the human situation that may differentiate man from the surrounding world. In those chapters we spoke about man's freedom and man's intellectual capacities, without considering one of the main goals of those capacities, the acquisition of truth and knowledge. In the next two chapters, we will discuss those two fundamental concepts.

There are people who would claim that there is nothing to discuss under these topics of truth and knowledge. They might claim that there is no such a thing as the truth and as our knowledge of that truth. Already in ancient times, the Sophist Protagoras claimed that man is the measure of all things, that things are in reality as each person perceives them to be, and that there is no such a thing as the one way things really are, or an intersubjective knowledge of reality.

Why do people advance these claims? I think that their major argument is a negative one. Their major argument is that no one has ever put forward a satisfactory account of what knowledge and truth really are, and that this cannot be done because these concepts are incoherent. It is always possible to meet this kind of challenge by turning the skeptical doctrines on themselves. One can always say that if these people are right, then their own doctrines cannot be described as true and they cannot claim to know that their doctrines are true. This is an old strategy. Plato employed it in one of his dialogues, the *Theaetetus*, to criticize the views of Protagoras:

Socrates: And what is the consequence for Protagoras himself? Is it not this? Supposing that not even he believed in man being the measure and the world in general did not believe it either—as in fact it doesn't—then this *Truth* which he wrote would not be true for anyone. If, on the other hand, he did believe it, but the mass of mankind does not agree with him, then, you see, it is more false than true by just so much as the unbelievers outnumber the believers.

Theodorus: That follows, if its truth or falsity varies with each individual opinion.

Socrates: Yes, and besides that it involves a really exquisite conclusion. Protagoras, for his part, admitting as he does that everybody's opinion is true, must acknowledge the truth of his opponents' belief about his own belief, where they think he is wrong.

Theodorus: Certainly.

Socrates: That is to say, he would acknowledge his own belief to be false, if he admits that the belief of those who think him wrong is true?

Theodorus: Necessarily.

Socrates: But the others, on their side, do not admit to themselves that they are wrong.

Theodorus: No.

Socrates: Whereas Protagoras, once more, according to what he has written, admits that this opinion of theirs is as true as any other.

Theodorus: Evidently.

Socrates: On all hands, then, Protagoras included, his opinion will be disputed, or rather Protagoras will join in the general consent —when he admits to an opponent the truth of his contrary opinion, from that moment Protagoras himself will be admitting that a dog or the man in the street is not a measure of anything whatever that he does not understand. Isn't that so?

Theodorus: Yes.

Socrates: Then, since it is disputed by everyone, the *Truth* of Protagoras is true to nobody—to himself no more than to anyone else.

We cannot simply stop with this rhetorical point. In the next two chapters, we will set forth a theory both of truth and of our knowledge of the truth. Of course, this theory will not be complete. But it will,

I believe, be sufficient to show that there is nothing incoherent about the ideals of truth and knowledge, and that there is no reason why we should not pursue those ideals.

One final remark about the order in which we are covering these two subjects. There is a good reason for examining truth before knowledge. As we shall see more fully in chapter 10, knowledge is knowledge of the truth, so the concept of truth is therefore more fundamental than the concept of knowledge. Another way of seeing the same point is to remember that there may well be many truths that we don't yet know to be truths and may never come to know. So truth is more extensive and more fundamental than knowledge and should be considered first.

We shall begin this chapter by considering a number of definitions of truth. Each of them will turn out to be inadequate, but what we learn from discovering their inadequacies will help us to see the nature of truth.

9.1 SOME INADEQUATE DEFINITIONS

Suppose that we consider the following accounts of the truth of my belief p:

1. p is true just if I believe that p
2. p is true just if most people believe that p
3. p is true just if there is evidence for p
4. p is true just if there is overwhelming evidence for its truth

The first two definitions are, presumably, what Protagoras had in mind when he said that man is the measure of all things. They may also be what people have in mind when they talk about certain beliefs being true for themselves but not true for others. Sometimes such people seem to mean nothing more than the common notion that not everybody agrees on what is true and that different people have different beliefs. But sometimes such people seem to have in mind something more controversial. In particular, they sometimes seem to have in mind the subjective definitions of truth embodied in 1 and 2. Let us turn then to an examination of 1 and 2.

The first of these definitions is the most subjective; it makes truth consist merely in the fact that I (the thinking subject) believe the particular belief. But this subjectiveness leads the definition into a number of serious difficulties. To begin with, it breaks down the distinction between true belief and false belief. It says there can be no such disstinction, for all beliefs (or, at least, all my beliefs) are true. Secondly, it leads to the possibility that some contradiction is true. Suppose, for example, I believe (a) that George Washington was the first president of the United States, (b) that George Washington was very wise, and (c) that the first president of the United States was not very wise. (This won't happen very often, but such things can and do happen.) Then, according to our definition, it is true that the same person was wise and not very wise. Thirdly, this definition destroys the need for any serious inquiry into any question. We often think that we must work very hard to discover the truth. According to this definition, there is no point to doing so. All that I have to do is form some belief, any belief, and it will be automatically true.

There are some obvious lessons to be learned from the failings of this first definition. To begin with, any theory of truth must provide us with an explanation of the possibilities both of true belief and of false belief. Secondly, it must rule out the possibility that a contradiction is true. And finally, it must make it clear why truth is sometimes hard to obtain.

We turn then to the second definition of truth, the definition that p is true just if most people believe that p. It has some advantages when compared to the first definition. It provides us with an explanation of both possibilities, of true belief and of false belief. According to it, my belief is true when most people agree with it and false otherwise. And it does offer an account of why truth is sometimes hard to obtain. It's not enough, after all, just to make up my mind in order to have the truth; I must, at least, make sure that others agree with me. Nevertheless, it cannot be right because it still leaves open the possibility that a contradiction is true. Consider, once more, our case involving the beliefs about George Washington and suppose now that most people hold beliefs (a)–(c). Then, according to this second definition, it is true that the same person was both wise and not very wise, so this definition must be rejected.

There is one more lesson to be learned about truth from the shortcomings of these first two definitions. According to either of the above definitions, the truth of the claim that George Washington was wise has nothing to do with how he behaved, what he thought, etc. Even if he never had a serious idea, even if he always did the most inappropriate thing, it is true that he was wise so long as we believe it. Moreover, the truth of that claim about the past will change if we now change our beliefs. We can now literally change past history by changing our minds. Clearly, these consequences of the theory are unacceptable. Such subjectivist theories fail to establish any connection between truth and what is happening (or has happened or will happen) in the world. So the final lesson to be learned is that such a connection must be part of any adequate theory of truth.

We turn then to definitions 3 and 4, the definitions that analyze truth in terms of evidence. It is easy to see the motivation for such an analysis. Our basis, after all, for deciding what is true and what is false is the evidence that we have. When we have enough evidence for a belief, we conclude that the belief is true. So why shouldn't we simply define truth in terms of the possession of evidence?

These definitions have the additional advantage of incorporating all of the lessons about truth that we have already learned. They establish a connection between what is happening in the world (the evidence that we gather is part of what is happening) and truth. They explain why the truth is sometimes so hard to find. They provide for a difference between true belief and false belief (a false belief is one for which there is no evidence).

Do they rule out the possibility of a contradiction being true? Definition 3, unfortunately does not. There might, after all, be evidence both for some belief p and for its denial not-p. In fact, many cases, the truth is difficult to know precisely because there is some evidence for the truth of each of the contradictory beliefs. Since 3 would mean that p and not-p are both equally "true," 3 won't do as a theory of truth. Definition 4 is, in this way, much better off. It seems that there could not be *overwhelming* evidence both for p and for its denial, so 4 rules out, as any good theory should, the possibility of some contradiction being true.

Despite the initial attractiveness of a theory like 4, there are substantial reasons for rejecting it. The first objection is best understood if we begin with an example. Consider the belief that there is intelligent life elsewhere in the universe, and its denial, the belief that there isn't. I think that one can fairly say that there isn't overwhelming evidence for either of those beliefs. In fact, there is hardly any evidence at all. According to theory 4, then, neither of those beliefs are true. But surely this is wrong; at least one of them must be true. More generally, just as it cannot be the case that

p is true and not-p is true

so it must be the case that

p is true or not-p is true.

Definition 4 is inadequate precisely because it fails to guarantee that at least one of the beliefs is true.

There is a second difficulty with definition 4. Suppose there was a time when we didn't have any evidence for the belief that the earth revolves around the sun. According to 4, that belief was not then true. Suppose, moreover, that we now have overwhelming evidence for that belief. Then, according to 4 that belief is now true. So the belief has turned from false to true, while the behavior of the earth and the sun hasn't changed at all! Definition (4) hasn't then really established the right sort of connection between truth and what is going on in the world. So 4 has to be rejected.

The theories of truth that we have considered so far (with the exception of 4, which comes close to what John Dewey sometimes meant in his account of truth) have not been held by many philosophers of repute, though they are sometimes advocated by nonphilosophers. Our main purpose in considering them was to learn certain lessons about truth which we could use in trying to formulate a more adequate theory. The main lessons were:

1. Any theory of truth must rule out the possibility that p is true and not-p is true, and must therefore ensure that there is a difference between true beliefs and false beliefs.

2. Any theory of truth must guarantee that p is true or not-p is true.

3. Any theory of truth must establish the right sort of connection between the truth of a belief and what is happening in the world.

It is these lessons that will guide us as we examine some of the historically more important theories of truth.

9.2 THE PRAGMATIC THEORY OF TRUTH

Pragmatism is America's most famous contribution to philosophy. Its first leading exponent was Charles S. Peirce, and he was followed by William James and John Dewey. As a result of their teaching, American philosophy in the first half of this century was strongly influenced by pragmatic thought.

While it is easy to recount this historical story, it is harder to state exactly what the main teachings of pragmatism were. Indeed, its leading exponents often disagreed with each other's views (about truth, among other things). Pragmatism was, in fact, more an approach than a definite set of views, so the best that we can do is to set out one very famous presentation of a pragmatic theory of truth, the theory found in the sixth lecture of William James's famous book, *Pragmatism*.

James begins his presentation of the theory of truth with a fine statement of how a pragmatist approaches a problem like the analysis of truth:

> Pragmatism, on the other hand, asks its usual question. "Grant an idea or belief to be true," it says "what concrete difference will its being true make in any one's actual life? How will the truth be realized? What experiences will be different from those which would obtain if the belief were false? What, in short, is the truth's cash-value in experiential terms?

James turns to the question of the value of truth, and he begins with the following observation:

> Let me begin by reminding you of the fact that the possession of true thoughts means everywhere the possession of invaluable instruments of action; and that our duty to gain truth, so far from being a blank command from out of the blue, or a "stunt" self-imposed by our intellect, can account for itself by excellent practical reasons. . . . The practical value of the true ideas is thus primarily derived from the practical importance of these ideas to us. Their objects are, indeed, not important at all times. . . . Yet since almost any object may someday become temporarily important, the advantage of having a general stock of extra truths, of ideas that shall be true of merely possible situations, is obvious.

There are those who would object that James hasn't sufficiently considered the possibility of merely theoretical truths, of truths that do not and cannot have any practical implications. But let us leave that objection aside for now and see how this observation leads James to his definition of truth.

> From this simple cue pragmatism gets her general notion of truth as something essentially bound up with the way in which one moment in our experience may lead us towards other moments which it will be worthwhile to have been led to. Primarily, and on the common-sense level, the truth of a state of mind means this function of a leading that is worthwhile. When a moment in our experience, of any kind whatever, inspires us with a thought that is true, that means that sooner or later we dip by that thought's guidance into the particulars of experience again and make advantageous connexion with them.

By now, the reader will have acquired the impression that the heart of James's pragmatism (and not merely his theory of truth) is his emphasis on the practical evaluation of things. In a final very famous passage James himself draws this connection between his theory of truth and some of his other views:

'The true,' to put it very briefly, is only the expedient in the way of our thinking, just as 'the right' is only the expedient in the way of our behaving. Expedient in almost any fashion; and expedient in the long run and on the whole of course; for what meets expediently all the experience in sight won't necessarily meet all farther experiences equally satisfactorily. Experience, as we know, has ways of boiling over, and making us correct our present formulas.

Does James's theory of truth embody the lessons that we learned in the previous section? It does seem to rule out the possibility of both p and not-p being true, since we can plausibly suppose that both of these conflicting beliefs cannot be expedient ways of thinking in the long run. Moreover, it does seem to establish a plausible connection between the truth of a belief and what is happening in the world. After all, whether or not a belief will be expedient surely depends, at least to a very large extent, upon what is happening in the world.

But what about the third lesson? Does James's theory really guarantee that, in any case, either p will be true or not-p will be true? Consider, after all, a case in which neither of these beliefs is of any use. In such a case, neither belief can be expedient, so neither can be true according to James's theory. G. E. Moore was one of the philosophers who were led to reject James's theory because of its implication for such cases:

> We are all, it seems to me, constantly noticing trivial details, and getting true ideas about them, of which we never think again, and which nobody else ever gets. And is it quite certain that all these true ideas are useful? It seems to me perfectly clear, on the contrary, that many of them are not. Just as it is clear that many men sometimes waste their time in acquiring information which is useful to others but not to them, surely it is clear that they sometimes waste their time in acquiring information, which is useful to nobody at all, because nobody else ever acquires it. . . . It seems to me that there are many true ideas which occur but once, and which are not useful when they do occur. And if this be so, then it is plainly not true that all our true ideas are useful in any sense at all. ("William James' Pragmatism," *Proceedings of the Aristotelean Society,* 1907–8)

Much as James's pragmatic theory of truth faces an objection from the possibility of true beliefs that aren't useful, so it faces an objection from the possibility of useful beliefs that aren't true. Bertrand Russell was particularly opposed to the pragmatic theory of truth for failing to consider this second possibility. Russell felt this led the pragmatists to an unjustified favorable evaluation of religious beliefs:

> In another place James says: "On pragmatic principles, if the hypothesis of God works satisfactorily in the widest sense of the word, it is true" (p. 299). . . . The advantage of the pragmatic method is that it decides the question of the truth of the existence of God by purely mundane arguments, namely, by the effects of belief in His existence upon our life in this world. But unfortunately this gives a merely mundane conclusion, namely, that belief in God is true, i.e. useful, whereas what religion desires is the conclusion that God exists. (*Philosophical Essays*, chapter 5)

Russell was, in effect, pointing out that there were two different but good ways in which beliefs could be connected with what is happening in the world. The pragmatists emphasized one of them, namely, that the belief is an expedient one given what is happening in the world. In doing that, however, they failed to consider the other connection, namely, that what is believed actually obtains in the world, and it is this connection, said Russell, that is fundamental to truth.

Russell makes one final point about James's theory of truth that we should note here, although its significance will only emerge later on. Russell begins by introducing the notion of a criterion:

> A property A is a criterion of a property B when the same objects possess both; and A is a useful criterion of B if it is easier to discover whether an object possesses the property A than whether it possesses the property B. (*ibid.*)

Now the point that Russell wants to make is that usefulness might be much better as a *criterion* of truth than as a *definition* of truth. After all, given that usefulness and truth are so often connected with each other, usefulness may well be a very useful criterion of truth, even if it won't do as a definition of truth.

9.3 THE COHERENCE THEORY OF TRUTH

While the pragmatic theory of truth was being developed in America at the end of the nineteenth century, a very different theory of truth, the coherence theory of truth, was being developed in England. Its leading advocate was the British Idealist philosopher F. H. Bradley, and he was followed in this theory by H. H. Joachim and the American philosopher B. Blanshard.

Blanshard offered the following very clear exposition of this theory and the motivation behind it:

Thought aims at understanding, and to understand anything means, as we have seen, to grasp it as necessitated within a system of knowledge. If the system is fragmentary, it will itself require understanding within a more inclusive system. The end that thought is seeking, the only end that would satisfy it wholly, because the only end that would bring complete understanding, is a system such that nothing remained outside and nothing was contingent within. . . . Our test of any theory is its coherence with this larger whole to which the system of knowledge itself is seeking to approximate. Secondly, what supplies the test of truth supplies also the nature of truth. To say that a proposition which was completely intelligible and necessary within such an inclusive system was also false would be meaningless. Systematic coherence is not only the criterion we use for truth; it is what in the end we mean by truth. (*Nature of Thought*, chapter 27)

As we look over this account of truth and compare it with James's pragmatic theory of truth, a number of points seem to be especially noteworthy:

1. Like James, Blanshard tries to base his definition of truth on his conception of the goal of our intellectual activities. But while James emphasized as the goal the development of useful instruments of action, Blanshard emphasized the more theoretical goal of acquiring understanding. In general, idealist proponents of the coherence theory felt that pragmatism erred precisely because it emphasized in connection with truth these nontheoretical goals of thought. As Bradley said:

The criterion of truth, as of everything else, is in the end the satisfaction of a want of our nature. To get away from this test, or to pass beyond it, in the end, I should say, is impossible. But, if so (the suggestion is a natural one), why should we not set forth, or try to set forth, the satisfaction of our nature from all sides, and then accept and affirm this statement as truth and reality? . . . Truth seems to differentiate itself clearly from other satisfactions. And philosophy, I at least understand, has to meet specially this special need and want of truth. . . . If there is to be philosophy its proper business is to satisfy the intellect, and the other sides of our nature have, if so, no right to speak directly. (*Essays on Truth and Reality*, chapter 8)

2. For the idealists, one acquired understanding only when one could fit that which is understood into some comprehensive, coherent, and integrated system. In that way, the truth is one indivisible whole. An individual belief would be true only insofar as it would fit into (cohere with) such an ideal system. So the truth of any given belief is

integrally related to the truth of all other beliefs. This is why idealists would object to James's willingness to consider the truth of a single individual judgment as independent of the truth of other judgments.

3. There is no doubt that we often use something like coherence with a larger system of beliefs as our test for the truth of a single belief; we often accept as true a belief because it fits in with the rest of our beliefs. But Blanshard and the other defenders of the coherence theory of truth go further; they say that this coherence is what truth means. And the question that we must now consider is whether they too, like the pragmatists, made the mistake of taking a criterion of truth and turning it into the meaning of truth.

The most fundamental objection to the coherence theory is that it fails to maintain the proper connection between the truth of a belief and what is going on in the world. To see that this is so, consider the possibility of developing several different but totally comprehensive sets of beliefs. Imagine that they cohere together internally but are in conflict with each other. Given the coherence theory, what would be the basis for only one of these systems being true? And given that this question cannot be answered, isn't it clear that the coherence theory is totally disregarding what is actually going on in the world? Bertrand Russell put this objection as follows:

> There is no reason to suppose that only one coherent body of beliefs is possible. It may be that, with sufficient imagination, a novelist might invent a past for the world that would perfectly fit into what we know, and yet be quite different from the real past. . . . In philosophy, again, it seems not uncommon for two rival hypotheses to be both able to account for all the facts. Thus, for example, it is possible that life is one long dream, and that the outer world has only that degree of reality that the objects of dreams have. . . . Thus coherence as the definition of truth fails because there is no proof that there can be only one coherent system. (*The Problems of Philosophy*, chapter 12)

It is interesting to see how Blanshard responded to this form of criticism:

> If truth did lie in coherence, then, confronted with two worlds equally coherent, we should be unable to select one as truer than the other; on reflection we can see that such inability is just what we should find; hence the equation of truth with coherence is so far verified. (*Nature of Thought*, chapter 26)

At first sight, this reply seems to be a non sequitur. Even if, after all,

TRUTH

we couldn't select which system is true, why should we concede that there is no basis for one of them being true and the other false? Why shouldn't we say that the true system is the one that corresponds to what is going on even if we can't tell which system is true? I think, however, that we can best understand Blanshard this way: he is arguing here that since coherence is our criterion of truth, we should treat it as the meaning of truth as well, and reject the claim that only one of those systems is the truth.

Russell had another persuasive objection to the coherence theory of truth:

> Two propositions are coherent when both may be true, and are incoherent when one at least must be false. Now in order to know whether two propositions can both be true, we must know such truths as the law of contradiction. . . . But if the law of contradiction itself were subjected to the test of coherence, we should find that, if we choose to suppose it false, nothing will any longer be incoherent with anything else. Thus the laws of logic supply the skeleton or framework within which the test of coherence applies, and they themselves cannot be established by this test. (*The Problems of Philosophy, ibid.*, chapter 12)

In short, said Russell, all talk of coherence presupposes certain truths, the truths of logic, so their truth must be definable independently of coherence. Thus, he says, the coherence theory of truth cannot be a correct definition of truth.

9.4 THE CORRESPONDENCE THEORY OF TRUTH

In criticizing the earlier theories of truth that we have examined, we have emphasized their failure to establish the proper connection between the truth of a belief and what is happening in the world. The final theory of truth that we will be considering, the correspondence theory of truth, starts from this basic point that truth consists in the proper relationship between a belief and what is happening in the world. By starting there, its advocates hope to avoid the difficulties that other theories have faced.

Russell presents this theory as follows:

> If we take such a belief as 'Othello believes that Desdemona loves Cassio' we will call Desdemona and Cassio the object-terms and loving the object-relation. If there is a complex unity 'Desdemona's

love for Cassio', consisting of the object-terms related by the object-relation in the same order as they have in the belief, then this complex unity is called the fact corresponding to the belief. Thus a belief is true when there is a corresponding fact, and is false when there is no corresponding fact. (*ibid.*)

In short, Russell is claiming that the truth of a belief consists in the existence of the corresponding fact while its falsehood consists in the nonexistence of the corresponding fact.

This version of the correspondence theory has encountered a number of difficulties, some having to do with facts and some having to do with the relation of correspondence. Let us look at each of them separately.

Facts. There are many philosophers who are dubious about the existence of facts. While conceding that objects exist and have properties, they deny that there exists, in addition, the fact of the object in question having the property in question. Consequently, they must reject Russell's theory. Thus, P. F. Strawson once wrote:

> That (person, thing, etc.) to which the referring part of the statement refers, and which the describing part of the statement fits or fails to fit, is that which the statement is about. It is evident that there is nothing else in the world for the statement itself to be related to either in some further way of its own or in either of the different ways in which these different parts of the statement are related to what the statement is about. And it is evident that the demand that there should be such a relation is logically absurd. . . . But the demand for something in the world . . . to which the statement corresponds when it is true, is just this demand. ("Truth," *Proceedings of the Aristotelean Society*, 1950)

This kind of argument is of considerable philosophical importance, and it is worth elaborating on. There is an area of philosophy, metaphysics, that is concerned with, among other things, giving an account of the sorts of things that exist in the world. We all know that there are such things as physical objects and persons (though there have been philosophers who have felt otherwise). But what about such objects as numbers, events, and facts? Do such entities exist as well? And if they do exist, is their existence of the same type as the existence of physical objects and persons? These are the sorts of questions that metaphysicians worry about and which Strawson is raising in his objection to the correspondence theory of truth.

Strawson's point is really a very simple one. He begins by noting that the correspondence theory of truth asserts that a belief is true only if some corresponding fact exists. It is then a presupposition of the correspondence theory of truth that at least some facts exist. In this way, there is a metaphysical presupposition behind the correspondence theory of truth. Now what Strawson wants to claim is that this metaphysical presupposition of the theory is false. He claims that there are no such things as facts. If this claim is correct, then the correspondence theory of truth collapses.

Why is Strawson so dubious about the existence of facts? At one point in the above statement, he suggests that it is just "evident" that there are no such things. It is ironic that he says this, for in an equally famous passage, Bertrand Russell takes the existence of facts as being obvious. In that passage Russell says:

> The first truism to which I wish to draw your attention—and I hope you will agree with me that these things that I call truisms are so obvious that it is almost laughable to mention them—is that the world contains *facts,* which are what they are whatever we may choose to think about them, and that there are also *beliefs,* which have reference to facts, and by reference to facts are either true or false. I will try first of all to give you a preliminary explanation of what I mean by a 'fact.' When I speak of a fact—I do not propose to attempt an exact definition, but an explanation, so that you will know what I am talking about—I mean the kind of thing that makes a proposition true or false. If I say 'It is raining', what I say is true in a certain condition of weather and is false in other conditions of weather. The condition of weather that makes my statement true (or false as the case may be), is what I should call a 'fact'. If I say 'Socrates is dead', my statement will be true owing to a certain physiological occurrence which happened in Athens long ago. If I say, 'Gravitation varies inversely as the square of the distance', my statement is rendered true by astronomical fact. If I say, 'Two and two are four', it is arithmetical fact that makes my statement true. On the other hand, if I say 'Socrates is alive', or 'Gravitation varies directly as the distance', or 'Two and two are five', the very same facts which made my previous statements true show that these new statements are false.
>
> I want you to realize that when I speak of a fact I do not mean a particular existing thing, such as Socrates or the rain or the sun. Socrates himself does not render any statement true or false. . . . Socrates himself, or any particular thing just by itself, does not make any proposition true or false. 'Socrates is dead' and 'Socrates is alive' are both of them statements about Socrates. One is true and the other false. What I call a fact is the sort of thing that is expressed by a whole sentence, not by a single name like 'Socrates'. When a single word does come to express a fact, like 'fire' or 'wolf',

it is always due to an unexpressed context, and the full expression of a fact will always involve a sentence. We express a fact, for example, when we say that a certain thing has a certain property, or that it has a certain relation to another thing; but the thing which has the property or the relation is not what I call a 'fact'. (*The Philosophy of Logical Atomism,* lecture 1)

There is, I must confess, a considerable attractiveness to what Russell is saying, and it is very hard, in reading Strawson, to get clear on exactly what is the objection to the existence of facts. But perhaps we can approach the objection in the following way: if we suppose that there are facts whose existence makes certain beliefs true, then we will be committed to the belief in so many facts that we will ultimately prefer to give up facts altogether and find another theory of truth.

This argument can also be put as follows: suppose that one were initially inclined to agree with Russell that there are facts whose existence is responsible for the truth of certain beliefs. Now among the true beliefs are the following:

1. all men are mortal
2. either John loves Francine or he loves Matilda
3. it is not the case that John loves Francine

On Russell's account, at least as he initially presented it, it would seem that the truth of these beliefs would commit us to the existence of general facts, disjunctive facts (stated by using "or"), and negative facts. Even many of those who are initially prepared to accept the existence of facts might well hesitate about admitting all of these additional facts into existence. And that at least begins to suggest, although it certainly does not entail, that perhaps we were wrong to agree that there were facts. Perhaps we were wrong to accept the existence of any theory of truth that required the existence of facts.

Russell was well aware of these problems, and he and many of his followers tried to modify his theory of truth so that it would avoid a commitment to the existence of these troublesome facts while still accepting the basic idea that truth is based upon the existence of certain basic facts. Thus, for example, they argued that the truth of belief 2, above, is based upon the existence of the fact that John loves Francine or upon the existence of the fact that John loves Matilda, and there is no need to postulate the existence of the additional disjunctive fact. Now if they could have carried through their program for general and negative facts as well, they would have made the belief in facts far more plausible.

Unfortunately, however, they found it far more difficult to do without negative and general facts.

Let us look, as an example, at the problem of negative facts. What non-negative fact is such that its existence could account for the truth of belief 3? One obvious suggestion is that it is the fact that John hates Francine. But that suggestion can't be right, since belief 3 may well be true; it may well be the case that John does not love Francine, without the fact John hates Francine existing. (For example, John may be totally indifferent to Francine). We will need some more complicated disjunctive fact, something like 'John hates Francine or he dislikes her or he is indifferent to her or . . .' And then, of course, we might hope to get rid of that disjunctive fact in the same fashion that we eliminated the disjunctive fact in connection with belief 2.

Russell saw, however, that this will not do, and he stated his reasoning as follows:

> We have come now to the question, how are we really to interpret 'not-p', and the suggestion offered by Mr. Demos is that when we assert 'not-p' we are really asserting that there is some proposition q which is true and is incompatible with p ('an opposite of p' is his phrase, but I think the meaning is the same). That is his suggested definition:
>
> > 'not-p' means 'There is a proposition q which is true and is incompatible with p.'
>
> As, e.g., if I say 'This chalk is not red', I shall be meaning to assert that there is some proposition, which in this case would be the proposition 'This chalk is white', which is inconsistent with the proposition 'It is red', and that you use these general negative forms because you do not happen to know what the actual proposition is that is true and is incompatible with p. Or, of course, you may possibly know what the actual proposition is, but you may be more interested in the fact that p is false than you are in the particular example which makes it false. As, for instance, you might be anxious to prove that someone is a liar, and you might be very much interested in the falsehood of some proposition which he had asserted. You might also be more interested in the general proposition than in the particular case, so that if someone had asserted that that chalk was red, you might be more interested in the fact that it was not red than in the fact that it was white.
>
> I find it very difficult to believe that theory of falsehood. You will observe that in the first place there is this objection, that it makes incompatibility fundamental and an objective fact, which is not so very much simpler than allowing negative facts. You have got to

have here 'That p is incompatible with q' in order to reduce 'not' to incompatibility, because this has got to be the corresponding fact. (*ibid.*, lecture 3)

Similar difficulties were encountered when Russell and his followers tried to find a way to do without general facts. All of this then led many philosophers (though not Russell) to doubt the existence of facts, as well as any philosophical theory that presupposed their existence.

Correspondence. There is a second problem about the correspondence theory. According to Russell's theory, the truth of a belief is grounded upon the existence of some fact. Which fact? The corresponding fact. But which fact is that. What is involved in a fact's corresponding to some belief? Russell, in the quotation above, attempts to explain the relation of correspondence for the simple belief with which he is concerned. But can a general account of correspondence be offered? The answer seems unclear.

9.5 A RECENT THEORY

By the 1920s, many philosophers found themselves in the following unhappy situation. On the one hand, they were unwilling to adopt either the pragmatic or the coherence theory of truth because these theories failed to establish a sufficient connection between truth and reality. On the other hand, they found Russell's theory of truth, with its facts and its mysterious relation of correspondence, unsatisfactory. This situation led to the development of a new theory of truth, one which attempted to capture the merits of Russell's correspondence theory without its shortcomings.

This theory, the redundancy theory, is explained in the following passage by A. J. Ayer:

> Reverting to the analysis of truth, we find that in all sentences of the form "p is true," the phrase "is true" is logically superfluous. When, for example, one says that the proposition "Queen Anne is dead" is true, all that one is saying is that Queen Anne is dead. . . . Thus, to assert that a proposition is true is just to assert it, and to say that it is false is just to assert its contradictory. And this indicates that the terms "true" and "false" connote nothing, but function in the sentence simply as marks of assertion and denial. And in that case there can be no sense in asking us to analyze the concept of "truth". (*Language, Truth, and Logic*, chapter 5)

TRUTH

Ayer is making three main points: (1) There is no property of beliefs such as truth and falsehood. (2) When we say that a belief p is true, all that we are saying is that p. Thus, when I say "it is true that Queen Anne is dead," that is just a way of saying "Queen Anne is dead." (3) There is, however, this connection between truth and reality: when I say that a belief is true (that, for example, it is true that Queen Anne is dead), I am saying something about what is going on in the world (namely, that Queen Anne is dead).

In a very famous essay, P. F. Strawson extended this view. Strawson was concerned with understanding why we even bother to say "it is true that" since saying it is superfluous. He felt that it must make some contribution, even if it doesn't add to what it asserted. He offered the following account: "In general, in using such expressions [truth, is true, etc.], we are confirming, underwriting, admitting, agreeing with, what somebody has said; but . . . we are not making any assertion additional to theirs." ("Truth," *Analysis,* 1949)

Strawson's extension of Ayer's analysis is based upon an extremely important insight into the functioning of language that has been developed extensively by philosophers in recent years. According to many traditional conceptions of the role of language and language use, sentences in the declarative form are always used to assert that something is the case. On such a conception of the use of language, the natural question that arises is: exactly what are we asserting when we assert that 'p is true'? From this perspective, it is natural to conclude, as did Ayer, that 'is true' is superfluous, that it contributes nothing to what is being asserted. Although this conclusion may seem to go against our intuitions, it is forced upon us if we adopt the view that the declarative sentence is merely a mechanism for asserting that something is the case.

But there is no particular reason to accept that view about the use of language. It is fairly evident that there are other uses for declarative sentences. To quote J. L. Austin:

> Now it is one such sort of use of language that I want to examine here. I want to discuss a kind of utterance which looks like a statement and grammatically, I suppose, would be classed as a statement, which is not nonsensical, and yet is not true or false. These are not going to be utterances which contain curious verbs like 'could' or 'might', or curious words like 'good', which many philosophers regard nowadays simply as danger signals. They will be perfectly straightforward utterances, with ordinary verbs in the first person singular present indicative active, and yet we shall see at once that they couldn't possibly be true or false. Furthermore, if a person makes an utterance of this sort we should say that he is

doing something rather than merely *saying* something. This may sound a little odd, but the examples I shall give will in fact not be odd at all, and may even seem decidedly dull. Here are three or four. Suppose, for example, that in the course of a marriage ceremony I say, as people will, 'I do'—(sc. take this woman to be my lawful wedded wife). Or again, suppose that I tread on your toe and say 'I apologize'. Or again, suppose that I have the bottle of champagne in my hand and say 'I name this ship the *Queen Elizabeth*'. Or suppose I say 'I bet you sixpence it will rain tomorrow'. In all these cases it would be absurd to regard the thing that I say as a report of the performance of the action which is undoubtedly done—the action of betting, or christening, or apologizing. We should say rather that, in saying what I do, I actually perform that action. When I say 'I name this ship the *Queen Elizabeth*' I do not describe the christening ceremony, I actually perform the christening; and when I say 'I do' (sc. take this woman to be my lawful wedded wife), I am not reporting on a marriage, I am indulging in it. (*Philosophical Papers*, chapter 10)

Strawson would freely concede, of course, that asserting a sentence of the form '*p* is true' is not exactly like the cases that Austin is referring to. Strawson realized that one does assert something, whatever different assertion one would have made had one not added the words 'is true'. What Strawson wants to claim in his essay is that adding the words 'is true' means that you have also performed certain actions (e.g., admitting or agreeing).

In short, then, there exists a theory that captures the right sort of connection between truth and reality. And we can therefore say that the basic idea behind the correspondence theory can be successfully embodied in an adequate theory of truth.

9.6 TYPES OF TRUTH

We have, so far in this chapter, been concerned with trying to develop a general definition of truth, a general account of when some belief (or some sentence used to express that belief) is true. We have seen that there is an account of truth available which captures the important insights of the correspondence theory of truth without introducing any of the difficulties about facts and the correspondence relation. There is therefore no reason to accept the view that a theory of objective truth is incoherent.

In this final section, we will be concerned with introducing and discussing a number of important distinctions among truths. These dis-

TRUTH

tinctions have a certain intrinsic interest, but their main philosophical importance is in what they can tell us about how we can know what beliefs are true. Moreover, introducing these distinctions among types of truths will lay the foundations for our discussion of knowledge in the next chapter. It is important to remember that even if we have provided a coherent account of truth, we have not yet defended the claim that we have knowledge of the truth.

The first distinction that we need is the distinction between *necessary* truths and *contingent* truths. A necessary truth is a truth that has to be true, or that could not be false. Consider the sentence 'all bachelors are males'. It is a necessary truth, and it is so precisely because it could not be false. It is not merely the case that the world *happens* to be such that all bachelors are male. Rather, things could not be otherwise. On the other hand, a contingent truth is a truth that need not be true. It could be false. Consider the sentence 'all the coins in my pocket at this moment are nickles'. If it is true, it is a contingent truth, and it is so precisely because it could have been false. The world happens to be such that all the coins in my pocket at this moment are of a certain type, but it could have been otherwise.

We have seen so far certain clear examples of both necessary truths and contingent truths. There are certain claims, however, whose status is less clear. For example, if we suppose that every event has a cause, is that a necessary truth or a contingent truth? Is it merely a fact about how things are that every event has a cause, or is it in some sense necessary that every event have a cause? Or consider the truth that $2 + 2 = 4$. Is that merely a contingent truth or is its truth necessary? Philosophers have strongly disagreed about these examples and others like them.

We shall return to these disagreements in a while, but before doing so we have to look at some further distinctions. Let's begin with the distinction between *analytically* true sentences and *synthetically* true sentences. An analytically true sentence, roughly speaking, is a sentence that is true by virtue of its meaning. Thus, it is often said that the sentence 'all bachelors are male' is an analytically true sentence because if you understand the meaning of its constituent terms (and especially the meaning of 'bachelor') you will see that the sentence is true. On the other hand, a synthetically true sentence is one that is true, but not merely by virtue of its meaning. Thus, 'all the coins in my pocket at this moment are nickles' is usually said to be a synthetic truth precisely because its truth does not follow from the meaning of the sentence and its constituent terms.

In a famous passage, W. V. O. Quine (who, as a matter of fact, is himself skeptical about this distinction) set out the following more precise account of the distinction:

The problem of analyticity then confronts us anew. Statements which are analytic by general philosophical acclaim are not, indeed, far to seek. They fall into two classes. Those of the first class, which may be called *logically true,* are typified by:

(1) No unmarried man is married.

The relevant feature of this example is that it not merely is true as it stands, but remains true under any and all reinterpretations of 'man' and 'married'. If we suppose a prior inventory of *logical* particles, comprising 'no', 'un-', 'not', 'if', 'then', 'and', etc., then in general a logical truth is a statement which is true and remains true under all reinterpretations of its components other than the logical particles.

But there is also a second class of analytic statements, typified by:

(2) No bachelor is married.

The characteristic of such a statement is that it can be turned into a logical truth by putting synonyms for synonyms; thus (2) can be turned into (1) by putting 'unmarried man' for its synonym 'bachelor'. We still lack a proper characterization of this second class of analytic statements, and therewith of analyticity generally, inasmuch as we have had in the above description to lean on a notion of "synonymy" which is no less in need of clarification than analyticity itself. ("Two Dogmas of Empiricism," *Philosophical Review,* 1951)

The final distinction that we should introduce, and the one that is most directly related to questions about knowledge, is the distinction between *a priori* truths and *a posteriori* truths. An a priori truth is a belief whose truth can be known solely upon the basis of reasoning and without any appeal to experience. Thus, to use a familiar example one more time, 'all bachelors are male' is an a priori truth, and it is one precisely because you don't have to go out and check bachelors to see whether or not they are male in order to know that all bachelors are male. One can see this on the basis of reasoning alone, once one knows what the relevant terms mean.

On the other hand, an a posteriori truth is one whose truth can only be established upon the basis of experience; its truth cannot be known upon the basis of reasoning alone. Thus, to use another familiar example, 'all the coins in my pocket at this moment are nickles' is an a posteriori truth, and it is one precisely because the only way I can know it is true is for me (or someone else) to check and see that this is so, because mere reasoning will not enable me to determine its truth.

When we introduced the first of our distinctions, the distinction between necessary truths and contingent truths, we pointed out that there are truths (e.g., 'every event has a cause', and '2 + 2 = 4') about which it is not clear whether they are necessary truths or contingent truths. We can now add that it is also unclear as to whether they are analytic truths or synthetic truths. Moreover, it is unclear whether they are a priori truths or a posteriori truths. The reason why these examples have attracted so much interest is precisely because they raise questions about all of these fundamental distinctions.

The reader may by now have acquired the impression that these three distinctions come to the same thing, that there are, on the one hand, necessary analytic a priori truths and, on the other hand, contingent synthetic a posteriori truths. And it does in some ways seem natural to suppose this. Necessarily true sentences are necessarily true precisely because their truth follows from their meaning (and is, hence, analytic). And since we can see this without the aid of experience, they are a priori truths as well. On the other hand, contingently true sentences are true because of what is happening in the world (and which might not have happened), and the only way we can therefore find out that they are true is by checking and seeing that they are true. This natural tendency has greatly influenced many philosophers, explicitly or implicitly. A very clear indication of the way in which these distinctions have been run together is to be found in the following passage from David Hume.

> All the objects of human reason or inquiry may naturally be divided into two kinds, to wit, "Relations of Ideas," and "Matters of Fact." Of the first kind are the sciences of Geometry, Algebra, and Arithmetic, and, in short, every affirmation which is either intuitively or demonstratively certain. *That the square of the hypotenuse is equal to the square of the two sides* is a proposition which expresses a relation between these figures. *That three times five is equal to the half of thirty* expresses a relation between these numbers. Propositions of this kind are discoverable by the mere operation of thought, without dependence on what is anywhere existent in the universe. Though there never were a circle or triangle in nature, the truths demonstrated by Euclid would forever retain their certainty and evidence.
>
> Matters of fact, which are the second objects of human reason, are not ascertained in the same manner, nor is our evidence of their truth, however great, of a like nature with the foregoing. The contrary of every matter of fact is still possible, because it can never imply a contradiction and is conceived by the mind with the same facility and distinctness as if ever so conformable to reality. *That the sun will not rise tomorrow* is no less intelligible a proposition and implies no more contradiction than the affirmation *that it will*

rise. We should in vain, therefore, attempt to demonstrate its falsehood. Were it demonstratively false, it would imply a contradiction and could never be distinctly conceived by the mind. (*Inquiry Concerning Human Understanding*, section 4)

Since the time of Immanuel Kant (the late eighteenth century), philosophers have come to recognize the importance of making these three distinctions and leaving open the possibility that there might be such things as a *synthetic* necessary a priori truth. One of the reasons why they have done so is precisely because of the troublesome examples that we mentioned before. Kant himself thought that the truths of arithmetic were synthetic necessary a priori truths. Following this tradition, we will leave it an open question (whose significance will emerge more fully in the next chapter) as to whether these three oppositions ultimately merge into one.

10

Knowing and Believing

At the beginning of the last chapter, we considered the claim of the skeptic, the claim that truth and the knowledge of the truth are incoherent ideals. The skeptic claims that all that we can ever have are our own beliefs and prejudices. In chapter 9, we tried to develop a number of approaches to defining that ideal of truth. We were able to show, in any case, that the ideal of truth was something that could be defended and understood. In doing that, however, we did not fully respond to the challenge of the skeptic. Even if there is a coherent ideal of truth, the skeptic can still argue that it is irrelevant to us because there is no such thing as knowledge of the truth. And if the skeptic is successful in that argument, then our efforts in chapter 9 will really have been lost. What we shall try to do here, then, is (1) present an account of the nature of knowledge and (2) show that the skeptic is wrong, and that at least some knowledge is attainable.

Our concern in this chapter is not, however, merely that of meeting the challenge of the skeptic. We shall also be concerned with justifying much of what we have done in earlier chapters. In chapter 5, for example, we tried to discover whether or not we can know that God exists, presupposing that there is a coherent ideal of knowledge. Again, in chapter 6, we were concerned with whether or not moral knowledge was attainable independently of divine revelation. Once more, we presupposed the coherence of that concept of knowledge. On those occasions, we did not have the opportunity to examine more fully the general question of the nature and extent of human knowledge. It is just that question that we will consider here.

Two notes before we begin. It is one of the characteristics of modern philosophy since the time of Descartes (the beginning of the seventeenth century) that it has taken the problem of human knowledge as *the* fundamental philosophical problem. I think that this is not an accident. Rather, it reflects the immense growth of knowledge in the modern scientific era. That growth in knowledge has certainly made its impression on modern philosophy. It can, I believe, be said with much justification that, for many of the great modern philosophers (Descartes, Locke, Kant, etc.), the goal of the philosophical examination of knowledge is to defend science's claim to knowledge and to analyze the nature and extent of that knowledge. This theme emerges, for example, at the very beginning of Locke's *Essay Concerning Human Understanding*:

> Five or six friends meeting at my chamber, and discoursing on a subject very remote from this, found themselves quickly at a stand, by the difficulties that rose on every side. After we had a while puzzled ourselves, without coming any nearer to a resolution of those doubts that perplexed us, it came to my thoughts that we took a wrong course; and that before we set ourselves upon inquiries of that nature, it was necessary to examine our own abilities, and see what objects our understanding were, or were not, fit to deal with.

The other note is a methodological one. Following the lead of many of the classics in the theory of knowledge, we shall not begin by assuming the existence of knowledge. After all, our purpose is to refute the skeptic and not merely to assume that he is wrong. What we shall do instead is examine the nature of knowledge, and then, in light of that examination, consider the question of whether, and to what extent, knowledge is possible.

10.1 THE NATURE OF KNOWLEDGE

When philosophers have discussed the question of the nature of knowledge, they have traditionally put their problem as follows: Suppose that I believe that it is going to rain tomorrow. Suppose, moreover, that it will rain, so my belief is true. What more is required if my belief is to

KNOWING AND BELIEVING

be an instance of knowledge? More generally, what is the difference between knowledge and mere true belief?

A presupposition of this philosophical tradition is that knowledge cannot be identified with true belief. Why won't philosophers identify knowledge with true belief? Primarily, because there seem to be cases of true beliefs that are not cases of knowledge. Suppose, for example, that I have a wild hunch that Lucky Star will win the fifth race tomorrow, and suppose, moreover, that it turns out that he does. Then, my belief that Lucky Star would win was a true belief, but I certainly didn't *know* that Lucky Star would win. So knowledge must not be identical with true belief.

What is the difference between them? Let us begin our discussion of the difference by looking at a well-known passage in the *Republic*, where Plato tries to distinguish opinion (belief) from knowledge:

> I will begin by placing faculties in a class by themselves; they are powers in us, and in all other things, by which we do as we do. Sight and hearing, for example, I should call faculties. . . . In speaking of a faculty, I think only of its sphere and its result; and that which has the same sphere and the same result I call the same faculty, but that which has another sphere and another result I call different. . . . Would you say that knowledge is a faculty, or in what class would you place it?
>
> Certainly knowledge is a faculty, and the mightiest of all faculties.
>
> And is opinion also a faculty?
>
> Certainly, he said; for opinion is that with which we are able to form an opinion.
>
> And yet you were acknowledging a little while ago that knowledge is not the same as opinion?
>
> Why yes, he said; how can any reasonable being ever identify that which is infallible with that which errs? . . .
>
> Then knowledge and opinion having distinct powers have also distinct spheres or subjectmatters?

Plato seems to be saying here (1) that opinion (even when true) and knowledge differ from each other because they are concerned with different subject matters, and (2) that consequently, knowledge is not true opinion plus something, and that a true opinion (like my lucky hunch) cannot be turned into knowledge by the addition of anything.

Plato seems to have gone too far here. While he is certainly right in distinguishing true opinion and knowledge, he has separated them too much. After all, to return to our simple example, if I go to the track tomorrow and see Lucky Star win, then it seems that my belief will be turned into knowledge; so (1) and (2) seem to be false. It would seem therefore that the best approach is to distinguish knowledge and true belief but to say that knowledge is true belief plus something else. A true belief by this approach, can be turned into knowledge by the addition of the something else. Plato himself suggests this more plausible alternative in another passage:

> That is a distinction, Socrates, which I have heard made by someone else but I had forgotten it. He said that true opinion, *combined with reason*, was knowledge, but that the opinion which had no reason was out of the sphere of knowledge. (Theaetetus)

It is important to note that Plato does not say that we turn true belief into knowledge by perceiving through our senses that the belief is true. He had good reasons for not offering this as a general account of knowledge. Even if one supposes that one can sometimes turn a belief into knowledge by perceiving that it is true, there are other cases of knowledge in which the truth of the belief certainly cannot be perceived. These include some of the a priori beliefs we discussed at the end of the chapter 9. In connection with such beliefs, there must be other ways of turning belief into knowledge. To quote Plato once more:

> SOCRATES: How about sounds and colors: in the first place you would admit that they both exist?
>
> THEAETETUS: Yes
>
> SOCRATES: And that either of them is different from the other and the same with itself?
>
> THEAETETUS: Certainly.
>
> SOCRATES: And that both are two and each of them are one?
>
> THEAETETUS: Yes . . .
>
> SOCRATES: But through what do you perceive all this about them? For neither through hearing nor yet through seeing can you apprehend that which they have in common. (*ibid.*)

As we saw above, the suggestion that Plato does consider in the *Theaetetus* is that you must combine true belief with reason to turn it into knowledge. But he never offers in that dialogue a satisfactory account of what is involved in doing that. In more recent times, philosophers have understood that combination to mean that knowledge is *justified true belief;* knowledge is made up of beliefs for which we have good

KNOWING AND BELIEVING

reasons to believe that they are true. Thus, modern philosophers have said that 'A knows that p' should be analyzed as:

1. A believes that p
2. p is true
3. A is justified in believing that p

They have also pointed out that clause 3 may in some cases involve A's perceiving that p and may in some cases involve something else. So this definition is more general and flexible than the claim that true belief is turned into knowledge by perception.

This last point is extremely important and needs to be developed more fully. We saw in the previous chapter that there were considerable differences between various truths. In connection with the theory of knowledge, the most important of those differences is the difference between a priori knowledge and a posteriori knowledge. It is extremely important, in formulating a definition of knowledge, to make sure that one's definition leaves open the possibility of both of these types of knowledge. The adoption of clause 3 of the above definition does just this.

The account of knowledge as justified true belief is now known to be partially inadequate. There seem to be cases of justified true belief that we would not be prepared to treat as cases of knowledge. This difficulty was first pointed out by Edmund Gettier in the following passage:

> Suppose that Smith and Jones have applied for a certain job. And suppose that Smith has strong evidence for the following conjunctive proposition:
> (d) Jones is the man who will get the job, and Jones has ten coins in his pocket.
>
> Smith's evidence for (d) might be that the president of the company assured him that Jones would in the end be selected, and that he, Smith, had counted the coins in Jones's pocket ten minutes ago. Proposition (d) entails:
> (e) The man who will get the job has ten coins in his pocket.
>
> Let us suppose that Smith sees the entailment from (d) to (e), and accepts (e) on the grounds of (d), for which he has strong evidence. In this case, Smith is clearly justified in believing that (e) is true.
>
> But imagine, further, that unknown to Smith, he himself, not Jones, will get the job. And, also, unknown to Smith, he himself has ten coins in his pocket. Proposition (e) is then true, though proposition (d), from which Smith inferred (e), is false. In our example, then, all of the following are true: (i) (e) is true, (ii) Smith believes

that (e) is true, and (*iii*) Smith is justified in believing that (e) is true. But it is equally clear that Smith does not *know* that (e) is true; for (e) is true in virtue of the number of coins in Smith's pocket, while Smith does not know how many coins are in Smith's pocket, and bases his belief in (e) on a count of the coins in Jones's pocket, whom he falsely believes to be the man who will get the job. ("Is Justified True Belief Knowledge?" *Analysis*, 1963)

This example of Gettier's has provoked a great deal of discussion. Intuitively, it is clear what has happened in his case. Smith's true belief, that the man who will get the job has ten coins in his pocket, is indeed justified, but its justification is ultimately based on a false belief, the belief that Jones is the man who will get the job. This is why this is a case of justified true belief that is also not a case of knowledge. Unfortunately, however, it has turned out to be very difficult to rule out such cases on the basis of this intuition. Various attempts have been made to impose a fourth condition on what is required for a belief to be an instance of knowledge—a requirement that will rule out cases like the one proposed by Gettier—but none of them has won universal acceptance.

Although this counterexample to the claim that knowledge is simply justified true belief raises extremely important theoretical questions, we shall disregard them for now. The account of knowledge as justified true belief is a reasonable approximation for our purposes.

This definition naturally raises two questions. The first, what is it for a belief to be true, has already been discussed in chapter 9. There is, however, a second question that this definition raises: under what conditions is a person justified in holding some belief? This question is important enough to occupy us for the rest of this chapter.

If we keep this second question in mind, we can see a powerful strategy for defending skepticism. The skeptic need merely show that we are never really justified in holding some belief. If that is so, then it would follow from our definition that we never possess any knowledge. This is, indeed, the very way the skeptical argument goes. We shall present, in the next section, two arguments that purport to show that there is no such thing as knowledge precisely because our beliefs can never really be justified.

10.2 TWO SKEPTICAL ARGUMENTS

The first of these skeptical arguments was presented by René Descartes, the great seventeenth century French philosopher. Like us, Descartes wasn't really arguing for skepticism; he presented the skeptical argument in as strong as a fashion as possible so that, in responding to it, he could put forward a satisfactory theory of knowledge.

Descartes begins with a very plausible principle: "Reason already persuades me that I ought no less carefully to withhold my assent from matters which are not entirely certain and indubitable than from those which appear to me manifestly to be false." In our terminology, Descartes's principle says that one isn't justified in having a belief (and doesn't therefore know it to be true) unless there can be no doubt about its truth, unless its truth is certain. It is pretty clear, once the principle is put that way, how the skeptical argument will run: In order to know that p is true, the truth of p must be certain. But this can never happen; there is always at least some basis for doubting any belief. So there can be no knowledge.

A fundamental assumption of this argument is, of course, the claim that there is always some basis, however weak, for doubting any belief. How did Descartes defend that assumption? He began with those beliefs whose justification is based upon perception, and he argued that we can never rule out the possibility that things are different from the way in which we perceive them:

> It is sometimes proved to me that these senses are deceptive, and it is wiser not to trust entirely to anything by which we have once been deceived. But it may be that although the senses sometimes deceive us concerning things which are hardly perceptible, or very far away, there are yet many others to be met with as to which we cannot reasonably have any doubt, although we recognize them by their means. . . . At the same time I must remember that I am a man, and that consequently I am in the habit of sleeping. . . . I remind myself that on many occasions I have in sleep been deceived by similar illusions, and in dwelling carefully on this reflection I see so manifestly that there are no certain indications by which we may clearly distinguish wakefulness from sleep. (*Meditations, I*)

But perhaps there are some simple and fundamental truths whose justication is not based upon perception and about which we can be certain and have knowledge. Descartes argues that even here some doubt is possible:

> As I sometimes imagine that others deceive themselves in things which they think they know best, how do I know that I am not deceived every time that I add two or three, or count the sides of a square, or judge of things yet simpler, if anything simpler can be imagined?

In short, some doubt is always possible, so how can we know anything? Many readers of Descartes have been confused as to exactly what he was trying to show. They have understood him to be arguing that, since we are sometimes wrong when we judge on the basis of our perceptions or upon the basis of what seems evident to us, therefore we are *always* wrong when we make judgments on those bases. This is clearly not a satisfactory argument, but it is also not the argument that Descartes was using. Descartes's argument was, instead, that since we are sometimes wrong when we judge on the basis of our perceptions or upon the basis of what seems evident to us, we can never be *certain* when we form our beliefs that way. Such beliefs are then open to doubt and cannot be instances of knowledge. This then is the first skeptical argument.

The second of the skeptical arguments that we shall be considering begins with the very common and plausible assumption that all of our beliefs rest upon certain fundamental assumptions which cannot be justified. From this the argument concludes that no knowledge is possible. We might express this argument as follows:

a. suppose that A knows that p

b. by clause 3 of the definition of knowledge, A must be justified in believing that p

c. that can only happen if A knows the truth of some other belief q which makes p certain

d. by clause 3 of the definition of knowledge, A must be justified in believing that q

e. this argument can be repeated indefinitely, so in order for A to know that p he would have to know an indefinite number of other things

f. clearly, A does not

g. as a matter of fact, A's belief in p must ultimately rest upon some belief r which rests on no other belief and A is not therefore justified in belicving r

h. then, A isn't really justified in believing that p, and doesn't really know that p is true

This second argument, which is often called the *infinite-regress* argument, has been used for purposes other than the defense of skepticism. It is used, on occasions, to defend holding beliefs rather than to challenge doing so. Thus, religious fundamentalists often defend their own antiscientific beliefs by use of this argument. They claim that their beliefs rest upon certain unjustified religious assumptions just as scientific beliefs rest upon unjustified scientific assumptions. Their claim is that the religious beliefs are just as justified as the scientific beliefs.

If one goes back and looks at the infinite-regress argument that we presented above, one can see that this fundamentalist argument accepts all of the steps through *f* and then continues as follows:

g'. A's belief in *p* must ultimately rest upon some belief *r* which rests on no other belief

h'. we are entitled, as is A, to choose these ultimately unjustified beliefs which are the basis of all of our knowledge because they serve as the basis for all of the justifications of our other beliefs

i'. therefore, religious beliefs based upon unjustified fundamental religious assumptions are as justified as scientific beliefs based upon unjustified scientific assumptions

This argument might seem to some readers a desperate attempt to justify religious belief made by those who really know that religious beliefs cannot be justified. I think that this would be an unfair assessment of this argument. It is rather an attempt to justify religious belief upon the basis of a theoretical analysis of justification, and it should not be dismissed without careful examination.

In any case, our main concern is with the infinite-regress argument as an argument for skepticism. As such, it argues that we cannot have any knowledge because having knowledge requires an impossible, infinitely-long justification.

Can our two skeptical arguments be met or is the attainment of knowledge really impossible? The following traditional analysis of this question has been widely adopted: Suppose that there is a class of true beliefs that share two characteristics (1) they are absolutely certain (there is no way in which they can rationally be doubted), and (2) we can ascertain that this is so without having to appeal to any other beliefs that we have. Such beliefs can be called *self-justified* beliefs. The existence of such beliefs would resolve both of our skeptical challenges. Since they are absolutely certain, they meet even Descartes's stringent principle about when beliefs are justified. And since we can ascertain their certain truth without having to appeal to any other beliefs, we will have some bits of knowledge that do not require either any basic unjustified assumptions or our having to know an indefinite number of beliefs. In short, the existence of such beliefs would vindicate the claim that knowledge is possible.

As we see in the next section, there are two major variants of this analysis of knowledge, the *rationalist* and the *empiricist*. Both variants begin with a presentation of certain beliefs which they feel are self-justified. Both use the existence of these beliefs to refute the challenges of the skeptic. And both claim that all other knowledge is based upon these self-justified beliefs, that all of our other beliefs must be justified by reference to these self-justified beliefs. In this way, both variants agree that human knowledge is an edifice resting upon a foundation of self-justified beliefs. All that these variants disagree about is which beliefs are self-justified.

10.3 RATIONALISM VS. EMPIRICISM

Perhaps the best way to understand the rationalist variant of this analysis of knowledge is to look carefully at the following presentation of it by Descartes:

> We shall here take note of all those mental operations by which we are able, wholly without fear of illusion, to arrive at the knowledge of things. Now I admit only two, viz., intuition and deduction. . . . By intuition I understand, not the fluctuating testimony of the senses, nor the misleading judgment that proceeds from the blundering constructions of imagination. . . . Intuition is the undoubting conception of an unclouded and attentive mind, and springs from the light of reason alone. . . . Thus each individual can mentally have intuition of the fact that he exists, and that he thinks; that the triangle is bounded by three lines only, the sphere by a single superficies, and so on. . . . Hence now we are in a position to raise the question as to why we have, besides intuition, given this supplementary method of knowing, viz., knowing by deduction, by which we understand all necessary inference from other facts that are known with certainty. This, however, we could not avoid, because many things are known with certainty, though not by themselves evident, but only deduced from true and known principles. (*Rules for the Direction of the Mind*, Rule 3)

We see in this passage all of the main themes of the relationist analysis of knowledge: (1) the basic self-justified beliefs are those beliefs that our reason immediately judges to be certainly true; (2) all other beliefs that we know to be true are known on the basis of our ability to deduce their truth from the truth of the basic intuitive truths; (3) experience plays no role in the acquisition of knowledge.

We can also see here how Descartes hoped to meet the challenge of the skeptical arguments that we were considering in section 10.2. The intuitive beliefs are self-justified beliefs, so one can know their truth without having to know anything else. At the same time, they are absolutely certain, and as such, are not open to the other skeptical challenge. Therefore, concluded Descartes, they are perfectly suitable to serve as the foundation of knowledge. The rest of the edifice of knowledge is derived from them through the process of reasoning.

Why did Descartes believe that these intuitive beliefs really are certain? Hadn't he pointed out that however certain these simple and intuitive beliefs seem to be, they really aren't certain, they really can be doubted, since people have been mistaken about them in the past? Is, for example, the belief that a triangle is bounded by three sides only really certain? Are there no grounds (however weak) for the slightest doubt about that belief? In raising these questions, I do not have in mind any grounds for doubting that belief. I freely confess that I feel certain about that belief. But should I? As Descartes himself pointed out, how can I ever entirely rule out the possibility that, even in the case of this simple and obvious belief, I have made an error.

The following reflection might serve to strengthen this doubt. Descartes, elsewhere in his writings, gives as another example of a certain self-justified belief; the belief that the whole is greater than any of its parts. That belief also seems to be certainly true. But, as a matter of fact, it is sometimes false. In the case of infinite wholes, the whole is equal to some of its parts; there are, for example, as many positive numbers as there are numbers. Shouldn't we conclude from this that no intuitive belief is ever certain, that however sure we feel about any intuitive belief, we still have reasons for at least a slight doubt about its truth?

The answer to these questions is to be found in Descartes's classic work on the theory of knowledge, the *Meditations*. In that book, having proved, at least to his own satisfaction, that he exists and that God exists, Descartes tried to show that he could not be deceived about these self-evident beliefs. Their truth was, to him, intuitively evident. His argument was based upon the idea that the goodness of God ruled deception out. It ran as follows:

> For, first of all, I recognise it to be impossible that He should ever deceive me; for in all fraud and deception some imperfection is to be found, and although it may appear that the power of deception is a mark of subtilty or power, yet the desire to deceive without doubt testifies to malice or feebleness, and accordingly cannot be found in God.
>
> In the next place I experienced in myself a certain capacity for judging which I have doubtless received from God, like all the other things that I possess; and as He could not desire to deceive me, it is clear that He has not given me a faculty that will lead me to err

> if I use it aright. . . . But if I abstain from giving my judgment on any thing when I do not perceive it with sufficient clearness and distinctness, it is plain that I act rightly and am not deceived. But if I determine to deny or affirm, I no longer make use as I should of my free will, and if I affirm what is not true, it is evident that I deceive myself; even though I judge according to truth, this comes about only by chance, and I do not escape the blame of misusing my freedom; for the light of nature teaches us that the knowledge of the understanding should always precede the determination of the will. And it is in the misuse of the free will that the privation which constitutes the characteristic nature of error is met with. Privation, I say, is found in the act, in so far as it proceeds from me, but it is not found in the faculty which I have received from God, nor even in the act in so far as it depends on Him. (*Meditations, IV*)

In short, argued Descartes, as long as we do not misuse our rational capacities, as long as we only judge as intuitively evident the things which we perceive with sufficient clearness and distinctness, we are ensured by the goodness of God against error.

This Cartesian appeal to God as the guarantor of knowledge has not been widely accepted. There are a number of reasons for this. To begin with, there is considerable doubt about the arguments that Descartes (and others) used to prove the existence of God. We saw some basis for that doubt in our discussion in chapter 5. Since Descartes's argument presupposes that the existence of God has been proven, this doubt certainly undercuts Descartes's response to the skeptic. Secondly, there is a general feeling that Descartes is unjustified in assuming that a good God would certainly give us intellectual faculties that would lead us to the truth when properly employed. For all that we know, God may have good reasons for allowing us to be deceived even when we use our faculties of reasoning correctly.

There is, however, still a more fundamental objection to Descartes's whole argument. It was expressed in Descartes's own time by one of his most astute critics, Arnauld, who wrote:

> The only remaining scruple I have is an uncertainty as to how a circular reasoning is to be avoided in saying: the only secure reason we have for believing that what we clearly and distinctly perceive is true, is the fact that God exists.
>
> But we can be sure that God exists, only because we clearly and distinctly perceive that; therefore prior to being certain that God exists, we should be certain that whatever we clearly and evidently perceive is true. (*Objections to Descartes's Meditations*)

Arnauld's argument was really very simple. Descartes was trying to defend a certain conception of reasoning as a source of knowledge. In that defense, he *used* that very method of reasoning to prove the reliability of that method. Isn't that really arguing in a circle and begging the very question at hand, namely, the certainty of the results of that method of reasoning. We can conclude therefore that there is a serious difficulty with Descartes's rationalist conception of the foundation of knowledge, and that there are perhaps similar difficulties with rationalism in general.

Let us turn then to the empiricist conception. The following are the main theses of that analysis of knowledge: (1) There are some basic self-justified beliefs whose truth is immediately judged to be certain by our reason. These are analytic truths, beliefs (like 'all bachelors are males') whose truth follows from the meaning of the relevant terms. (2) But there are other basic self-justified beliefs about the direct findings of our senses. (3) All other beliefs that we know to be true are known on the basis of our ability to infer their truth, deductively or inductively, from the truth of these basic truths. (4) Experience therefore plays a significant role in the acquistion of knowledge.

We find these theses developed in the following passage by C. I. Lewis:

> Every statement we know to be true is so known either by reason of experience or by reason of what the statement itself means. There are no other sources of knowledge than on the one hand data of sense and on the other hand our own intended meanings. Empirical knowledge constitutes the one class; all that is knowable independently of sense experience—the *a priori* and the analytic— constitutes the other, and is determinable as true by reference to our meanings.
>
> Traditionally a statement which can be certified by reference exclusively to defined or definable meanings is called *analytic;* what is non-analytic being called *synthetic*. And traditionally that knowledge whose correctness can be assured without reference to any particular experience of sense is called *a priori;* that which requires to be determined by sense experience being called *a posteriori*.
>
> All analytic statements are, obviously, true *a priori;* whatever is determinable as true by reference exclusively to the meaning of expressions used, is independent of any empirical fact. That the converse relation also holds; that whatever is knowable *a priori,* including the principles of logic and all that logic can certify, is also analytic, is not so obvious. It has, of course, frequently been denied; most notably in the Kantian doctrine which makes *synthetic a*

priori truth fundamental for mathematics and for principles of the knowledge of nature.

The thesis here put forward, that the *a priori* and the analytic coincide, has come to be a matter of fairly wide agreement amongst logicians in the last half-century. (*An Analysis of Knowledge and Valuation,* chapter 3)

In our statement of the basic principles of the empiricist approach, we referred to "the direct findings of our senses." These findings are, for empiricism, as fundamental as are the intuitive self-evident beliefs for the rationalists. But empiricists have strongly disagreed about what they are. As this disagreement is so important, we must look at it more carefully.

There are those empiricists who believe that the foundation of all our knowledge is our perception of the external world: the basic findings of the senses are that certain external objects exist. There are, on the other hand, empiricists who are convinced that while the foundation of our knowledge is our perception, what we perceive are internal impressions and not external objects. For convenience, let's label these two empiricist approaches the *objective* approach and the *subjective* approach, respectively.

In order to understand this dispute, one should look carefully at the following passage drawn from the writings of George Berkeley:

> When I hear a coach drive along the streets, immediately I perceive only the sound; but, from the experience I have had that such a sound is connected with a coach, I am said to hear the coach. It is nevertheless evident that, in truth and strictness, nothing can be *heard* but *sound;* and the coach is not then properly perceived by sense, but suggested from experience. So likewise when we are said to see a red-hot bar of iron; the solidity and heat of the iron are not the objects of sight, but suggested to the imagination by the colour and figure which are properly perceived by that sense. In short, those things alone are actually and strictly perceived by any sense, which would have been perceived in case that same sense had been first conferred on us. As for other things, it is plain they are only suggested to the mind by experience, grounded on former perceptions. (*Three Dialogues*)

Berkeley was one of the leading exponents of the second (subjective) empiricist approach, and in this passage, he sets out the major reasons for adopting it: (a) It is important to distinguish between what I properly and directly perceive and what is suggested by what I perceive, even though we often loosely talk of perceiving that which is really only suggested. (b) When we think that we perceive an external object, we strictly and properly only perceive certain colors and figures. (c) The external object is, at best, suggested, it is not strictly perceived. Elsewhere in his writings, Berkeley identifies these colors and figures with sensations and treats them as entirely internal.

The crux of the argument is step (b). It is on this step that empiricists strongly disagree. There are those who agree with Berkeley, and who therefore ground the whole of empirical knowledge on our internal impressions. They then have to work very hard to claim any knowledge of the external world. There are those, on the other hand, who disagree with Berkeley, and who ground empirical knowledge on a direct perception of external reality. They have to justify, of course, the claim that there is such a direct perception.

This last point should be emphasized. It is extremely important. The empiricists are, after all, trying to find a foundation for empirical knowledge in what is directly perceived. Many subjectivists feel that they have no trouble finding a foundation in our internal impressions. The question that they have to consider is whether they can build on these foundations, using them as the basis for inferring that the external world exists and has certain features. Some of these philosophers feel that there is no difficulty in doing so. John Locke, for example, felt that we could justifiably infer the existence of the external world as the cause of our internal impressions. He put his argument as follows:

> But besides the assurance we have from our senses themselves, that they do not err in the information they give us of the existence of things without us, when they are affected by them, we are further confirmed in this assurance by other concurrent reasons:
>
> (I) It is plain those perceptions are produced in us by exterior causes affecting our senses: because those that want the *organs* of any sense, never can have the ideas belonging to that sense produced in their minds. This is too evident to be doubted: and therefore we cannot but be assured that they come in by the organs of that sense, and no other way. The organs themselves, it is plain, do not produce them: for then the eyes of a man in the dark would produce colours, and his nose smell roses in the winter: but we see nobody gets the relish of a pineapple, till he goes to the Indies, where it is, and tastes it.
>
> (II) Because sometimes I find that *I cannot avoid the having those ideas produced in my mind.* For though, when my eyes are shut, or windows fast, I can at pleasure recall to my mind the ideas of light, or the sun, which former sensations had lodged in my memory; so I can at pleasure lay by *that* idea, and take into my view that of the smell of a rose, or taste of sugar. But, if I turn my eyes at noon

toward the sun, I cannot avoid the ideas which the light or sun then produces in me. So that there is a manifest difference between the ideas laid up in my memory, (over which, if they were there only, I should have constantly the same power to dispose of them, and lay them by at pleasure) and those which force themselves upon me, and I cannot avoid having. And therefore it must needs be some exterior cause, and the brisk acting of some objects without me, whose efficacy I cannot resist, that produces those ideas in my mind, whether I will or no. Besides, there is nobody who doth not perceive the difference in himself between contemplating the sun, as he hath the idea of it in his memory, and actually looking upon it: of which two, his perception is so distinct, that few of his ideas are more distinguishable one from another. And therefore he hath certain knowledge that they are not *both* memory, or the actions of his mind, and fancies only within him; but that actual seeing hath a cause without.

(III) Add to this, that many of those ideas are *produced in us with pain*, which afterwards we remember without the least offence. Thus, the pain of heat or cold, when the idea of it is revived in our minds, gives us no disturbance; which, when felt, was very troublesome; and is again, when actually repeated: which is occasioned by the disorder the external object causes in our bodies when applied to them: and we remember the pains of hunger, thirst, or the headache, without any pain at all; which would either never disturb us, or else constantly do it, as often as we thought of it, were there nothing more but ideas floating in our minds, and appearances entertaining our fancies, without the real existence of things affecting us from abroad. The same may be said of *pleasure*, accompanying several actual sensations. (*Essay Concerning Human Understanding*, Book IV)

Not all empiricists have been satisfied by Locke's arguments. Berkeley himself thought that the inference from what is directly perceived to the external world could not be justified:

It remains therefore that if we have any knowledge at all of external things, it must be by reason inferring their existence from what is immediately perceived by sense. But (I do not see) what reason can induce us to believe the existence of bodies without the mind, from what we perceive, since the very patrons of Matter themselves do not pretend there is any necessary connexion betwixt them and our ideas? I say it is granted on all hands (and what happens in dreams, frensies, and the like, puts it beyond dispute) that it is possible we might be affected with all the ideas we have now, though no bodies existed without resembling them. Hence it is evident the supposition of external bodies is not necessary for the producing our ideas; since it is granted they are produced sometimes, and might possibly be produced always, in the same order we see them in at present, without their concurrence.

But, though we might possibly have all our sensations without them, yet perhaps it may be thought easier to conceive and explain the manner of their production, by supposing external bodies in their likeness rather than otherwise; and so it might be at least probable there are such things as bodies that excite their ideas in our minds. But neither can this be said. For, though we give the materialists their external bodies, they by their own confession are never the nearer knowing how our ideas are produced; since they own themselves unable to comprehend in what manner body can act upon spirit, or how it is possible it should imprint any idea in the mind. Hence it is evident the production of ideas or sensations in our minds, can be no reason why we should suppose Matter or corporeal substances; since that is acknowledged to remain equally inexplicable with or without this supposition. If therefore it were possible for bodies to exist without the mind, yet to hold they do so must needs be a very precarious opinion; since it is to suppose, without any reason at all, that God has created innumerable beings that are entirely useless, and serve to no manner of purpose. (*Principles of Human Knowledge,* I)

There are then certain difficulties associated with the subjective version of empiricism which insists that the basic findings of our senses are internal impressions and not external objects. In the end, these difficulties come down to the question of whether one would be able to go beyond the impressions to the external objects. These difficulties would, of course, be avoided if one adopted the position that it is the external objects themselves that are directly experienced. This is, indeed, what most people believe. We think, after all, that we directly perceive chairs, trees, people, etc. and these all seem to be standard examples of external objects. Why have many empiricists been reluctant to adopt this objective version, which simply holds that we directly perceive external objects? There are a number of major reasons for this reluctance:

1. *The argument from illusion.* We are all familiar with the situation in which we have illusory experiences. In such a situation, we cannot be directly experiencing an external object, since the external object just doesn't exist. The only thing that we can be experiencing is an internal impression. But since these experiences are no different from the experiences that we normally have even when we believe that the external object is present, shouldn't we conclude that what we normally experience is only the internal impression, and that the existence of the external object is at best inferred?

2. *The argument from perceptual relativity.* What we experience on a given occasion is not merely determined by the nature of the external object. It is also in part determined by our relations to that object. If we are, for example, closer to an object, what we see is different from what we would see if we were further away. The external object, however, does not change as we move closer to it or further away from it. Therefore, what we perceive cannot be identical with the external object. To quote David Hume:

> It seems also evident that when men follow this blind and powerful instinct of nature, they always suppose the very images presented by the senses to be the external objects, and never entertain any suspicion that the one are nothing but representations of the other. This very table which we see white, and which we feel hard, is believed to exist independent of our perception and to be something external to our mind which perceives it. Our presence bestows not being on it; our absence does not annihilate it. It preserves its existence uniform and entire, independent of the situation of intelligent beings who perceive or contemplate it.
>
> But this universal and primary opinion of all men is soon destroyed by the slightest philosophy which teaches us that nothing can ever be present to the mind but an image or perception, and that the senses are only the inlets through which these images are conveyed, without being able to produce any immediate intercourse between the mind and the object. The table which we see seems to diminish as we remove further from it; but the real table, which exists independent of us, suffers no alteration. It was, therefore, nothing but its image which was present to the mind. These are the obvious dictates of reason; and no man who reflects ever doubted that the existences which we consider when we say *this house* and *that tree* are nothing but perceptions in the mind and fleeting copies or representations of other existences which remain uniform and independent. (*An Inquiry Concerning Human Understanding*)

3. *The time-gap argument.* Suppose that you are looking at the sun. The light rays that impinge upon your sensory organs actually left the sun about eight minutes earlier. At best then, you can be seeing an object that only existed in the past (the sun of eight minutes ago). But clearly you are perceiving an object that exists now. So what you must be perceiving is a subjective impression. The same thing is true in all cases of perception, although the time-gap in normal cases is considerably smaller.

There are, then, serious difficulties with either version of empiricism. It seems difficult, on the one hand, to claim that we directly experience external objects. If, however, we conclude that all that we directly experience are private and subjective impressions and sensations, how can we use our knowledge of their existence as the basis for knowing about the external world? Defenders of both of these versions of empiricism have attempted to meet these objections, but we need not consider their attempts any further. There is yet another reason for objecting to empiricism, for concluding that the foundations of our knowledge cannot be the direct findings of our senses. The trouble is that, on either version of empiricism, we lack certain knowledge about the findings of our senses. Our beliefs about them are not certain.

Let us consider this question from the point of view of the objective version, the theory that says that what we directly experience are external objects. Do we have certainty about the resulting beliefs that those objects exist? Would such a certainty be justified? I think that it is easy to see that it would not. Suppose that we had carefully examined the object we think we see, and we conclude that there is a physical object in front of us. Can we ever be certain that the object is really there? How can we rule out the possibility that it is just a complicated realistic illusion as improbable as that might seem? These are the sorts of considerations that have led many philosophers to conclude that if what we want is certainty, then empirical knowledge must be founded on judgments about our impressions and sensations. This view fits in, of course, with the second, "subjective," version of empiricism. Thus, the first "objective," view of empiricism won't do as an account of the certain foundations of knowledge.

But there are also reasons for doubting that we can have as the certain foundations of knowledge reports about our impressions and sensations. Is it really clear that we can't be wrong about them? Suppose, for example, that I report that I am having a table experience (whether or not there really is a table in front of me). Couldn't I be wrong about such a report? Couldn't it be possible for me to correct my report and claim that I had misdescribed the nature of my experience ("I really wasn't thinking when I said that"). There are philosophers who would insist that this could not happen, but the basis of their insistence is certainly unclear.

10.4 SOME SUGGESTIONS

What seems to be happening here is very similar to what happened when we examined rationalism. Both rationalism and empiricism seem to be in trouble precisely because the beliefs that they put forward as the certain foundations of knowledge really aren't certain and cannot therefore serve in that capacity. Is this, correct, however? If we go back and look at the arguments that we offered against the certainty of the various basic beliefs, we can see that they are all of the following form: For any one of these beliefs it is possible that it can be false; therefore, we are not certain of its truth. But is this form of argumentation valid? Perhaps we can be certain of the truth of these beliefs even if it is possible that the belief is false. This, at least, is the suggestion made by Norman Malcolm:

> Now is it possible that every perceptual statement is false in any sense of "It is possible" from which it follows that it is not certain that any perceptual statement is true? . . . Any perceptual statement may be false in the sense that the contradictory of any perceptual statement is not self-contradictory; but it does not follow that it is not certain that any perceptual statement is true. It is true, I believe, that the evidence that one could offer in behalf of any perceptual statement does not entail that the statement is true; but, again, it does not follow that it is not certain that any perceptual statement is true. . . . Nothing remains to be meant by the statement "It is possible that every perceptual statement is false" except the claim that the grounds for accepting any perceptual statement are never conclusive. . . . The philosophical claim that those grounds are not conclusive does not rest on evidence. On what does it rest? On a confusion, I believe. One is inclined to argue "It is not conclusive that that perceptual statement is true because it is possible that it is false." But examination of this statement shows that the words "It is possible that it is false" do not mean that there is evidence that it is false. They mean that it is logically possible that it is false. But the fact that it is logically possible that it is false does not tend to show in any way that it is not conclusive that it is true. ("The Verification Argument" in M. Black's *Philosophical Analysis*)

Is Malcolm right? And if he is right, how much of either the rationalist's or the empiricist's foundation of knowledge can be kept as certain? And finally, whatever is kept, is that enough to build the rest of our knowledge upon? These are the many questions raised by Malcolm's provocative remarks about certainty. It is not unreasonable to conclude, I think, that Malcolm's reflections on certainty is one of the most promising ways of trying to save a view of knowledge based upon certain foundations. We shall not, however, explore this option further, for we shall explore a more fundamental alternative, an alternative that would do without certain foundations at all.

One of the original sources for this view is to be found in the following passage by W. V. O. Quine:

The totality of our so-called knowledge or beliefs, from the most casual matters of geography and history to the profoundest laws of atomic physics or even of pure mathematics and logic, is a manmade fabric which impinges on experience only along the edges. Or, to change the figure, total science is like a field of force whose boundary conditions are experience. A conflict with experience at the periphery occasions readjustments in the interior of the field. Truth values have to be redistributed over some of our statements. Reëvaluation of some statements entails reëvaluation of others, because of their logical interconnections—the logical laws being in turn simply certain further statements of the system, certain further elements of the field. Having reëvaluated one statement we must reëvaluate some others, which may be statements logically connected with the first or may be the statements of logical connections themselves. But the total field is so underdetermined by its boundary conditions, experience, that there is much latitude of choice as to what statements to reëvaluate in the light of any single contrary experience. No particular experiences are linked with any particular statements in the interior of the field, except indirectly through considerations of equilibrium affecting the field as a whole.

If this view is right, it is misleading to speak of the empirical content of an individual statement—especially if it is a statement at all remote from the experiential periphery of the field. Furthermore it becomes folly to seek a boundary between synthetic statements, which hold contingently on experience, and analytic statements, which hold come what may. Any statement can be held true come what may, if we make drastic enough adjustments elsewhere in the system. Even a statement very close to the periphery can be held true in the face of recalcitrant experience by pleading hallucination or by amending certain statements of the kind called logical laws. Conversely, by the same token, no statement is immune to revision. Revision even of the logical law of the excluded middle has been proposed as a means of simplifying quantum mechanics; and what difference is there in principle between such a shift and the shift whereby Kepler superseded Ptolemy, or Einstein Newton, or Darwin Aristotle?

For vividness I have been speaking in terms of varying distances from a sensory periphery. Let me try now to clarify this notion without metaphor. Certain statements, though *about* physical objects and not sense experience, seem peculiarly germane to sense experience—and in a selective way: some statements to some experiences, others to others. Such statements, especially germane to particular experiences, I picture as near the periphery. But in this relation of "germaneness" I envisage nothing more than a loose association reflecting the relative likelihood, in practice, of our choosing one statement rather than another for revision in the event of recalcitrant experience. For example, we can imagine recalcitrant experiences to which we would surely be inclined to accommodate our system by reëvaluating just the statement that there are brick houses on Elm Street, together with related statements on the same topic. We can imagine other recalcitrant experiences to which we would be inclined to accommodate our system by reëvaluating just the statement that there are no centaurs, along with kindred statements. A recalcitrant experience can, I have urged, be accommodated by any of various alternative reëvaluations in various alternative quarters of the total system; but, in the cases which we are now imagining, our natural tendency to disturb the total system as little as possible would lead us to focus our revisions upon these specific statements concerning brick houses or centaurs. These statements are felt, therefore, to have a sharper empirical reference than highly theoretical statements of physics or logic or ontology. The latter statements may be thought of as relatively centrally located within the total network, meaning merely that little preferential connection with any particular sense data obtrudes itself. ("Two Dogmas of Empiricism," *Philosophical Review*, 1951)

The following seem to be the main theses of this Quinean approach:
1. There really is no difference *in kind* between our supposedly diverse types of beliefs—no difference in kind between analytic and synthetic, between a priori and a posteriori.
2. The justification of all of our beliefs ultimately rests upon the experiences that we have.
3. None of our beliefs are certain, and they are all open to revision in the light of further experiences.
4. The most that we can say by way of distinguishing our beliefs is that some of our beliefs are more likely (as a matter of psychological fact) to be given up in the light of certain experiences rather than others.

In short, this view depicts a web of uncertain revisable beliefs rather than an edifice of knowledge resting upon certain unrevisable foundations.

On this account, to behave rationally is not to act upon beliefs that are certain; it is to act with greater or lesser personal risk in proportion to the probability of the beliefs upon which the actions are based. To quote Keith Lehrer:

> We can offer a theory of reasonable belief and action that does not presuppose that we know for certain that any contingent statement is true. The broad outline of such a theory may be sketched in a few words. Whether a belief or action is reasonable depends on two factors. One factor is what one values. The other factor is the proba-

bility of obtaining what one values. Once both values and probabilities are assigned, the reasonable belief or reasonable action may be calculated. The reasonable belief or action is the one that gives you a maximum of expected value. ("Skepticism and Conceptual Change" in Chisholm and Swartz's *Empirical Knowledge*)

The differences between this model and the model of knowledge based upon foundations are immediately evident. To begin with, rather than requiring the existence of some certainty, this model explicitly claims that there is no such thing. Secondly, rather than requiring something upon which all of our knowledge is based, this model explicitly claims that any one of our beliefs might at one time or another be challenged on the basis of some others. Because of these differences, the skeptical challenges which we were examining do not rise for this model. That there is no certainty, as the skeptic says, is no challenge for this model because it presupposes none. That there is no base of knowledge, as the skeptic says, is also no challenge for this model for it once more presupposes none.

There is naturally much more that has to be said by way of elaborating upon and defending this model. I believe, however, that it offers one of the most promising approaches to avoiding the muddles of traditional epistemology.

Conclusion

Students of philosophy often come to the conclusion that no issues are ever resolved in philosophy, that at the end philosophy consists of nothing more than lots of positions and arguments but no resolutions. It is not surprising that students (particularly introductory students) come to this conclusion because textbooks (particularly introductory textbooks) often do nothing more than that.

We have tried in this book to avoid this. We have tried to set out the various positions on a number of issues and to argue that some of them are correct. In particular, we have tried to establish the truth of the following claims:

1. Morality consists of following a set of moral rules, and not of trying to do the action that has the best consequences. These rules are based upon our moral intuitions, both about the rules in question and about what is right or wrong in given cases. While not infallible, these intuitions are adequate as a foundation for morality.

2. It cannot be shown that morality and self-interest are always compatible. Nevertheless, we have a reason for doing what is right even if it is not in our own self-interest. This reason is based upon our desires to do what is right and to be benevolent. But we have no reason for preferring to follow these desires over the desires of self-interest; which we will follow is determined by the strength of our desires.

3. Justice is a special virtue, and one that is not identical with

CONCLUSION

equality. There are just inequalities much as there are unjust inequalities. No general theory of justice is forthcoming. The best that we can say is that justice consists in each person having that to which he has a right—where these rights are determined by the past and present situation, character, and actions of the agents involved. There is therefore no one overall pattern of the distribution of goods in society that is the uniquely just pattern.

4. Although the state is a mechanism of coercion, its existence can be justified on the grounds of the consent of its citizens. This consent is not, however, an actual explicit consent. This consent is based upon certain expectations about the behavior of the state, and if the state violates enough of them, civil disobedience or revolution may be justified.

5. None of the traditional arguments for the existence of God succeeds in proving that God exists. At the same time, even the powerful argument from evil against the existence of God fails to prove that God does not exist. Because of the special nature of what is at stake in the area of religion, faith (as well as agnosticism) is a reasonable course of action.

6. Religious beliefs have a variety of concrete implications for human life. To begin with, although they are not needed as a foundation for morality in general, they do serve as the foundation for certain special moral beliefs and practices. They also serve, although in a more problematic fashion, as the foundation for certain ritual practices. Finally, on certain models of the meaning of life, but not on others, they help to provide such meaning.

7. The dualistic model of man can meet most of the traditional challenges raised against it. Nevertheless, it does not seem to fit into the scientific picture of the origin of man in the way that the materialist conception of man does. Although the behaviorist version of materialism is unacceptable, there are other versions, especially the brain-state theory, that are acceptable.

8. The ascription of responsibility is a difficult matter, partially because of the difficulties in the relevant concept of causality and partially because of the difficulties in understanding the relevant excuses. In any case, there is a further challenge to such ascriptions based upon the thesis of determinism. That challenge can easily be met if one holds the teleological theory of punishment, but it cannot if one holds the retributive theory.

9. The various subjective definitions of truth are inadequate. The pragmatic and coherence theories of truth while better, still run into difficulty, and we must therefore adapt some form of the correspondence theory of truth. That theory, as traditionally presented, encounters

serious metaphysical difficulties, but there are versions of it that can avoid them.

10. Just as it is possible to give a coherent account of truth, it is also possible to give a coherent account of knowledge. The crux of that account is that knowledge is justified true belief. Various skeptical arguments can be raised on the basis of that definition, but they can be met so long as we are prepared to give up either the idea that justification requires certainty or the idea that certainty requires the impossibility of error.

Although I believe that these claims are true, and that we have provided good arguments for them in this book, I would not want claim that they have been established conclusively and that all alternatives have been ruled out. Obviously, this is not so—and could not be in an introductory text for an introductory course. But there is much philosophy, both of the past and the present, that deals with each of these problems, and the reader who is interested in a particular problem is urged to pursue his inquiry, starting with those discussions. If reading this book caused you to do so, then I will be very satisfied.

Questions for Further Thought

CHAPTER 1—THE NATURE OF PHILOSOPHY

1. A system of moral rules that contained only one rule would not have to deal with the problem of conflicting moral rules. Try to construct a number of such systems and assess their adequacy.

2. Can you think of any moral rule to which there are no exceptions? If so, state and defend it. If not, show the exceptions to rules that might have been considered exceptionless.

3. Why do people believe that the end does not justify the means? Has Fletcher shown that it does?

4. Does the rejection of egoism really mean that we must be means to the ends of others?

5. What arguments could be advanced against considering the consequences to animals? To members of future generations?

6. Are there types of knowledge that are not extrinsic goods? If so, are they goods at all?

7. What goods should be recognized as goods in a satisfactory version of ideal utilitarianism?

8. Try to formulate a version of utilitarianism that allows us to consider more than the consequences of particular actions and apply it to the question of voting.

9. Do our special obligations always take precedence over our general obligations? If not, when do they?

10. Are there any rights which one couldn't give up? Could one, for example, waive one's right not to be enslaved?

CHAPTER 2—MORAL RULES AND THEIR EXCEPTIONS

1. "How can you decide for sure whether some action will be in your long-range interest? After all, circumstances may change. So it's best only to worry about the short run." Critically evaluate this argument.

2. How can a system of punishment be made efficacious enough to provide us with good reasons for doing what is right?

3. Are there any ways of explaining self-conflict while retaining the idea that the psyche is a unified entity?

4. Does reason conflict with desire in the case of the errant spouse or is this a conflict between the desire for sex and the desire to preserve the marriage?

5. Is a person in whom reason rules necessarily a person who neglects his emotional life?

6. Is a pleasure truly better because it would be chosen over other pleasures by those who have experienced both? Perhaps it only means that those people prefer that pleasure?

7. How powerful a government is required for Hobbes's purposes?

8. Is a sense of duty identical with a desire to do what is right (as Prichard seems to think)? Or is it independent of any desire?

9. How does Kant understand a sense of duty?

10. Are you satisfied with the conclusion that we ultimately have no reasons for preferring one basic desire over another?

CHAPTER 3—JUSTICE AND EQUALITY

1. "All men are created equally and are endowed by their creator with certain inalienable rights." In what ways does this differ from radical egalitarianism?

2. What arguments could be offered for radical egalitarianism?

3. Can we measure what people produce, or their abilities, or their needs, etc.? If not, in what way can we use the classical formulas of justice?

4. Can you account for the fact that the different formulas of justice seem appropriate in the different cases?

5. Can you justify rewarding people in proportion to their abilities given that these abilities are accidents of birth?

6. How do we determine whether people really need something or whether they would just be better off if they had it?

7. Is it really true that people with low incomes value extra income more than people with high incomes? Can you think of any possible exceptions?

8. What does equality of opportunity mean? Do we have that equality just if everyone has an equal legal right to pursue their goals? If not, what more is required?

9. Is freedom from coercion more or less important than the positive types of freedom?

10. How can we decide which rights take precedence when not all can be satisfied?

CHAPTER 4—THE EXISTENCE OF THE STATE AND THE OBLIGATION TO OBEY ITS LAWS

1. Would we object to coercion even if people were being coerced into doing what they ought to do anyway? If so, why?

2. Now do we decide which groups of people can be treated paternalistically? How, for example, can we decide when children are old enough so that paternalistic treatment is no longer justified?

3. Can some of our paternalistic laws be justified by reference to other considerations of a nonpaternalistic nature?

4. Can someone object to the theory of tacit consent on the grounds that people remain in the state only because they have no place else to which they would prefer to go?

5. Have we met Rousseau's objections to the social contract theory?

6. How would you resolve the questions about the right to emigrate that are raised in this chapter?

7. Is Rawls really right in supposing that hypothetical consent is politically relevant?

8. What document or documents in our society define the contract between the citizen and the state? What could take the place of such documents in a society that lacked them?

9. Has Locke really met the objection that his theory of revolution would lead to anarchy?

10. What considerations are relevant to determining whether we have reached the point at which civil disobedience is justified?

CHAPTER 5—THE EXISTENCE OF GOD

1. Are there any common features of the deities that men have worshipped or the ways in which they have worshipped them?

2. If God is omnipotent, then he should be able to swim the English Channel. Since he is incorporeal, he cannot. How would you resolve this apparent contradiction in the conception of God?

3. Is it possible to limit the Deity in any way without disrupting the main strands of the Judao-Christian tradition?

4. What reasons can be offered against believing in an infinite series of causes? Are they sound?

5. Is the case of the universe like Edwards's case of the Eskimos or is there a special legitimacy in asking for the cause of the total universe?

6. Could the universe have evolved in the fashion described by modern science while still emerging as part of some Divine Plan?

7. How can we decide whether the fact that mystical experiences can be drug-induced is evidence for their illusory nature?

8. Are there any circumstances in which one could reasonably conclude that a miracle has occurred?

9. Is the "Job theodicy" a solution to the problem of evil or a desperate attempt to avoid having to deal with it?

10. Does James's defense of faith justify holding any religious beliefs that may appeal to one or are there some constraints left?

CHAPTER 6—THE IMPLICATIONS OF RELIGIOUS BELIEF

1. What are the clearly objectionable elements in the classical beliefs concerning survival, and what remains for serious consideration and evaluation?

2. Can one be a saint while hoping for divine reward and salvation?

3. Is there any satisfactory way of determining which, if any, purported revelation truly is a divine revelation?

4. Why do most people reject Edwards's conception of an arbitrary deity? Are they right?

5. Can one reasonably claim that the fear of God is morally different from, and does not involve the same attitudes as, the fear of an earthly power?

6. Are there any nonreligious reasons for rejecting the Lockean tradition about property?

7. Are there any nonreligious moral objections to suicide?

8. What connection, if any, is there between a religious ethics and an ethics that admits of no exceptions?

9. How would you decide between the two models of a meaningful life?

10. How would you reconcile the conflicting demands of tradition and innovation in rituals?

CHAPTER 7—MAN AND HIS PLACE IN NATURE

1. Are there good reasons for taking the cessation of brain functioning as central in the definition of death? What are the alternatives?

2. Are there any features of human beings that can be used to distinguish their moral status from the moral status of animals and fetuses?

3. What arguments can be offered for and against that form of dualism that denigrates the body?

4. Do you see any grounds for preferring occasionalism to pre-established harmony or vice versa?

5. What might have led dualists to rule out the possibility of interaction between different types of substance?

6. Can any analogical argument be reinterpreted as an inference to the best explanation?

7. How would a believer in the soul fit its emergence into the scientific picture of the evolutionary emergence of man?

8. Develop a behavioristic account of believing that it is raining outside. Do the difficulties that you encounter shed any light upon the shortcomings of behaviorism?

9. Why is simplicity an advantage in a metaphysical theory? In a scientific theory?

10. Is Rorty's proposal a real improvement over Smart's original thesis?

CHAPTER 8—RESPONSIBILITY FOR OUR ACTIONS

1. What arguments can be offered for and against the claim that an omission can be a cause?

2. Try to construct a theory of proximate causation. What difficulties do you encounter? Are they different from the ones mentioned by the court in Palsgraf?

3. What does it mean to say "B had to occur given that A occurred previously?"

4. What are the major practical differences between adopting Bentham's theory of excuses and Hart's theory of excuses?

5. Critically compare the two classical accounts of intentions, the one based upon desire and the other based upon expectation.

6. How would you decide whether the addict was compelled to aid in the robbery?

7. Critically compare the retributive and teleological theories of punishment.

8. Is deterrent punishment really an instance of treating a person as a means rather than as an end, and, if so, is it therefore wrong?

9. What arguments can be advanced for and against the truth of determinism?

10. Can Schlick's theory be defended against Hospers's objections?

CHAPTER 9—TRUTH

1. What reasons can be offered for and against Protagoras's claim that things are to each person as they perceive them to be?

2. Why must a theory of truth rule out the possibility that a contradiction is true?

3. Defend the claim that either p is true or not-p is true.

4. Does pragmatism allow for the theoretical as well as the practical role of truth?

5. Is Russell correct in objecting to the pragmatic theory of religious truth?

6. What did the idealist mean by the coherence of a body of truths? Does the concept of coherence really presuppose the truth of the laws of logic?

7. Is there a difference between the event "The French Revolution" and the fact that the French Revolution occurred? If not, is Strawson denying the existence of that event as well?

8. Why do people find negative facts more troublesome than positive facts?

9. If there is no such property as truth, what are people talking about when they say such things as "the truth is hard to find"?

10. Do you think that 2 + 2 = 4 is analytic or synthetic, a priori or a posteriori, necessary or contingent?

CHAPTER 10—KNOWING AND BELIEVING

1. Why do you think Plato concluded that knowledge and belief have different objects?

2. How would you try to solve the problem raised by Gettier's example?

3. What considerations can be offered in defense of Descartes's claim that justification requires certainty?

4. Can we ever know for sure whether or not we're just dreaming?

5. How would you attempt to meet the argument raised by the religious fundamentalist?

6. Descartes treats as intuitive beliefs both the belief in our own existence and the belief that the triangle is bounded by three lines. Are there important differences between these beliefs?

7. What exactly is the distinction between what we directly perceive and what is suggested by those perceptions?

8. Assess the strengths and weaknesses of the views of Locke and Berkeley about the possibility of inferring the existence of the external world.

9. Do the arguments from illusion and perceptual relativity really prove that we don't directly perceive external objects?

10. Can we, as Malcolm suggests, have knowledge without certainty?